WHAT MORE IN/FOR SCIENCE EDUCATION

NEW DIRECTIONS IN MATHEMATICS AND SCIENCE EDUCATION
Volume 27

Series Editors
Wolff-Michael Roth
University of Victoria, Canada
Lieven Verschaffel
University of Leuven, Belgium

Editorial Board
Angie Calabrese-Barton, *Teachers College, New York, USA*
Pauline Chinn, *University of Hawaii, USA*
Brian Greer, *Portland State University, USA*
Lyn English, *Queensland University of Technology*
Terezinha Nunes, *University of Oxford, UK*
Peter Taylor, *Curtin University, Perth, Australia*
Dina Tirosh, *Tel Aviv University, Israel*
Manuela Welzel, *University of Education, Heidelberg, Germany*

Scope

Mathematics and science education are in a state of change. Received models of teaching, curriculum, and researching in the two fields are adopting and developing new ways of thinking about how people of all ages know, learn, and develop. The recent literature in both fields includes contributions focusing on issues and using theoretical frames that were unthinkable a decade ago. For example, we see an increase in the use of conceptual and methodological tools from anthropology and semiotics to understand how different forms of knowledge are interconnected, how students learn, how textbooks are written, etcetera. Science and mathematics educators also have turned to issues such as identity and emotion as salient to the way in which people of all ages display and develop knowledge and skills. And they use dialectical or phenomenological approaches to answer ever arising questions about learning and development in science and mathematics.

The purpose of this series is to encourage the publication of books that are close to the cutting edge of both fields. The series aims at becoming a leader in providing refreshing and bold new work—rather than out-of-date reproductions of past states of the art—shaping both fields more than reproducing them, thereby closing the traditional gap that exists between journal articles and books in terms of their salience about what is new. The series is intended not only to foster books concerned with knowing, learning, and teaching in school but also with doing and learning mathematics and science across the whole lifespan (e.g., science in kindergarten; mathematics at work); and it is to be a vehicle for publishing books that fall between the two domains—such as when scientists learn about graphs and graphing as part of their work.

What More in/for Science Education

An Ethnomethodological Perspective

Wolff-Michael Roth
University of Victoria, Victoria, BC, Canada

SENSE PUBLISHERS
ROTTERDAM / BOSTON / TAIPEI

A C.I.P. record for this book is available from the Library of Congress.

ISBN 978-94-6209-252-5 (paperback)
ISBN 978-94-6209-253-2 (hardback)
ISBN 978-94-6209-254-9 (e-book)

Published by: Sense Publishers,
P.O. Box 21858, 3001 AW Rotterdam, The Netherlands
https://www.sensepublishers.com/

Printed on acid-free paper

Contents

Preface

> The first rule and the most fundamental is to *consider social facts as things.*
> (Durkheim 1919: 20, original emphasis)

Has science education covered all avenues for doing research on topics of its interest? *What more* might there be available in the methodological domain that would open up (radically) new possibilities for research topics? For years, I thought that there was little else to be explored and that our methodological tools were well developed. I only realized rather recently that despite cultural-historical and socio-cultural turns in science education, very little has changed in the way we look at learning and that the very research methods are inappropriate for making claims about the *social* nature of facts and the thing-like nature of social facts in everyday conduct. This is so because, for example, the analysis of conversation is guided by *psychological perspectives,* which emphasize what one individual says and how another individual responds. The unit of analysis is the individual so that the social is theorized to emerge from the collaboration or *inter*action of individuals. But this is reducing *social* events into the sum, addition, or interaction of psychological events rather than treating social events as irreducible phenomena sui generis. The second major phenomenon I came to recognize is the absence of theories that can take into account social and life processes *from the inside.* Educational theories tend to theorize states – knowledge before and knowledge after a science curriculum unit; and the transition between these states is somehow caused by forces outside that which has changed. For example, students are said to 'construct' 'knowledge', 'conceptions', or 'meaning' where the nature of the things involved and the relations between them – subject of knowing and constructing, transitive activity that changes, and object being acted upon – are not articulated.

There exists a form of sociological research that not only has yet-to-be-explored possibilities but also constitutes a radical, 'asymmetrical alternate' to existing forms of research, both quantitative and qualitative: ethnomethodology (e.g., Roth 2009b). Researchers in the social sciences see their work to consist in extracting Durkheim's patterned social facts by drawing on this or that formal analytic apparatus – which, in most instances, requires methods courses and special training. Ethnomethodology re-specifies Durkheim's aphorism presented in the introductory quotation in the sense that it exhibits how those who staff social settings actively and endogenously produce and orient to this order. That is, ethnomethodology understands social structure very differently from the way standard quantitative and qualitative research treat it. Whereas in these forms of research, special methods are required to reveal the structures in social phenomena, ethnomethodological studies assume the social structure to be *accountably* produced, made visible, taught, and otherwise explicitly addressed by the members of society themselves. That is, the members themselves draw on, recognize, and deploy for each other the methods for producing social structure. However, despite its decided potential for making contributions to the social sciences, ethnomethodology is probably the least understood, most misunderstood, and most difficult approach in the social sciences generally and in science education specifically. I know about this personally, for recently one editor returned a manuscript to me asking the ethnomethodological part to be taken out prior to entering the manuscript to the review process; and in mathematics education, an article was accepted because/although the editor recognized its innovative way of describing mathematical learning and its difficult/unaccustomed way of writing. To assist in reading, a glossary at the beginning of the book contains the main technical terms.

Yet the ethnomethodological approach presented here has something to offer that would be of tremendous advantage to the development of science education research. In part, the difficulties derive from ethnomethodological texts, which require more than superficial readings. These texts require different writing and reading practices. One has to be familiar with such texts to understand them; but to become familiar with such texts, one has to read them understandingly. There is therefore a dialectical tension, because the only way to become familiar with these texts is by reading them; and their reading requires this familiarity, which the texts presuppose. The purpose of the extended study of science learning presented in this book is to bring ethnomethodology and the affiliated conversation analysis closer to science educators. I provide an account of where the approach has come from and its fundamental position. Materials from a science inquiry lesson are then used to articulate concretely how ethnomethodological analysis works, what sort of phenomena it targets, and what may be obtained using this approach to the understanding of social facts.

What should make ethnomethodology interesting to science educators is the fact that it can be used in conjunction with Vygotsky's cultural-historical project of founding a *concrete human psychology*, which is entirely based on irreducible human relations and the constitution of society. To Vygotsky, all higher psychological functions are soci(et)al relations prior to the instant that we may want to ascribe these functions to individuals. Analysts do not therefore attempt to get into the individual human mind. They do not have to, *for mind is in society to the extent that society is in the mind.* In growing up, we contribute to the endogenous production of societal relations whereby everything needed to exhibit order and orderly things is done so that anyone can observe them right then and there in situ where they need it. The approach presented here is also consistent with the Marxist sociological approach to language, which considers systems of ideas, ideologies, to be available to speakers of natural language acting in concrete situations (Vološinov 1930). The co-occurrence of references to these bodies of work in this book therefore is not coincidental.

The Australian Research Council Discovery Grant DP0984394 (PI S. Ritchie), on which I was an international collaborator funded the research reported in this study. Ken Tobin provided an extensive reading of an early fragment of this text, which led me to realize that a much expanded version is required to answer the question 'What more?' in and for the context of science education. I was inspired to write this book especially because of his comments about readability of research and my reply about the contradiction of innovative language, which may be rejected precisely because it jars with common ways of describing and explaining phenomena of interest to science educators. Stephen Ritchie also read and provided feedback on the first text in which the overall themes for this book where articulated. My thanks go to him for providing access to these materials and the transcription assistance provided by his graduate students.

In this text, I draw on and quote texts published in languages other than English. Unless marked otherwise, all translations are mine. I explicitly draw on the original texts, where available, and on my own translations because the problems *inherent* in translations. The Italian language has a diction that names and describes the problem: *traduttore traditore* – translator traitor. This is so because all translation requires interpretation, as no two natural languages can be mapped onto each other in a one-to-one fashion. Translators make choices according to their ways of understanding the world; and these choices frequently are inconsistent with the fundamental theoretical, epistemological, ontological, and axiological underpinnings of the original work. My translations, while being subject to the same problematic, at least render in English my reading of the original rather than someone else's reading. My reading is consistent with the theoretical framework underpinning this book.

Victoria, BC
March 2013

Glossary

Accountable. People act in ways that they can subsequently describe and explain when they are held to account for their actions. That is, they can provide reasons for what they have done. For example, one person may note that she is insulted by what her counterpart said, who, in saying that 'he was only joking' provides an explanation of what he was really doing.

Bracketing. This term denotes the act of the social scientist to put at bay their own preconceptions that might come into play trying to understand a phenomenon. Thus, rather than accepting 'power' as a social construct, the brackets in the expression '{power}' indicate that the investigation concerns the very production of conduct that leads social scientists to use the term 'power'. That is, bracketing orients the social scientist to study the work that makes 'power' an observable social fact.

Conversation analysis. This is the name for a particular analytic method that Harvey Sacks originated and developed. It is *not* simply the analysis of conversations, as novices in the field of educational research often assume. That is, conversation analysis always is the analysis of conversation, but not all analyses of conversations in fact do conversation analysis. Conversation analysis takes the turn pair as its minimum unit. This decenters the analysis from the psychological to the *social* level.

Documentary method. The documentary method was introduced by Karl Mannheim and subsequently used by Harold Garfinkel to explain how, based on concrete examples from our lifeworld, we get a sense of something like a 'worldview' or a 'queue'. Concrete incidences are taken to be documents of something, like a 'worldview' or 'queue', which, though general, only exists in and through the manifold concrete experiences that we have with events that deserve these names. Neither addition nor synthesis nor abstraction can explain the relation between the concrete document and the whole of which it is a document.

Dope (cultural, psychological). The term is used to denote the human being in the way it appears in the psychological and sociological literature, 'who produces the stable features of society by acting in compliance with preestablished and legitimate alternatives of action that the common culture provides' (Garfinkel 1967: 68). In sociology, school performance *is explained by* socio-economic status; and in (Piagetian) psychology, schemas *explain* what a person sees and does. Thus, the person's *reasoned* and *justified/justifiable* evaluations, judgments, and decision-making are treated as epiphenomena.

Durkheim's aphorism. The 'father' of sociology, Émile Durkheim, established what we now know as sociology in stating that the first rule and the most fundamental is to *consider social facts as things*. As *things*, social facts therefore are observable. Ethnomethodology is concerned with the work involved in making social facts observable and accountable to every member to the setting.

Endogenous. From the inside. The term is used in ethnomethodology to insist on the fact that actors themselves produce conduct in such a way that produces the social facts and social conditions that in turn determine what they do. The social facts are not abstract schemas, rules, or practices. They are the results of performances that the actors hold each other accountable for.

Ethnomethodology (EM). Literally the science of the methods everyday folk use to accountably produce social facts and situations.

First-time-through. The adjective 'first-time-through' is used to characterize a form of analysis where the researcher takes the perspective of the members to the setting (or cohort, staff of the phenomenon) studied. That is, researchers then have no way to use future states, the outcomes of actions, to analyze earlier happenings in a teleological fashion. This changes the way in which researchers can work, for it is no longer possible, for example, to say what a statement does, because what it will have done is apparent only through its effects available in and from subsequent talk and actions.

Formal analysis (FA). All forms of social research that have to specify the special (scientific) methods of how they identified the reported social facts fall under this category. Studies using formal analytic methods differ from ethnomethodological studies in the sense that the latter employ and demonstrate competence of precisely the same methods that are used to produce social facts. Formal analysis and ethnomethodology therefore are asymmetrical alternates with respect to the study of social facts. The former focus on facts, using special methods to extract them from data, whereas the latter study the actual work that produces what formal analysis identifies. Knowing the ethnomethods always will allow us to get at the social facts, whereas formal analytically identified social facts do not get us to the ethnomethods that produced them.

Formulating. Speakers of natural language frequently *formulate* what they are doing with language. For example, a speaker might say 'Let me ask you this, "How ...?"' Here, the actually intended question is prefaced by the note that a question is forthcoming rather than a statement, invitation, or order. The speaker has *formulated* an aspect of the ongoing conversational work.

Glossing, glossing practices. In the ethnomethodological literature, this term is used to refer to the fact that speakers always 'mean differently' than they can say in so many words. After many years of absence from Hattiesburg, MS, where my alma mater is located, I was invited there to give a talk at the 100th anniversary of the school. While driving through the center of town, I say to my host 'It certainly has changed since I was here', and my host responds, 'Yes, they revitalized the entire city center to bring people back here'. In this situation, the first sentence is treated as a gloss and in the second sentence my host elaborated what I was really saying without having said so.

IRE. This acronym stands for '*i*nitiation, *r*eply, *e*valuation', a sequence that describes a particular way of taking turns in classroom talk. In this sequence, teachers tend to take the first and third position (initiation, evaluation) and students take the second, middle position.

Lebenswelt. This term denotes the world as it appears to us and that we inhabit. It is the self-evident, inherently shared world *given* to us in our experience. It is not a world that we construct, because construction (e.g., using language) is possible only as the result of inhabiting and evolving in/with a Lebenswelt. Much of the initial research concerning the Lebenswelt was done by the German philosopher Edmund Husserl during the 1920s and 1930s. Alfred Schütz extended this work into the sociological field. Harold Garfinkel, the founder of ethnomethodology, recognizes the contributions of both to his own work.

Members (to the setting). Ethnomethodological investigations concern the endogenous work by means of which social structures are observably and accountably produced. Because the phenomena are social, they are independent of the particular individuals (or *cohort*) that '*staff*' the phenomenon in any particular case. Thus, although a researcher may use the queue in front of a movie theater as an example, the phenomenon denoted by the gloss {queue} *is independent of the particular cohort* presently observed.

Method. The way in which something is actually done.

Methodology. This term often is used in the sense of method, even though, in structural equivalence with all other sciences that include the word ending *-logy*, methodology is the *science* of method. Ethnomethodology is such a science, because it is concerned with the different methods used in everyday situations to produce the order of things. The term is misused in scientific journal articles, which state methods rather than engage in the work of 'doing {methodology}'.

Phenomenology. Literally the science of phenomena, focuses on the work that makes the phenomena appear in the ways they do, that is, the work by means of which phenomena phenomenalize themselves. The term is often mistakenly used to refer to the study of personal (psychological) experiences rather than to the fundamental processes of phenomenalization that lead to this or that experience. Thus, we might see this or that cube looking at a flat drawing (experience). Phenomenology is not interested whether we see one or the other cube or something else altogether. Rather, it is interested in the underlying processes – a matter of eye movement in individuals (Roth 2012) or a matter of complex social representation practices in the case of science (Roth and Bowen 1999b) – that lead to one or the other experience.

Sheffer stroke. The Sheffer stroke '|' is used in logic to denote the logical conjunction 'not and' or NAND. In a truth table, the 'not and' conjunction of two logical variables, each of which can be true or false, is true only if at least one of the two variables is false. This allows the construction of concepts with inner contradictions. For example, the dialectical concept 'margin | center' embodies an inner contradiction, which is equivalent to saying that it embodies difference, or movement. When analytically applied in static fashion, a situation manifests itself as marginal, central. When applied in a dynamic fashion, the concept points to and theorizes continuous change, which may also be one that manifests itself in transitions from centrality to marginality and vice versa.

Staff. Ethnomethodological investigations concern the endogenous work that accountably produces, for participants themselves, the surrounding social situation and its facts. Because such phenomena are widespread, those who figure in a particular example are but staff that in any *this* case bring the phenomenon to life. Any other situation would involve different staff but the same *social* phenomenon. A good everyday example is a queue. We *find* queues 'everywhere'. Science lessons, independently of who teacher and students are, constitute another case. We can walk into a classroom and *know/see* that there is a science lesson independent of its current staff. Ethnomethodological studies ask, 'What is the endogenous work that makes a lesson recognizably a science [rather than mathematics, reading, social studies] lesson?'

Sympraxis. An expression Lev S. Vygotsky and Alexei N. Leont'ev borrowed from the linguist Karl Bühler to point to the irreducible joint labor of producing social praxis. Bühler used this expression to underscore that a conversation is a *social* phenomenon requiring at least two voices. Like a two-handed clap, which is the interplay of two hands from which something *new* emerges rather than the addition of two single-handed claps, the conversation cannot be understood as the addition of two voices.

Umwelt. A word that has entered the English language from German, where it literally denotes the world (*Welt*) surrounding (*um-*) an organism. The *Umwelt* inherently implies the world as attended and relevant to the organism. Thus, a pine beetle, a bird eating pine beetles, and a human climbing pine trees relate to the bark in very different ways. That is, the bark of a pine tree is very different and has different roles in the Umwelt of the pine beetle, the bird hunting its prey, and the human being (who may use the rough bark as handholds).

We ask what it is about natural language that permits speakers and auditors to hear, and in other ways to witness, the objective production and objective display of commonsense knowledge, and of practical circumstances, practical actions, and practical sociological reasoning as well? What is it about natural language that makes these phenomena observable–reportable, i.e., *account-able* phenomena? For speakers and auditors the practices of natural language somehow exhibit these phenomena in the particulars of speaking, and *that* these phenomena are exhibited is itself, and thereby, made exhibitable in further description, remark, questions, and in other ways for the telling.

The interests of ethnomethodological research are directed to provide, through detailed analyses, that account-able phenomena are through and through practical accomplishments.

(Garfinkel and Sacks 1986: 163)

1

Ethnomethodology in/for Science Education

In science education, as in most other fields of social science inquiry, special quantitative and qualitative methods are used to extract structure from situations of interest. For example, one recent study – which investigates and theorizes discourse during the writing of analogies in chemistry (Bellocchi and Ritchie 2011) – specifies how a fine-grained analysis identified the 'hybridization of everyday discourse and chemical discourse' and how the researchers arrived at identifying the 'fluidity of meanings, signs, symbols, and practices' in this way:

> We began by listening and reviewing all audio and video material and artifacts either on the day of the lesson or within a few days after observations for each student group. Audio and video data that offered insights relevant to our research question were immediately transcribed. Starting from the hybridization of everyday and chemical discourse, we coded the data sources. As common themes emerged from each student group, comparisons of the three student groups allowed the refinement of our coding categories; for each group, transcripts and artifacts were re-coded based on the new themes. (ibid: 778)

The fact that the researchers offer this description of method points us to its special nature; they would not have to describe method if what they were doing had been done by the routine, everyday, unremarkable methods people use to endogenously produce everyday situations. If the method by means of which the 'hybridization of everyday discourse and chemical discourse' is specified, then there is a reason for this textual move in the research article. It might be that the phenomenon, the hybridization of two different forms of discourse, would not be visible other than by means of the special method. An analogy would be the staining procedures microbiologists use to make visible the presence of certain kinds of bacteria (Gram positive, Gram negative). In this case, the question would be this: 'Does the identified pattern matter in the production of the social situation that these researchers observed?' That is, do the research participants *actively* orient to the production and presence of the pattern? If they do not, what is the role of such a pattern? How are the authors' 'coding categories' related to the social situations they observed – i.e., the conversations among students in a chemistry class? Do participants act according to such patterns (i.e., to the categories that emerged from coding) without knowing it, just as human beings are said to act out certain 'schemas' without knowing that they act according to these 'schemas'? If this were the case, then human beings would be no more than psychological or cultural dopes, acting out schemas that they themselves are not aware of. Human beings – students, teachers, and even researchers – would be nothing other than animals who act without knowing why they do what they do. Human beings would be no more than machines acting according to innate or learned psychological and sociological programs – i.e., invisible psychological and sociological schemas – that drive what they do. But is this the case?

The fact that we do things with and for reason is observable in the specification of special social science methods that are found in research articles. The researchers in the quotation listened and reviewed the data *because* they were interested in patterns, *because* they were interested in understanding the hybridization of different discourses, and *because* they were interested in the 'common themes' that they anticipated to 'emerge from each student group'. But it is not only researchers who behave in ways so that they can provide reasons and rationales for it. All human beings – unless handicapped in this or that way – act in accountable ways: They are able to provide, when asked, accounts for their actions. This is so even for younger children, who will have a reply when asked 'Why did you hit your brother?' by saying, for example, 'He hit me first' or 'He took my teddy'. Actions, because these have *intended* outcomes, can be accounted for in terms of what they were to achieve and why.[1]

The exergue of this book presents a different approach to the analysis of social phenomena. It states as the driving question: 'what it is about natural language that permits speakers and auditors to hear, and in other ways to witness, the objective production and objective display of commonsense knowledge, and of practical circumstances, practical actions, and practical sociological reasoning as well'. 'What is it about natural language', the authors of the text in the exergue question, 'that makes these phenomena observable–reportable, i.e., *account-able* phenomena?' To sketch some first tentative answers to questions such as these, let us take a look at a lesson excerpt to identify the difference between what people *actually* do and what researchers *say* they do. The following excerpt and its analysis are provided in the same study from which the quoted description of methods was taken.

> Everyday discourses did feature in the other observed lessons. For example, during one episode when the class was solving stoichiometry problems, Trev's group was working on a solution to a problem. As Trev was looking over Mal's shoulder, he noted that Mal had incorrectly spelt the word 'whether'. Trev intervenes as seen in Extract 1 to correct Mal's spelling. This led to a brief exchange with a play on the word whether as also meaning a sheep.

---

[1] There are serious problems with the cause–effect reasoning, which has not been found in nature but has been invented based on the observation that human actions are related to effects: an observation made *after the fact* (Nietzsche 1956). The gap between plans and situated actions can be traced to cause–effect fallacy, which is based on teleological reasoning.

```
37  Trev:   Shouldn't that whether have a 'H' after the w?
38  Mal:    Trev let's not worry about grammar in chemistry
39  Louise: But yes it should
40  Trev:   Cool
41  Mal:    A wether is a male sheep
42  Trev:   No that's a ram
```

The full exchange consists of six turns relating to the sheep. The discussion on the spelling ends after Turn 42 and the topic of sheep does not feature again in the remainder of the exchanges. (Bellocchi and Ritchie 2011: 779)

In their text, these authors provide a reading of the conversation that is separate from what the overheard student group actually does and what the participants to the setting make available to each other and to themselves. This begins with the transcription that does not render what is available on the tape – e.g., the sounds – but the *authors'* hearing rather than the hearings of the participants. For example, there is a capital 'H' in turn 37 enclosed in quotation marks. Did Trev produce a sound that the International Phonetics Alphabet transcribes as /ˈeɪtʃ/ (like 'age') or as /ˈheɪtʃ/ (like 'hage')? The latter pronunciation of the letter 'h', while being non-standard in many Anglo-Saxon countries, is a feature of Irish-English. In fact, in Northern Ireland it is a shibboleth, a feature distinguishing Protestants from Catholics, where the schools of the former teach the pronunciation /ˈeɪtʃ/ whereas the latter teach the pronunciation /ˈheɪtʃ/. It could have political implications with repercussions on the events in the classroom. In Australia, where the study was conducted, an estimated 60% of the population uses the latter pronunciation. The question of pronunciation would tremendously matter if the *con*versation were to orient towards it.

That pronunciation and its relation to writing matters clearly is at issue in this excerpt where the researchers transcribe the same sound-word /ˈwɛðə(r)/ as both 'wether' (turn 41) – a male sheep, ram, especially when it is a castrated male sheep – and 'whether'. In fact, the transcription of turn 37 appears to be incorrect, for Trev would not have said 'shouldn't that whether have a "h" after the w?' if the word 'whether' had been spelled as shown in the transcription. Rather, the issue arose because the spelling likely was 'wether', so that asking whether there should be an 'h' is a plausible, reasoned thing to do in the situation. Trev could have provided a reason for asking the question – i.e., he could have provided an account for his discursive action – that any one present would have understood as a legitimate reason. In the following paragraphs I provide an initial analysis of the transcript from the perspective of the *con*versation, which is a social phenomenon.[2] I achieve taking this perspective by taking the turn-pair as the minimum unit of analysis. In

---

[2] We know and in fact experience daily that conversations are *social* phenomena that exceed, that is, transcend, individual intentions. For example, in a department meeting, a meeting of a tenure and promotion committee, or meeting during which research proposals are assessed, the decisions made collectively exceed the sum total of what individuals bring to the meeting. If it were not like this, the meeting would be unnecessary. Members to a committee could send in their individual appraisals and some algorithm would compute a final result. However, I personally have sat in meetings where an initially favorable sum total of recommendations about a research grant turned into a rejection; and an initially unfavorable sum total of recommendations in a tenure decision turned into a favorable recommendation for tenure and promotion.

so doing, I transcend what one *individual* says and how another 'interprets' or is otherwise affected by it.

The authors claim that 'Trev ... noted that Mal had incorrectly spelt the word "whether"' and that the 'full exchange consists of six turns relating to the sheep'. We have to ask whether these claims matter to understanding the unfolding of the event and whether there was a six-turn discussion of the topic of sheep. The authors also state that the discussion ends as if there was a mysterious event that brought itself to a close independent of the social relation and independent of the sympractical work of the participants to the setting. What is it that *these* participants orient to, make available to each other, and thereby accomplish in the setting? What is it that drives this event qua *social* event, that is, something that is first and foremost a *collective* phenomenon produced in and through *collectively* accomplished work?

The student did orient toward a matter of grammar, here, of orthography, that is, the spelling of the word phonetically transcribed as /'wɛðə(r)/. *In this situation*, turn 37 is heard as an issue of grammar (turn 38); and this hearing constitutes the nature of the preceding turn. Or more abstractly, rather than talking about speakers, we may ask how one turn treats the one preceding it. We can then ask questions about how two speaking turns related to each other and how, in fact, two consecutive turns reify each other. Thus, although the authors placed a question mark at the end of turn 37 – *their* interpretation of what has been done here – turn 38 is not actually a reply to a question. From the perspective of the conversation, a statement has been made about grammar; and this nature of the statement (turn 37) is available only in the next turn. For this reason, the two turns are mutually constitutive, the former preceding and giving rise to the latter, but the latter determining what the preceding turn has done. I therefore use the Sheffer stroke '|', which marks both conjunction and negation typical of dialectical terms that embody an inner contradiction.

A proposal | rejection pair of turns follows: the statement of an issue of grammar is not to be worried about (turn 38) is followed by the statement that 'it should' (turn 39). The beginning of turn 39 employs a contrastive connective 'but yes', which both sets up and emphasizes the different orientation to the presence or absence of 'h' following the 'w' in the 'wether' that appears on the page in front of Mal. A proposal | acceptance pair follows taking the form 'yes it should' | 'cool', the first part constituting an assertion that grammar should matter and the latter its acceptance. In contrast to the authors' claims, there is nothing about sheep up to this point. What matters in and to the situation, collaboratively exhibited as such in the members' actions, is the role of grammar in chemistry. There is then a statement | rejection pair: 'a wether is a male sheep' | 'no that's a ram' (turns 41 | 42). The first part of this pair, itself a second part of a preceding pair, in fact is a reply to the 'wether' on the paper. Grammatically, 'wether' is the subject of a statement and 'is a male sheep' the predicate. Predicates tell us something about the subject. The second part of the turn pair makes the preceding predicate problematic, 'no, that's a ram' (turn 42). The rendering problematic, the negation, is achieved by means of a negation, 'no', the statement of the subject using the pronoun 'that' to denote what just has been mentioned, the 'male sheep', and the statement of a new predicate. In this turn pair, two alternative statements are offered, which may be glossed in this way: 'a wether is a male sheep' and 'a male sheep is a ram'. There are therefore only two turns or, more precisely, only one turn pair that is concerned with sheep.

In the present instance, as the authors write, there are no further statements that they hear as being related to the issue. There is an apparent contrast between the two statements that is not taken further by the *conversation*. The contrast therefore is a non sequitur, is not being taken up and, therefore, does not shape the conversation in its future unfolding. In fact, the two statements can be heard as complementary rather than as contrast: Both statements are valid simultaneously: 'a wether is a male sheep' and 'a male sheep is a ram'. From the perspective of the conversation, any speculation is mote, as 'non sequitur' means that there is no follow up, there is a break between the statement and what follows.

In this analysis, we therefore see that the authors have *imputed* aspects to the events that are irrelevant to *this* conversation in its unfolding and, therefore, to the members to the setting. To understand a conversation, that is, to understand its *unfolding* and its *trajectory*, the authors' interpretations are irrelevant. Their method does not reveal what the members to the social settings *actually* do and the ways in which they render their public the accountable nature of their actions. What really matters is made thematic in a question stated in the exergue: 'What is it about natural language that makes these phenomena observable–reportable'? We have to ask, 'How does natural language exhibit phenomena in the particulars of speaking?' 'How are phenomena made exhibitable in the further descriptions, remarks, questions, and in other ways of telling that the speakers mobilize *for* each other?' The alternative hearing I offer follows the social process and, therefore, the ways in which accountable phenomena – accountable on the part of the actors that the research follows through their lives – '*are through and through* practical *accomplishments*'. This alternative hearing is based on the assumption that social actors behave in reasonable and reasoned ways, who can always state what they do and why. The alternative reading takes the perspective of the social actors who, at a particular instant in time (e.g., turn 37), do not know what will happens only seconds hence (e.g., in turn 38). Thus, in turn 37, these actors provide *no* indication that the conversation is about sheep. Even if one or the other actor were silently thinking about sheep, it would not matter to the *social* situation from the perspective of the social, that is, from the perspective of an analytic unit that is social. The sheep are articulated and oriented to *only* in turns 41 and 42. My reading follows what the actors exhibit to each other and, therefore, how they understand *this* conversation and the manner in which it unfolds. Thus, in this conversation, turn 37 comes to be treated as a statement rather than as a question that the researchers mark it to be (by using a question mark). The response does not indicate that a question has occurred but rather that a statement about grammar has been made.

The kind of reading I provide has evolved for me, in its particular form, from my engagement with a literature not commonly referred to in science education: ethnomethodology. As a field, ethnomethodology belongs to sociology, concerned as it is with the way in which it orients to commonsense knowledge, and of practical circumstances, practical actions, and practical sociological reasoning. But it practices sociology in a very particular way, a way that is a radical alternate to going quantitative and qualitative, 'formal analytic' approaches. Whereas the latter report and take as fact social order, the preoccupation of ethnomethodology 'is to find, collect, specify, and make instructably observable the local endogenous production and natural accountability of immortal familiar society's most ordinary organizational things in the world, *and to provide for them both and simultaneously as objects and procedurally, as alternate methodologies*' (Garfinkel 1996: 6). That is, ethnomethodology is concerned with how social situations are structured endogenously, from the *inside*, so that the social structure as much as its production becomes visible to the actors themselves and to the social scientists, who use this or that method for extracting structure. Although these scientists specify a different, formal method for doing so, their own seeing of structure in a social situation *requires* the same competencies that allow social actors to perceive and act towards it. This is so because 'the ur-materials of the first sense-formation, the ur-premises so to speak, exist *prior to all science* in the world of life, which is not merely material Umwelt but already shaped cultural Umwelt' (Husserl 1939: 219). That is, what is scientific and logical in both natural and social sciences has its origin in the pre-logical, fundamental experiences of the world. This first world that we encounter before making contact with any formal science is the irreducible condition for any scientific knowledge, practice, and understanding. Thus, 'everything "logical" emerges from a pre-logical sphere, which has its own rationality, its own, everything bearing/carrying truth' (Husserl 1993: 154). This pre-logical world is the only true world, 'the only one that we can talk about, into which each new science grows and fits itself, just as any other praxis and its newly generated formations' (ibid: 140).

Garfinkel, in one of his last texts, credits Husserl for helping him understand the foundational function of our everyday lifeworld. This leads us to the fundamental methodological issue and to the watershed between formal analytic and ethnomethodological approaches: '*The point:* Formal methods – formal analytic methods of generic representational theorizing – do not adequately and evidently describe the methods and practices of social analysis that identify in their discipline-specific worksite details ways in which human knowledge makes instructable, witnessable contact with an objective world in the sciences, natural or social' (Garfinkel 2007: 48). But those actors do not employ special methods: they use the methods that every competent member of society is learning and has learned by participating in the daily production of social order. Because this method of the people is so ordinary, their ethno-method, it does not have to be specified. This method is available in the very ways in which social settings are organized and produced from the inside. This does not prevent the existence of determinations over which social actors have no control. Thus, for example, a sociologist who understands herself as a single mother and participates in the relevant discourse of the 'single parent family' and the problems thereof is subject to an ideological determination that penetrates her lifeworld from the outside, so to speak (Smith 1990).

Ethnomethodology and Science Education

> Ethnomethodology's standing task is to examine social facts, just in every and any actual case asking for each thing, what makes it accountably just what that social fact is? (Garfinkel 2002: 251)

Very little work has been conducted in science education from the perspective of ethnomethodology, which may be in part attributable to the fact that the science education community does not readily accept and appropriate the methodological stance and in part of the disinterest the members of the field of ethnomethodology have shown for traditional concerns of science educators. In fact, issues such as open-inquiry and the pursuit towards more 'authentic' forms of science education have become the explicit critique from the perspective of ethnomethodology (e.g., Sherman 2004). One study that did take the approach reanalyzed a set of data that had originally led to claims about convergent conceptual change, but were used later to exhibit how, from the participants' unfolding transaction, the discovery of the relation between velocity and acceleration in a simulation environment was discovered (Koschmann and Zemel 2009). The authors show – comparing this discovery with that of the audiotaped discovery of the first optical pulsar – how the object discovery can be located within the ongoing talk itself. They further show that the discovery is not something preordained but rather constitutes an occasioned production that the participants themselves treat as something new. The second study, also pertaining to physics education, exhibits how the lessons constitute 'familiar, observable, and routinely organized activities that exhibit, for participants and analysts alike, how science can be produced through a manipulation of ordinary objects' (Lynch and Macbeth 1998: 269). The emphasis here is on how these activities exhibit for *participants* how science can be produced. These participants do not have the formal analytical technology, quantitative or qualitative, that science education journals display.[3] Rather, they 'merely' have their *ethno*methods; and it is these ethnomethods that produce the order that other research, with its formal analytic technologies that methods sections in journal articles specify, reports and theorizes in ways irrelevant to the social actors.

The interest of such work lies in how social structure generally and those pertaining to science specifically are produced within the activity itself, that is, in and as part of (i.e., *endogenously*) the integrality of the ongoing affairs. This then leads to very different thinking about existing science education topics, such as conceptual change, which can be shown to arise from the way in which interviews themselves are structured to produce misconceptions even when there is evidence that a person has not ever thought about an issue before and cannot have a conception (Roth 2008b; Roth et al. 2008). Such ethnomethodological work can then be used

---

[3] By articulating the need of specifying scientific method, by holding authors to account for the methods they used to arrive at the social facts they report, social scientists in fact are 'administering an in-principle difference between common sense knowledge of social structures and scientific knowledge of social structures' (Garfinkel 1988: 104). The application of special methods presupposes that there is no endogenous order and that 'there is no orderliness in concrete activities' (ibid: 105). In this way, 'real immortal society is *only* specifiable as the achieved results of administering the policies and methods of formal, constructive analysis' (ibid: 106).

in designing settings so that conceptual change is allowed to emerge from sets of existing, naïve practices that embody all the competencies required to make change accountably visible rather than relegating it to invisible mental processes (Macbeth 2000). Such studies may show how, for example, knowledgeability is up for grabs, where those in the institutional positions of 'teacher' may turn out to be less knowledgeable than those who are in institutional positions of 'students' so that the roles become actually reversed (Roth and Middleton 2006). The ethnomethodological approach is suited ideally for investigating the work that brings about such role inversions and how those who staff an instructional setting endogenously produce the event.

Inquiry has been a mainstay of science education at least since the 1960s, when there was an increasing interest in 'hands-on' experience subsequent to the impact of Jean Piaget's work. Most hands-on experience tended to be in the form of prepared laboratory tasks, whereby students implemented experiments for which they had received detailed instructions. The purpose was to get students develop some ('basic process') skills in manipulating laboratory equipment and materials, to develop an orientation towards appropriate laboratory behaviors, to collect data such that they could be analyzed to exhibit the known scientific laws or illustrate major scientific concepts. Thus, for example, students might do an experiment with carts moving on a slightly inclined air track to verify that acceleration is constant, velocity increases linearly, and distance traveled increases quadratically with time. The same laboratory task could be used to verify that there is a relation between the acceleration and the angle of the incline such that the maximum acceleration would be at 90° and would equal that of free fall. Students could thereby find out something about Galileo's effort to understand motion and learn about the history of science.[4]

The ethnomethodological orientation is different in that it seeks to understand how participants themselves discovered or learned, and how such noticing itself is a product of the locally produced, witnessable, accountable phenomenon of order in the setting. Whereas some ethnomethodological scholars argue that there are radical differences between laboratory science and school science – e.g., with respect to conceptual change (Greiffenhagen and Sherman 2008) – others show that there are numerous similarities between the two fields, for example, in the way that discoveries emerge from the endogenous organization of the activities themselves (Koschmann and Zemel 2009). For instance, in both instances initially vague 'its' evolve into definitive objects – a pulsar, the velocity of an object – in and through the situated inquiry of the parties involved. The authors thereby overcome the dichotomy between the work of scientists (who are said to do science authentically producing 'hot discoveries') and the work of students doing laboratory exercises (producing 'cold discoveries'). This research approach therefore acknowledges the tremendous, generally hidden order-producing work accomplished in the realization of laboratory exercises (Lynch et al. 1983). This work is no less authentic than the one of scientists. Given that there already exist some important and widely cit-

---

[4] However, see Garfinkel (2002, chapter 9) on the many things that students will not find out about the work of Galileo, for example, all those things Galileo has done or might have done when he lost his phenomenon.

ed ethnomethodological investigations of scientific laboratory practices (e.g., Lynch 1985), there is a wide open field for cognate investigations in science education that could lead to an elaboration of the similarities and differences between the practices and structures of work in the two settings.

Throughout this book, I use examples from an episode in an inquiry science lesson. Science educators became somewhat disillusioned with ready-made laboratory tasks, because students and teachers tended to take this part of the science course as motivational and less serious than the normal lessons characterized by teacher-dominated lectures. Even though '[l]aboratory activities appeal as a way of allowing students to learn with understanding and, at the same time, engage in the process of constructing knowledge by doing science' (Tobin 1990: 405), students often fail to understand *why* they are manipulating equipment in certain ways; and fixing the data to get the anticipated results and therefore good grades predominated over taking whatever was measured and trying to make sense of it.[5] The approach often was denigrated as 'cook book science'.

In an explicit attempt to give students opportunities to experience the vagaries of a discovery science and to learn about the nature of science in the ways it plays itself out in everyday scientific laboratories, some science educators began to promote, implement, and research 'open-inquiry' approaches (Roth 1995). In open inquiry, students designed investigations of their own interest, collected data, interpreted what they had collected, and reported their findings back to the collectivity (peers, teacher). In the process, students learned powerful data fitting procedures based on the least-square method, evaluated their findings with respect to those of other students doing similar experiments, and explained any deviations from anticipated findings by making reference to experimental design, data collection, or other sources of systematic error (e.g. Roth and Bowen 1994). One study that compares open and guided inquiry shows significantly higher performance levels on such factors as changes during inquiry and procedural understanding, whereas no differences were detected on other variables such as learning as a process and affective points of view (Sadeh and Zion 2009). In the face of high-stakes testing, with a primacy on recall and paper-and-pencil formats, which require competencies for success that are very different from those that are required for success in open inquiry science, it is not surprising that teachers and school exhibits little preference for this format of science learning.

An important finding of such research tends to be that motivation does not have to be introduced as an external factor in explaining what students do and teachers do not have to do to motivate students.[6] This is so because having chosen a particular motive for an inquiry, students experience a high degree of ownership over the research problem, process, and outcome as well as over the difficulties encountered. Students who often do not well in other approaches to learning tend to do well in open-inquiry, as shown in several studies where students who were desig-

---

[5] As one research study among undergraduate students showed, trying to fix the results are experiences that may shape what people do when they enter more advanced studies, such as conducting independent research for honors projects (Roth and Bowen 2001). 'Fibbing' and coming up with 'creative solutions' may become a way of life.

[6] In cultural-historical activity theory, the motive is a characteristic of collective activity; by participating in the activity, the individual subject subscribes to the motive (Roth 2004a; Roth and Lee 2007).

nated and treated as 'learning disabled' were among the most successful (e.g., Roth and Barton 2004). Thus, those students who do poorly when instruction and assessment emphasize written forms tend to do well when dealing with uncertainty, access to social and material resources, ownership over nature of problem and solution finding process are at a prime. In one open-inquiry physics course for upper elementary students – sixth- and seventh-grade students – five of the nine 'learning disabled' students ended up in the top quartile of the 25-student class in terms of their conceptual understanding as evaluated across different assessment formats (written, interview, discussion, practical) (Roth et al. 1999).

In many jurisdictions, inquiry is as an important dimension of the science curriculum. Because there is also a focus on learning specific content, the physics syllabus of Queensland, for example, also states that the students do not identify and define their own problems but 'negotiate' problems with the teacher, or students are asked to pursue research questions that the teacher designs. According to the syllabus, teachers 'must' provide scaffolding 'to help students complete the assessment' (QSA 2007: 22). However, 'the scaffolding provided should not specify the physics, or lead the student through a series of steps dictating a solution' (ibid: 22).

Bracketing

> To construct a scientific object also demands that you take up an active and systematic posture vis-à-vis 'facts'. To break with empiricist passivity, which does little more than ratify the preconstructions of common sense, without relapsing into the vacuous discourse of grand 'theorizing', requires not that you put forth grand and empty theoretical constructs but that you tackle every concrete empirical case with the purpose of *building a model*. (Bourdieu 1992: 233)

In the introductory section, I point to the fact that the everyday attitude and the everyday world surrounding world is the precondition for any science to emerge. It is therefore not surprising that preconstructions, expressions of a natural attitude, are pervasive in the sciences concerned with the everyday world (Bourdieu 1992), which it enters in the forms of preconstructions that the social scientist is not even aware of that it constitutes the pre-constructed. One of these pre-conceptions is to take the science teacher as imbued with 'power' 'over' students. Holding teacher accountable for a lesson, as if they, individual participants, were the causal determinants of what a living curriculum produces, is but another one of the preconceptions that a scientific science education has to question rather than accept. Preconstructions are dangerous because they become 'instruments of construction' (p. 233).

To practice a really scientific science of the natural world – the science classroom for science educators – the natural attitude has to be bracketed (Husserl 1976; Vygotskij 2005). Bracketing involves holding in abeyance the researcher's 'natural attitude', beliefs, experiences, understandings, and assumptions. It stops science educators short from using pre-constructed concepts without questioning them in the attempt to understand some aspect of the world of interest: the science classroom. The researcher continues to accept what is being bracketed – e.g., 'teacher power', 'student motivation', or 'interest' – but does not use it when attempting to understand and explain some aspect of the natural world. Once bracketed, the researcher focuses on *how* this or that aspect of the world *phenomenalizes* itself, that is, becomes a phenomenon such that his or her natural attitude or natural concepts include and index it. In this way the world is not negated, but the method merely counteracts the functioning of the natural attitude by rendering it temporally inoperative.

In the following, I provide a historical background of bracketing, explicate the ethnomethodological re-specification of Durkheim's aphorism about the thingy nature of social phenomena, provide a tutorial example exemplifying the ethnomethodological approach, contrast and compare formal analytic approaches and ethnomethodology, and articulate some phenomena science educators might want to bracket to specify the 'what more' there is to order in science classrooms.

Historical Origins of Bracketing in Phenomenology

Concretely, when science educators research events in a classroom, they accept the desks, chairs, chalkboards, writing implements, computers, or equipment as part of the natural world, as the background to anything that belongs to teaching science. But they also tend to accept the presence of other 'things' that are not quite as tangible: {knowledge}, {intentions}, {beliefs}, {power}, {motivation}, and the likes. All these 'things' are taken as really existing and explaining a world. To understand this world 'better and more completely than is possible in any way we see it by means of the naïve conception of experience' (Husserl 1976: 61), we require something like a 'science of the natural attitude' (p. 61). This science has to bracket, eliminate, the presuppositions that come from and with the natural attitude towards the situations that researchers tend to take for granted when they spend time to understand what is happening in science classrooms.

Even the natural sciences have their grounding in the Lebenswelt (Husserl 2008) or lifeworld. Bracketing therefore has to be applied to what the (social) sciences might have said about this phenomenon: 'So I *eliminate all of the sciences relative to this natural word*, as well as they are founded for me, as much as I admire them, as little as I think about objecting the least to them; I *make absolutely no use of their validity. I appropriate not a single proposition that belongs to them, even if there is perfect evidence for them; I use none of it, do not take it as a ground. ... I may only accept it after having dealt with it in the brackets'* (Husserl, 1976: 65, original emphasis). Here, as before, the results of the natural sciences, social sciences, and philosophy *are* accepted as other social facts: but not as explanatory resources. For Husserl the distinction between the different forms of consciousness and what to do to conduct really scientific research on the phenomenalization of the world in consciousness is so important that he returns at length to the issue of bracketing and why it is necessary.

In the natural attitude, people simply act in and towards a world. It is a form of everyday, unreflected, ordinary perceiving and experiencing the world. The character of the things that populate this lifeworld is that of things that are 'really' 'present at hand' (Husserl 1976: 107). People do not doubt those things that are given to them and serve them well in everyday life. The natural sciences and philosophy can be distinguished from the natural attitude in the sense that they produce logically ordered acts of thought; but, the objects of scientific research are the realities given in the natural attitude are determined and researched in a rigorous way. These realities therefore are disclosed in new ways to the inquiring spirit. The sciences, philosophy, and the natural attitude, therefore, share the way in which they accept the presence of the world in and to consciousness. They differ in the way they seek to understand this naturally given world.

Phenomenology, which is a radically different approach to a very different problem, begins by bracketing and locking out as a matter of principle the 'effectuation of all cogitative theses' (Husserl 1976: 107). That is, those theses that have already been accomplished in the natural attitude and the natural sciences are not allowed into the new science. Rather than living in these theses, rather than reproducing these theses, phenomenology engages in acts of reflection with these theses as their intentional object. Any explanatory device that serves the natural attitude and even the sciences – e.g., the notions of 'power', 'agency', 'structure' – are excluded, merely taken as other facts that the natural attitude and the sciences have produced. In his essay on the crisis of psychology, Vygotskij (2005) entirely sides with Husserl both on the nature of the problem and its resolution: 'I undertake to prove ... that only Husserl's and Feuerbach's formulas give a consistent solution to the problem' (ibid: 163).

Bracketing in Ethnomethodology

Throughout his work, Husserl was concerned with questions of consciousness, and, because of his focus on intentions and ideas, has been referred to with some legitimacy to be a metaphysical philosopher. However, his program of establishing a science of the natural attitude all the while bracketing it (its concepts) has found its way into sociology in a lineage that includes Husserl → Schutz → Garfinkel and has led to the emergence of ethnomethodology (Garfinkel 1967). Whereas Husserl's (1976) examples of phenomena are those of the natural world – his desk and the objects that are placed on it, his office/library – ethnomethodology takes Durkheim's aphorism as its point of departure and then proceeds with the social facts in a manner not unlike Husserl with material things. Just as Husserl bracketed the natural attitude with respect to investigations of our consciousness with respect to the things in the natural world, ethnomethodology brackets the natural attitude with respect to social facts by re-specifying and working out Durkheim's aphorism (Garfinkel 1991). Just as Husserl bracketed the natural attitude in his research of human consciousness, ethnomethodology brackets the natural attitude in the way it can be found in the everyday world and in the social sciences.

Ethnomethodology has emerged as a phenomenologically grounded reaction to the formal analytic approach in sociology. An important accomplishment in the theorizing of social phenomena that accompanied sociology, in its inception, is the recognition of social facts as phenomena sui generis that cannot be reduced to the individual. 'A thought that can be found in all particular consciousnesses, a movement that repeats itself in all individuals, are not because of that social facts' (Durkheim 1919: 11–12). Doing so would be confusing the manifestation of social facts in the individual person. Social facts are constituted by tendencies and practices of some group or community 'taken collectively' (ibid: 12). Social phenomena sui generis and their refraction in individuals are two things of very different kind. Social facts thereby 'take in this way a body, a sensible form that is particular to them, and constitute a reality *sui generis*, very distinct from the individual facts that manifest them' (ibid: 12, original emphasis). The point then is to describe, theorize, and understand social facts as such, not to reduce them to a composite of individual facts. The *documentary method* – designed to capture the 'interrelatedness of the different' and the 'existence of unity in the differences' (Mannheim 2005: 127) – accomplishes precisely that goal.

Ethnomethodologists refer to the work in the social sciences that identifies and explains social facts using quantitative or qualitative methods, the accomplishments of which are gathered under the notion of 'Formal Analysis (FA)' (Garfinkel 2007). FA technology describes and explains social facts. These are undisputed and accepted. However, ethnomethodology 'is proposing and working out 'What More' there is to the unquestionable corpus status of formal analytic investigations than formal analysis does, did, ever did, or can provide' (Garfinkel 1996: 6). Thus, '[e]thnomethodology's fundamental phenomenon and its standing technical preoccupation in its studies is to find, collect, specify, and make instructably observable the local endogenous production and natural accountability of immortal familiar society's most ordinary organizational things in the world, *and to provide from them both and simultaneously as objects and procedurally, as alternative methodologies*' (ibid: 6).

By means of the adverb 'procedurally', ethnomethodologists do not indicate their interest in process but their emphasis on the actual labor and living work that produces the phenomenon. This focuses us on important issues not generally taken into account in current science education research. Thus, a study may focus on the 'merged discourse' (Bellocchi and Ritchie 2011) that chemistry students displayed in their lessons. Whereas the researchers used their special methods – as per the above-quoted methods description – to identify 'merged discourse', they do not articulate the work of merging discourses or communicating by means of merged discourses or how participants' discourses when *novel* mergers are produced. To use an even simpler example, the same study states that 'the discussion on the spelling ends after Turn 42' (ibid: 779). But if the discussion, qua conversation, is a *social* phenomenon that *social* actors produce, then work is required to bring the event to an end. In fact, the researchers note that there is an beginning and an end, but there are no indications in the transcript fragment that the social actors themselves oriented to something like a beginning or an end. If there were an end from the perspective of the conversation, then it would be possible to specify the work that produces the ending; but if actors themselves do not orient towards an end, then it will be impossible to specify any work precisely because it has not been done. A legitimate beginning and end is produced when, for example, a teacher requests a student to take his turn and, once the student has completed the task, he is asked to take a seat and the next student is called upon (Roth and Thom 2009). In this case, the 'episode' is entirely identified, started, conducted, and ended *endogenously*, that is, from the inside. Not only did the student have a turn but that it is *his* turn is clearly demarcated from the preceding and following turns and in the way the transaction ritual of his turn unfolds (e.g., he responds before anybody else may respond to a teacher question).

In ethnomethodological studies, bracketing is effectuated by explicitly excluding 'the use of mental mechanisms, psychological actions, clinical psychological biographies, signed objects, and hermeneutics' (Garfinkel 1996: 13). Bracketing has been formally described in the following way. As example, we take what might be glosses on the part of formal analysis or based on the natural attitude on the parts of those who visit the science classroom under investigation throughout this book. Researchers or science teachers might gloss what they see by saying 'students are *investigating a phenomenon by means of self-directed inquiry'*, they may observe an instance of 'a teacher *using the triadic dialogue form'*, they appreciate 'the teacher's effort in *helping a weak student'*, or they might observe that 'Jane, she is only interested in *making a nice Chinese lantern but not in learning physics'*. It is indisputable that existing science education research has established a large and steadily growing body of work of this kind. To understand what it has not done, by and large, can be better understood after the following example of bracketing related to the stated glosses. Thus, whether a gloss is or has been made by a layperson or a researcher, it is formalized in the following way using one of the preceding glosses:

'doing {investigating a phenomenon by means of self-directed inquiry}'

Here, the gloss is placed in brackets; it constitutes a natural account ('notational particulars') (Garfinkel and Sacks 1986). 'Doing' refers us to the actual, living, *collective, sympractical* labor from which the social fact named in the gloss emerges. What is it people do in a science lesson, I ask, so that the members in the setting as much as observers *see* that students 'investigate a phenomenon by means of self-directed inquiry'. What is it the collective work of a teacher–student pair so that 'a science teacher using the triadic dialogue form' is a gloss that science educators might use to denote the situation. That is, bracketing does not mean that we make the contents that appears between brackets disappear; it does not mean that it is disputed. Rather, the question concerns the 'collective doing', 'collective labor', or 'sympractical work' from which whatever appears in the gloss emerges as an observable fact to which social actors orient themselves. Thus, in the mentioned study concerning the beginning and ending of a turn, beginnings and endings of a turn are produced in accountable ways: everyone present can hear the teacher's 'thank you' and see the student's returning to his seat, which co-occurs with the teacher's naming another student, who gets up and takes his turn. Ethnomethodology is interested in the *collective* 'doing', that is, the natural methods by means of which phenomena are produced and recognized by participants and observers

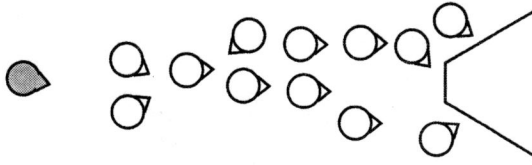

Fig. 1.1 Queuing for movie tickets is an example of an endogenously organized social event. A newcomer (grey) may be confused about the end of the line for one rather than the other movie.

alike. Here *collective* doing means that something is done that cannot be reduced to individual doings that then are added up or made to interact. Collective doing are irreducible social actions that require a unit of analysis that already is *social*.

A Tutorial Example: Queuing

Queuing is a good introductory example because it is such a pervasive but uninteresting *social* fact; ethnomethodologists use queuing as a prime tutorial example (e.g., Livingston 1987). We learn to queue and to recognize queues even without being taught explicitly because of the many concrete experiences of queuing we have in our lives by employing Mannheim's documentary method (see Garfinkel 2002). Queues are recognized daily, at a traffic light, on the motorway to work, at the supermarket checkout counter, at the movie ticket counter (Fig. 1.1), at the bus station, and so on. Queues are both pervasive and, despite the tremendous variations that exist among them, quite ordinary and unworthy of our attention. We 'automatically' and without trouble line up; and if the nature of the queue is problematic we do what it takes to get into line frequently without becoming aware of our doing. In such cases, we might ask, 'Is this the end of the line to movie X or movie Y?' or 'Are you waiting for …?' Similarly, when the first person in line is not walking up to the counter, the teller might repeat the call, 'the next one please!' or someone further back in the line might say 'there is an *open* one'. Those who staff a queue see and know when someone is attempting to 'cut in', whether an excuse is or may be legitimate or not (e.g., 'my plane leaves in a few minutes'). Those who staff a social phenomenon recognize when a newcomer is unaware that there is a lineup in the works, for example, in the local fishmarket (Fig. 1.2), and might tell the person to 'You got to take a number'. That is, the queue is a *social* phenomenon, requiring *collective* work, and this work provides the features required for recognizing the factual nature of what it brings about. That is, the work of queuing is *naturally* and *endogenously accountable* in and through its locally achieved product: the queue. The 'persons arrange themselves to exhibit the line that appear as the real existence of an order of service' (Garfinkel 2007: 15). They exhibit an orderliness that is 'produced and exhibited by <u>all</u> parties to the line that appears'. We can further see the social nature of the queue from the fact that it works even though within a few minutes or parts of an hour its staff has been completely exchanged. Moreover, a passer-by may note the 'same queue' in front of

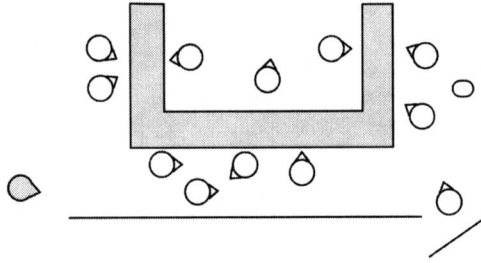

Fig. 1.2   Queuing in a fish market with a long counter (grey) may be confusing for the first-time shopper (grey) until he finds out that a next turn is organized by the number of a ticket to be taken from a dispenser to the right (small oval).

the blockbuster movie ticket window or at the cash register that they had seen when passing by or when entering the supermarket. That is, *the queue has a life of its own*, which has led to the expression of the 'immortal society', which continues in its ways even though its staff (i.e., citizens) are more or less completely exchanged within a certain number of years. 'Now we are getting into the WHAT MORE of the exhibited order of service's properties than that it is transcendental; specifically, that it is exhibitedly prior to and independent of any method or lexical device that is used to describe it. The existence of an order of service exhibits *itself* as the objective reality of the queue' (Garfinkel 2002: 254).

Formal Analysis Versus Ethnomethodology

The relationship between the labor that produces endogenously recognizable social patterns, social science methods, and social facts is displayed in Fig. 1.3 (e.g., Garfinkel 2002). Science educators, as other social scientists, report social facts. They employ special methods (Fig. 1.3, column 3) to tell readers how they arrived at the facts they describe (Fig. 1.3, column 4) from the data that they have collected (Fig. 1.3, column 2). Ethnomethodologists operate differently. They take the natural attitude and ethno-methods as all there is required to recognize the endogenous work that underlies the endogenously produced pattern. That is, ethnomethodologists never leave nor claim to leave column 2 (Fig. 1.3). They assume that social order is endogenously produced and made available by the participants themselves (note the '=' signs crossing the brackets versus the brackets appearing alone in column 4). This is also why they are not required to specify methods, because the very methods they describe are those that are used in producing and recognizing the local order. Social science methods need to be specifically described because the nature of the social facts reported in scholarly journals depends on the methods used; but these methods of producing order differ from those that the people studied themselves use. Issues such as 'reproducibility', 'quality', 'reliability', of the social fact and its prevalence depend on what social scientists do, because the social facts, to be observable, often depend on precisely what has to be done to re-

	How people do what they do (ethno-methods)	*Social science methods*	*Social facts ('researcher construction')*
Abstract pattern	( )	→	( )
Example 1: Social fact	(queuing)	ethnography	(queue)
Example 2: individual consciousness	(following instructions for a laboratory task)	Interpretive method, describing how pattern was extracted	(construction of the meaning of an instruction)
Example 3: Social fact	(telling Jane that we've changed her topic)	→	(Jane requires more guidance than other students)

Fig. 1.3   Relationship between ethno-methods, social science methods, and social facts.

produce an observation. The important point is that to employ social science methods requires the competencies mobilized in situation, a fact that is not generally acknowledged by formal analysts (Garfinkel 1967). For this reason, ethnomethodological studies, focusing on the actual endogenous order-generating work, produce 'incommensurable, asymmetrically alternate phenomena of order' (Garfinkel 1996: 9).

Formal analyses assume that the structures (patterns, themes, concepts, and categories) reported in scientific research articles are not self-evident or, to use a phenomenological term, 'apophantic', standing out and showing themselves from themselves. Rather, special methods – indicated in Fig. 1.3 by means of '→' signs – are required to identify patterns and, in their methods sections, social scientists specify what needs to be done to ascertain that the patterns reported can reliably be seen if the descriptions provided in the methods section are followed. The assumption is that '*only* methods of constructive analysis could provide – *only and entirely* – for any and every orderliness whatsoever, for every one of the endlessly many topics of order, meaning, reason, logic, or method' (Garfinkel 1988: 106). Moreover, these '*topics* of order*' had to be 'prepared for inquiry by formal analytic' (p. 106) methods and theory. Ethnomethodology, which includes conversation analysis, in contrast, begins with the observation that everyday practical affairs are '"naturally organized ordinary activities"' (p. 107), which not only produce order but also exhibit this order to participants. The phenomena of order, therefore, 'are immortal, ordinary society's common place, vulgar, familiar, unavoidable and irremediable *and* uninteresting "work of the streets"' (p. 108). The phenomena 'cannot be recovered with *a priori* representational methods. They are not demonstrable in the established terms of classical studies' (p. 107). They can only be observed in the details of the actual concrete achievement of the order itself, as available to, and used by, the members to the setting (or those who staff the social phenomenon in any particular case). In the ethnomethodological approach, therefore, Durkheim's social facts are 'society's locally, endogenously produced, naturally organized, reflexively accountable, ongoing, practical achievement, being everywhere, always, only, exactly and entirely, members' work, with no time out, and with no possibility of evasion, hiding out, passing, postponement, or by-outs' (Garfinkel 1988: 103). The social phenomena cannot be recovered from psychological interpretations of social facts or if 'ethnographic descriptions are explicated as psychological activities' (Garfinkel 1996: 18).

For Garfinkel (1996), the lesson of ethnomethodological studies is clear: to lose your phenomenon of order, all you have to do is use formal analytic methods. 'And in order to assure their loss in any actual case, do so with the methods of generic representational theorizing' (p. 18). Thus, rather than attempting to get at the general through abstraction of cases from their context, doing counting of the prevalence of their occurrence, and using abstract general descriptions, the ethnomethodological approach displays the making of order in the actual, concrete case of their application. Ethnomethodology is different, because it draws on the natural attitude, the natural competencies people deploy in the production of such things that social scientists denote as 'queue', 'power relation', 'excuse', 'interest', 'motivation', that is, the ethno-methods required for producing and recognizing the phenomenon of interest. For ethnomethodology, the recognition of the social fact and its production are but two manifestations of the same social phenomenon. Queuing, finding the end of the queue, taking one's turn, cutting in, pointing out an empty service slot etc. all are based on the recognition of the queue as queue or troubles in the queue. No additional method is required for understanding the work that phenomenalizes the queue. Knowing the structure of the work will allow us to know, in any particular case, what will be observed as a social fact. Knowing the social fact, however, does not allow us to understand the work that has led to its production (phenomenalization). We may gather all the different ways in which queuing might be observed, in all the variations of the irreducible social phenomenon, but all of these observations together do not get us at the work that makes queues come about and expressions of which staff members use in the maintenance of the queue.

What Science Educators Might Want to Bracket

A 'natural way' to think about what science educators (teachers, professors of science, science educators) may talk about what they do in their classes, irrespective of their epistemologies, could include 'trying to get a point across'. Bracketing means literally placing this gloss in brackets, '{trying to get a point across}', and asking questions about the work that is being done so that any one in the lesson or vicarious observers of a videotape thereof can see that 'trying to get a point across' is currently happening.

For science educators, the things of the natural world are unquestioned. When an oscilloscope is hooked up to a particular electrical circuit and exhibits a sinusoidal signal, constructivist science educators might talk about the signal constituting a representation or particular construction of whatever natural phenomenon there is. But they do not tend to question the presence of the signal itself. In the social sciences, the situation is different because social phenomena are not present in the same way as natural phenomena. Yet – and this is one of the foundations of sociology – the natural attitude does accept social phenomena as things.

Saying that some phenomenon is socially constructed does not implement Durkheim's notion of the social fact sui generis, and it does not focus on the *collective* work that is being done to make whatever is glossed a social fact. This is what ethnomethodologists understand as the 'What More?' to which its field orients over and above what every other formal analytic methods orients, whether these other studies are of the quantitative or qualitative kind. The distinction between EM and FA approaches further appears in the fact that FA approaches have to specify the method by means of which they reliably extract patterns from their data, whereas in the EM approach, the very natural attitude that allows us to see the social phenomenon is accepted as the only method required. Because it is the method of the people, emerging from the natural attitude, no further methodological specification is necessary.

Research Policies

This book is designed to look at *social* facts in/of science classrooms *sui generis*, that is, that inherently are of a collective nature and therefore cannot be explained beginning with the individual as the unit of analysis such that their contributions are added up or made to somehow *inter*-act to get out of the trap of individual and individualistic intentions. In such research that studies *inter*actions, the individualistic perspective has already been accepted; and research begins with individual actions that somehow are brought together to produce a social phenomenon. Conceiving of social phenomena where the minimum unit of analysis is *social* requires an approach that studies *trans*actions (Dewey and Bentley 1949/1999). In transaction, the parts cannot be identified independent of the whole and, therefore, one part cannot be understood independently of the other. We cannot therefore begin research by identifying something that will be a part of a whole (social) that could be isolated and understood in isolation. If we accept a conversation to be a social phenomenon, then we require a social unit of analysis to understand it. The *individual* speaker is not such a unit. The minimum unit of a conversation, to be social, requires at least a pair of turns at talk; and this pair of turns must be irreducible if the unit is to be a social one.

Both conversation analysis (Levinson 1983) and dialogical analysis (Vološinov 1930) make the turn or adjacency pair the minimal unit of analysis. Adjacency pairs or more complex forms of sequentially organized turn taking cannot be reduced to the individual speaker because each part of a pair (whole) requires the other and is intelligible only as a part of the whole. For example, in the following excerpt from the transcript (see Appendix B), there are four turns but only three full sequentially organized turn pairs. The first turn never is a true beginning but rather already constitutes a replique to a conversation in a historical context (Chrétien 2007). The first turn pair (turns 129–130) constitutes a question | reply unit, where the reply actually constitutes an affirmation of the assertion co-articulated in the locution ('I turn it off'). That is, we cannot know the nature of the locution in turn 129 until its 'social evaluation' in the situation is known, which comes with the next turn that also implicitly or explicitly (takes up) reports the preceding locution (Vološinov 1930). Similarly, we do not know the function of the second turn in a pair outside its relation with the preceding locution or situation, by which it has been addressed and to which it is a replique. At the same time, turn 130 also constitutes the opening of the next pair, which here is an assertion | question. Turn 130, which may be glossed in the expanded form as 'yes, you turn it off', constitutes the first part of a unit where the second part questions part of the preceding one. The question can be glossed as 'You turn it off *after you add the air?*' The next adjacency pair (turns 131 | 132) is again a question | affirmation. (Transcription conventions are provided in Appendix A.)

```
Fragment 1.1
   129 J: do I turn it off you turn it off
   130 C: yea.
   131 J: after you add the air?
   132 C: yea.
```

Adjacency or turn *pairs* are units that meet Durkheim's requirement of social facts to be irreducible 'things'. Adjacency pairs then cannot be viewed as being staffed by specific individuals but, as units, are social things. Turn or adjacency pairs constitute a reality that exceeds that of the individual; and these have the further advantage in that the dynamic of life is contained, for the unit is diastatic: spread across time and people.

Using the turn pair as unit also takes into account that the interlocutor currently not speaking is also active rather than inactive (e.g., Roth 2013). Take turn 129 as an example. For there to be a reply, Carrie has to actively attend to, listen to, Jane to be affected by the speech in order to appropriately reply. In fact, while listening, there is an active take-up in inner speech, whereby the words of the speaker are received (witnessed), commented upon, and retorted to simultaneously as the opening, forming part of the outward reply in the subsequent turn (Vološinov 1930). That is, Carrie is not inactive while Jane is speaking in turn 129. Her own locution in turn 130 is only the (external) expression of the complete response. Even though it contains only one word, turn 130 therefore implies reported speech and reporting context. Between these two exist a 'complex and tight dynamic relations. Without taking this into account, it would be impossible to understand one thing of the problem of reported speech' (ibid: 117). Similarly, for Jane to take an appropriate next turn requires attending to, listening, receiving, commenting, and 'retort' (add) to the locution so that in the course of turn 130, she is as active as Carrie. The turn pair therefore meets the requirement of capturing the *sym*practical work. Each locution is *joint* work rather than the work of only one person. Each word belongs to all interlocutors rather than only the speaker.

An immediate upshot of this discussion is that we cannot ever say what an individual locution *is*, for – as any part is always a part of a whole – locutions specify each other in a pair-wise fashion. Take the following turn from the latter part of the inquiry science lesson analyzed throughout this book:

```
Fragment 1.2a
   150 J: kay. but wouldnt that heat the air thats around the
          ouside?=
```

Because it has the grammatical structure of a question and because it is intonated in the way questions frequently are, researchers might be tempted to suggest that Jane asked a question and develop all sorts of implication from this. Attending to the intonation and other prosodic cues is important to the analyst, for these are the ways in which speakers provide their audiences with information about *how* a locution is to be taken: as quotation, literal speech, metaphor, commentary, critique, analogy, and so on (Vološinov 1930; Vygotskij 2005). Therefore, even if, as in the same example that these two authors discuss, the same word is said six times in a row, its function is never the same – not in the least because each new instance is heard against all the preceding ones as the indexical ground. To understand the *internal* dynamic of *this* conversation, we have to hear the word in the ways that the participants hear it. Consistent with our interest in *social* facts, the turn has to be considered as part of the minimum analytic unit of *social* phenomena. In the case of a *con*versation this minimum unit is a turn pair (Schegloff 2007). As the turn pair shows, the second part treats the forgoing as an 'interesting point' (turn 151). From the perspective of the conversation, therefore, turn 150 makes the point that is acknowledged in turn 151. This then is the new state of affairs that *the conversation has to deal with* rather than an individual.

Fragment 1.2b
```
150 J: kay. but wouldnt that heat the air thats around the
       ouside?=
151 C: ^NN. thats an interesting pOINt you mIght lIke to (.)
       commENT on that.
```

In this book, I am concerned with exhibiting the ethnomethodological approach with empirical materials, for which we seek to provide an ethnographically *adequate* description (McDermott et al. 1978). This means that I 'must articulate the same hesitant and momentary contexts that the natives are displaying to each other and using to organize their concerted behavior' (ibid: 246). In the present instance, 'the natives' are members of a physics classroom, staffing the particular social phenomenon that we, qua science educators, are interested in. Social phenomena of order exist in and are the retrospective result of transactive, sympractical, collective work that makes explicit everything required for noticing both order and deviation from it. The same competencies underlying the production of order endogenous to social phenomena are required competencies for us, qua analysts, who then *'can use the ways members have of making clear to each other and to themselves what is going on to locate to our own satisfaction an account of what it is that they are doing with each other'* (ibid: 247, original emphasis). The intent is to provide descriptions and explications that allow readers to take our analyses and, for every instance described, find the same order producing work in the science classrooms that they have access to.

A lot of (science) education research currently is caught up in detailing the special methods by means of which researchers develop patterns – i.e., (social) structures – from their qualitative data. The methods need to be detailed because they are assumed to be different from those that the research participants themselves use in making sense of, orienting towards, and acting in their lifeworld. A secondary problem immediately arises, for when these methods differ from those that participants themselves use, then a method can be judged adequate or inadequate to the particular research question that drives the research. In ethnomethodological work, this question does not appear at all, because the methods of the research participants for structuring the social events are the same that they use for perceiving them. When researchers use the same methods, then there no longer is a need to specify it, for the very research project exhibits the methods in use. There no longer is a question of the authenticity of research findings, whatever the type of authenticity.[7]

This approach is sometimes charged with objectivism. But this is not so. Rather, the researchers do everything so that the work that structures practical action is exhibited in and by research so that the specification of method becomes unnecessary because it is available in the account itself. The account is no more and no less objectivist than the research object, which is the work by means of which participants exhibit structuring work and its results – social structure as sociology's fact – *in and through their own actions*.

How, from within this framework, should we understand language as it is displayed in the science classroom not only for the other but also for the speakers themselves? In what consists mastery of natural language, where this 'mastery' is to be understood at the level and through the eyes of the participants? From an ethnomethodological perspective, natural language consists in this: 'In the particulars of his speech a speaker, <u>in concert with others,</u> is able to gloss those particulars and is thereby meaning differently than he can say in so many words; he is doing so over unknown contingencies in the actual occasions of interaction; and in so doing, the recognition *that* he is speaking and *how* he is speaking are specifically not matters for competent remarks. That is to say, the particulars of his speaking do not provide occasions for stories about his speaking that are worth telling; nor do they elicit questions that are worth asking, and so on' (Garfinkel and Sacks 1986: 165, original emphasis, underline added). The 'particulars' that the authors refer to are {glossing practices}, that is, the 'methods for producing observable and reportable understanding, with, in, and of natural language' (ibid: 164–165). These glossing practices serve to 'exhibit-*in*-speaking' and 'exhibit-*for*-the-telling' that speaking is understood and how it is to be understood. Thus, it is in speaking that the what Jane has said is exhibited as being an 'interesting point', and, it is exhibited-in-the-telling in the sense that I (or anyone else) can now report ('tell') that 'Carrie remarked on Jane's idea as an "interesting point"'.

---

[7] Constructivist research has to pose the question of authenticity (e.g. Guba and Lincoln 1989), because there cannot be a guarantee that members to a setting find anything recognizable in research results. This is so because research methods are different from the methods people use to produce social phenomena.

2

Glosses and Glossing Practices

> [T]alk itself, in that it becomes a part of the selfsame occasion of interaction becomes another contingency of that interaction. It extends and elaborates indefinitely the circumstances it glosses and in this way contributes to its own accountably sensible character. (Garfinkel and Sacks 1986: 165)

In science education, the predominant way of considering language is to look at its content, that is, what some saying is about. In chapter 1, I discuss the example from an Australian classroom where a student comments on a word spelled as 'wether', where an 'h' is missing to make it 'whether'. A typical analysis focuses on the spelling or on 'the play of words'. Accordingly, language is about spelling, about the fact that students talk about sheep in a chemistry classroom, or about using everyday language to make play on words. But language first and foremost is a means to conduct social intercourse (Vygotskij 2005). In the course of conducting such intercourse, language itself becomes part of the occasion. This is shown precisely in the episode, where the spelling of a word becomes an issue. The unhearable difference between /'wɛðə(r)/ ('whether') and /'wɛðə(r)/ ('wether'), one that could have been extended to include /'wɛðə(r)/ ('weather'), not only is another contingency of that trransaction but itself a topic of discussion. Whether /'wɛðə(r)/ is to be heard as 'wether', 'whether', or 'weather' does not tend to be a problem in competent natural language use, for it is not the sound-word that 'means' but the situation as a whole. It is the situation itself that makes for, allows, and affords the distinctive hearing. What the researchers do, in their paper, is this: they work up an analysis designed to overcome the indexicality of the language. They write, for example, that Trev … noted that Mal had incorrectly spelled the word "whether"' (Bellocchi and Ritchie 2011: 779). But this, as I suggest in my brief re-analysis of the extract in chapter 1, is not what Trev notes or does. Grammatically there is a query about whether there should be an 'h' after the 'w', which is heard as a 'worry about grammar in chemistry'. It is that worry about grammar in chemistry that becomes an issue *from within the situation* rather than the spelling that the researchers are writing about. We may therefore take the authors' analysis as a *gloss* of the kind that tends to characterize qualitative research generally and ethnographic research specifically (Have 2004).

On Glossing

Glossing is not something specific to researchers; we uses glosses every day and all of the time. However, it is not the contents of the glosses that is of interest to ethnomethodological studies. Rather, everyday {glossing practices} themselves are the central issue in and research interests of ethnomethodology. The term {glossing} is used to denote the fact that we cannot ever state in so many words, that is, directly, what we mean to say. In fact, as readers we make out what a text says even when and precisely because the text does not actually say it. For example, a reader of an early text of mine introducing an ethnomethodologically oriented study noted 'There is something about the text that seems to communicate that most folks are not aware of ethnomethodology and those who are aware of it have not used it correctly'. That is, the reader communicated to me that there was 'something about the text' that 'seems to communicate' what it did not itself state: 'most folks are unaware of ethnomethodology' and 'those who are aware of it have not used it correctly'. That is, something in the text was such that that reader could attribute all sorts of attitudes and intentions. In fact, authors of such statements recognize this possibility of the disjunction between intention and their own impressions: 'You may not intend this and you might not be surprised that I am reading it this way'. The fact that we always say more than we mean to say, more than what we intend to say, can be seen from this last quotation. Thus, its author also communicates that I know him/her sufficiently well so that it makes sense to state that I would not be surprised that s/he was reading my text in the way s/he read it.

We learn from these examples that social actors use words to denote states of affair but precisely what the words denote is clarified to some extend through the extended use of the word. In the ethnomethodological literature, brackets are often used – here '{...}' – to enclose such terms.

Etymologically, the term derives from the ancient Greek γλῶσσα [glõssa] and Latin *glõssa*, tongue, language, foreign language, a foreign or obscure word. One of its present-day senses is precisely that: an obscure word. In another sense, *gloss* denotes a word inserted on a page (between lines, in the margins) that explains, translates, elaborates, or otherwise renders a difficult or foreign word of the text. In a more extended sense, *gloss* may denote a comment, explanation, or interpretation. *Formulating* what is happening, has happened, or will happen in social events constitutes one way of employing glosses. For example, in Fragment 2.1, Carrie does not just begin to talk to Jane but she *formulates* that talking to Jane is the event, which, in this case, is supposed to be happening: 'I better talk to Jane first' (turn 001).

Fragment 2.1
```
→ 001   C:    okay. (0.24) OH; ((moves toward Jane)) i better talk
→             to JAne first. (0.24) okAY:. (1.63) changef plA:Ns.
```

Fig. 2.1 The teacher Carrie, in walking towards Jane *formulates* what is going to happen: 'I better talk to Jane first' (turn 001).

```
002       (0.26)
003   J:  U::M::: ((head sideward, gloss: disappointment on
           face, Fig. 2.1))
```

Here, there is a future orientation in the formulation even though grammatically the future tense is not employed. In part, this move *may have been* occasioned by the fact that Carrie actually moves from the back of the classroom towards Jane, who is oriented to the front and side (Fig. 2.1). But this formulation is part of the sym-practical and transactional work accomplished by the two participants that opens a classroom episode, *marked as such by the members to the setting themselves.* That is, the 'episode' is not defined as such by an excerpt that the researchers extract from their data sources but rather, the episode is defined by the members them-selves. As shown below, the teacher (Carrie), the student (Jane), and the researcher present each provides a gloss of what *has happened* after the two have closed out this segment of the lesson.

There is a pause and then a statement: 'change of plans' (turn 001). This may elaborate the 'better' that has preceded, because – if heard as an announcement of future things to come, that is, as a change in what has planned apparently in refer-ence to Jane – what the latter would be doing during this lesson that just started would change. Carrie not only articulates what is anticipated to happen, here real-ized because, *after the fact*, we can say that it *actually* happened, but also says 'I *better* talk to Jane first'. *What* she says by using 'better' is not evident in the saying itself. But it may be disclosed in the talking that happens, or in a gloss (descrip-tion) that Carrie might provide after everything has been said and done. Even without taking recourse to subsequent parts of the events – illegitimate in and for the process of establishing a *first-time-through* account – we may want to try and anticipate what might be coming by investigating the next few seconds. Following a brief pause (turn 002), there is an interjection ('u::mm::'), the second part of a turn pair that expresses the social evaluation of what has preceded.

Fragment 2.2
```
003   J:   U::M::: ((head sideward, gloss: disappointment on
```

```
            face))
004         (0.76)
005    C:   uMM::tmake dlIfe EA:sier; (0.31) <<all>okay>; ..HHH
            UUm (0.42) <<len>it has (0.22) bin=decided that it is
            too dIFficult.> kAY:? ((187→300 Hz) ((head sideward,
            gaze down))
006    J:   <<plaintive>i=just=found=out=a=way=to='dO=`it.>
            ((318Hz))
```

The pitch begins with a high value of 408 Hz and, after being sustained for a while, descends to 194 Hz. The transcriber noted that the interjection can be heard as 'disappointment'. In fact, the next speaking turn responds both to the change of plans, providing a reason for it, and a reply to the interjection: 'to make life easier'. That is, what the formulating gloss in Turn 001 really says, in describing that the talk to Jane 'better' occurs 'first', might anticipate a possible disappointment; but it also anticipates the 'change of plans', which, the earlier it is enacted, the better it is for Jane, because, as the subsequent talk shows (see chapter 3), Jane would not be 'losing more time' on something that 'has been decided that it is too difficult' (turn 005).

Ethnomethodology is less interested in the particular glosses used than it is in the work that glossing practices achieve in the setting. That is, in this approach, glossing practices are a topic of research. Glossing practices, therefore, are recognized to be integral aspects of practices by means of which social structure is produced and recognized, and these practices, as the introductory quotation to this chapter shows, become part of the situation as but another of its contingencies. In the present situation, it is part of the opening of a talk about a change of plans. This glossing talk 'extends and elaborates indefinitely the circumstances it glosses' (Garfinkel and Sacks 1986: 165), that is, there is a reflexive nature in that the gloss both *is about* the circumstances and *(becomes) part of* the circumstances. In so doing, the gloss 'contributes to its own accountably sensible character' (ibid: 165). Thus, for example, the statement 'I better talk to Jane first' not only formulates what is to come but in itself becomes part of the context for whatever comes next. This is consistent with the sociological approach to language that has arisen in the Bakhtin circle, whereby a word, when repeated, no longer 'means' or functions in the same way as during its first articulation in the situation (Vološinov 1930). This is so because, in having been uttered for a first time, the word, in its second occurrence, can be heard *as a second* rather than a first occurrence: the context now includes the first occurrence so that the very fact that the word is uttered for a second time becomes significant.

Glosses may be used to point to complex processes and events. For example, when asked later about some aspects that stood out to her in the lesson, Carrie explicitly referred to the exchange with Jane: 'I had to tell Jane that we've changed her topic'. This phrase glosses what had been an exchange between the two that lasted over 5 minutes. Below, following a brief description of the setting, I provide and elaborate on the glosses that different members to the setting – teacher, student, and researcher – provided afterwards.

Setting

The social facts described in this book were derived from 16 video-recorded lessons (2 hours each) of one 11th-grade physics class in which individuals and paired groups each worked at completing one from about six possible extended experimental investigations (see chapter 8 on some of their specification in the state syllabus). The statement for each extended experimental investigations was deliberately general and open to interpretation. For example, the rising bubble extended experimental investigations simply stated: 'A vertical tube is filled with a viscous fluid. On the bottom of the tube there is a large air bubble. Study the bubble rising from the bottom to the surface'. Students were asked to design a set of experiments that was expected to lead them to a deeper understanding of the phenomenon, in this case, the conditions under which an air bubble would rise to the surface of the fluid, and the details of its trajectory to the surface. They had to write and submit a report of their extended investigation at the conclusion of the 10-week term. The grade they received would be the only form of formal assessment for the entire term.

The class in which the video recordings were made was one of three physics classes at this grade level in the school. All members of this class from an independent school for girls had encountered a similar, though less demanding, form of open inquiry in their previous year of general science. Their teacher Carrie was a beginning teacher in her first year at the school. She was a former research engineer with considerable commercial product-development experience in Australia and Europe.

Even though the final reports varied in quality, the physics teachers who shared responsibility for assessment decisions across the classes judged all but one report from this class to be satisfactory. In this book I focus on the exchange between this student (i.e., Jane), her teacher (i.e., Carrie), the researcher, and other students to show how bracketing is effected in studies that invoke ethnomethodology. Jane selected the lantern investigation, which required students to 'Design and make a [paper] lantern powered by a single tea-light that takes the shortest time (from lighting the candle) to float up a vertical height of 2.5 m. Investigate the influence of the relevant parameters. (Please take care not to create a risk of fire!)'. The major reason for selecting Jane's exchanges with the teacher and peers was that her extended experimental investigations was modified just two weeks into the project due to unanticipated complications with burning candles required to raise the lantern, as experienced in the other classes, and the work done by the teacher and student in these transactions was observable. At this early stage, Jane had not yet attempted to elevate her lantern design, despite purchasing materials to build a lantern. The episode selected for analysis focuses on an exchange between Carrie and Jane that begins with Carrie breaking the news of the modification required.

Participants' Glosses

The analyses reported and elaborated in the subsequent chapters of this book concern one 5'11" episode as defined, produced, and later pointed to by the members to the setting as something that had stood out for them. The direct (rather than vicarious) witnesses talk about it as the 'change of plans' from the original to a revised task definition for a self-directed inquiry project. After having approached Jane from behind (Fig. 2.1), Carrie sits next to her at the laboratory table on which there are many of the materials that the student had prepared (and bought) for her investigation (Fig. 2.2). Throughout the event, the two sit in this way, face-to-face, talking about what Carrie formulated as a 'change of plan'. In this section, I present different glosses that are associated with these events, including that the teacher (Carrie), the student (Jane), and the researcher provided. I add a fourth type of glossing for parts of the event, which were produced by the person producing the raw transcript. In the subsequent account of the event, which takes a first-time-through approach, these glosses are explicitly bracketed, that is, eliminated as having any explanatory value and existing merely as social facts next to all other social facts within and surrounding the episode. The analysis then specifies the lived work by means of which the order described in the after-the-fact provided glosses has been achieved. Each gloss, though pertaining to the same sympractical work, constitutes a concrete index to the event that is experienced and manifests itself in different ways.

Gloss 1: 'I had to tell Jane that we've changed her topic ... and Jane did balk at it all'

Following the lesson from which the fragment to be analyzed was extracted, the researcher had an interview with the teacher. In response to the question whether 'anything stands out from that session', Carrie responded, as stated above, 'I had to tell Jane that we've changed her topic'. The researcher and teacher then engaged in a conversation in which this gloss of the lesson segment was elaborated. Carrie explained what she was doing and why in the following words:

> Jane is sort of, towards the bottom of the list as far as physics achievement in that class goes. [So what would that be?] Scraping a sound. Technically Linda has a lower mark but she was ill and almost didn't do a piece of assessment but did it. So discounting that, which was sort of abnormal, Wanda and Jane are lower down. So Jane is really just scraping through. And she's doing physics because her dad wants her to do physics, I think, really and she struggles with it, which is, I always thought that that topic wasn't the best for her because it's not as straight forward and the other groups doing the same topic in other classes have also had a lot of trouble getting anything to work at all. They're meant to be making a lantern rise through light candles. We have simplified the problem and adding hot air to the lantern, seeing how quickly it can rise. ... Andrew [department head] changed [the wording of

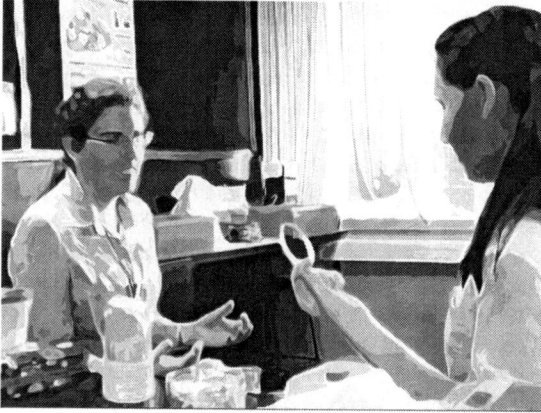

Fig. 2.2   Artistic rendering of the instant when the teacher Carrie talks to Jane about a 'change of plans'. The laboratory desk is littered with the materials Jane has purchased and brought to complete her project.

the problem] because there's a dozen other classes doing that problem who haven't been able to get anything done so Andrew decided that something had to be done about it, so changed the kind of direction of it all. Yes it was very specific what now is the direction and her variables are still up to her. Whether she changes the volume of the lantern or the shape of it or the temperature which she gets the air to before she lets it go or whatever. ... So adding hot air through a hairdryer or something like that. Or heating it by passing air over a hot element which is a hairdryer. We haven't specified using a hairdryer but how else do you heat air without using a flame. ... So and Jane did balk at it all. As much as it's making life easier for her, she wants to do her own thing so hopefully it doesn't put her off too much and she does get on with it. She's also not working with anyone. ... I don't think she is as interested in physics as she is in singing, music and ... when she does do a little bit of something she'll let you know, 'cause it's rare. Anyway so that was probably a fairly important thing that happened today and yes, I'll try and give her more guidance to try and get her doing things so she can get to ... It appears to me that she doesn't want to be seen to not know things. This is the whole point, they don't know things and they're meant to be trying to find things out and the other girls will say, I don't know. Whereas she spouts all these words that, when you add them up, don't say much at all. I was, I sort of knew that she wouldn't be particularly happy with it and I guess I approached her with the idea that I wanted her to feel that it was a good thing rather than meaning she'd done all this work and it was wasted etc. ... That was the aim of the conversation to let her know that this was what was happening but have her feel that it was okay.

In the end, Carrie summarized and glossed the notable character of the event by saying: 'Yes, it was different to the run of the mill kind of trouble shooting type things that are going on'. Elsewhere during the interview, she also said about the exchanges she has had with Jane: 'I guess I feel, I feel a bit more aware of making sure I say things that won't, I guess, upset her in a way, whether it's how I say it or how I try and put things to make sure she doesn't get off track. ... Not so much upset Jane, but not have Jane upset'.

I take this to be a natural, after-the-fact account of what has happened, as one of the two participants and witnesses provided it. Neither the phenomenological nor the ethnomethodological approach criticizes members for their accounts. In neither approach do researchers belittle or ironize members for the contents or the methods of their accounting. Thus, researchers do not evaluate a student statement as being a 'misconception' or states what a student or teacher should have done. This kind of research, in phenomenology or ethnomethodology, simply brackets such accounts seeking to understand what the structure of the labor (practical action) is that goes into producing the episode that the teacher here accounts for in her natural-attitude based discourse. These are precisely the kinds of descriptions in the social domain that Husserl (1976) develops a method for researching at the level of the individual. Carrie tells us a lot about intentions, understanding, knowledge about the students, presuppositions, guesses, and the likes that 'underlie' doing what she had to do: tell Jenny that we've changed the topic.

This kind of account is not uncommon. In fact, I watched the video first with the researcher and graduate students working on the project, the researcher, who had videotaped the classes and interviewed teacher and students, used the same kind of explanations for what happened and why. In the analyses I advocate and employ here, nothing of the things that appear in the glosses can be used to construct an explanation. 'Everything' has to be subject to be placed in brackets, and, thereby, taken out of playing a role in the analysis other than being among the range of facts in the case. Even 'teacher', 'student', 'power', or 'identity' cannot be used as explanatory resources, for, in an approach that takes social facts sui generis, any unit of analysis cuts across these categories. This is why they require bracketing.

Gloss 2: 'Is that back to the drawing board for you?'

The researcher, who had videotaped the exchange, expresses his understanding of the episode he had just witnessed in the question he posed to Jane immediately after the teacher has left. He asked, 'Is that back to the drawing board for you, Jane?' He subsequently offers an assertion and question, 'You can still do it at home, can't you?', which affirms as possibility to continue the project but that comes with some unstated drawback. The original assertion and question is in fact a social commentary (Vološinov 1930), a response to the witnessed scene. That is, in this situation and in the language of the teacher (Carrie) and student (Jane) there is something that provides for the possibility of hearing and seeing the scene as one that has consequences circumscribed by the gloss 'going back to the drawing board'. This description is 'authentic' in the sense that Jane replies by providing an affirmative. The descriptions turns out to be recognizable *within* the situation and as an account of an event that multiple members to the setting have witnessed and do/can provide accounts for.

If we had had the opportunity to ask the researcher afterwards what he had meant by the statement 'going back to the drawing board', or, rather, what in the situation was such that he – and in fact Jane and he – found it appropriate to use the expression, then he might have elaborated further, told us about the 'change of plans', about 'Jane trying to continue with her project', and so forth. When we watched the videotapes together, he did talk about Jane {doing poorly}, about {not really wanting to do physics}, or about {being more interested in how things look rather than in the physics concepts}. That is, he did provide something of the 'more' that he did not originally say in the expression 'going back to the drawing board'. But this 'more' has been in the form of more glosses to elaborate an initial gloss. We can clearly see how even researchers use everyday ways of talking to do what we might gloss as {lay sociology} or {lay psychology}. In fact, natural language provides us with all the resources required to do just that. But, and this is a central point in this book, to move towards a more rigorous form of research, we might bracket for a while this or that gloss and investigate what the work is by means of which members to the setting make available to others, for example, that they {do not really want to do physics} or that they are {more interested in how things look rather than in the physics concepts}.

Gloss 3: 'Yea, it's back to the drawing board, I don't know what to do now'

When the researcher asked Jane, immediately following the exchange with Carrie, whether that is back to the drawing board for her, Jane noded. We might render what Jane said during the interview in this way:

> It sucks. … It's really annoying, because I had everything planned and I knew what exactly I wanted to do. And it's like when I first got it, I was like 'Yes this is the one that I want to do out of all of them', and now it's sort of, you know, but … [the main problem] was trying to get the right weight so that the candle could lift it off. And I found something that would do it last night but – I mean, mum and I went shopping and bought all these stuff, and it was fun and like, yea. [You can still do it at home, can't you?]. Ea, like, now that it's sort of you know, I don't know. I have to come up with a good reason for a science experiment so, I mean I can do it at home but like I just – I don't know what to do now, so.

In this gloss of the situation, Jane describes to/for/in-the-language-of the researcher the impact the meeting has on her project, that she has found a solution and designed an experiment, that she already had bought the equipment and materials needed. There clearly is an emotional quality in her description, too, disappointment not being able to do the experiment that she wanted to do out of all those offered. We find the articulation of coming up with a good reason for the science experiment, and such a reason appears to have existed in her initial project, such as finding the right weight so that the lantern could lift off with the candle.

Whereas the gloss sort of gives us the gist of what was said, it does ascribe what was said to Jane, which actually has not been the case. As any social situation, the one in which the researcher talks to Jane is the result of the sympractical engagement of members to the setting. That is, the gloss ascribed to Jane is the result of an transactionally produced relation with the researcher (R) the full transcript of which is given in Fragment 2.3.

Fragment 2.3

```
001   R:   is that back to the drawing board for you jane.
002   J:   ((nods.))
003   R:   how is that.
004   J:   its sucks.
005   R:   how does this make you feel.
006   J:   its really annoying because i had everything planned
           and i knew what exactly i wanted to do, and its like
           when i first got it i was like YES this is the one
           that i want to do out of all of them and now its sort
           of () you know () but
006   R:   what was the main problem.
007   J:   well i was trying to get the right weight so that the
           candle could lift it off
008   R:   ah yea yea yea
009   J:   and i found something that would do it last night but
           i mean, mum and i went shopping and bought all these
           stuff, and it was fun and like yea
010   R:   i guess you can still do it at home cant you.
011   J:   yea like now that its sort of you know i dont know i
           have to come up with a good reason for a science ex-
           periment so i mean i can do it at home but like i
           just i dont know what to do now so
012   R:   you know they have a lantern festival in taiwan
           ((Stop of tape.))
```

Jane did not just dump some contents of her mind onto a sheet of paper or record-ed, through her voice, on a tape. Rather, what is attributed to Jane has been occa-sioned by questions, which again had been occasioned by the preceding events. This account, here, clearly is the product of a social relation – a researcher and a student who had signed up for the research. What is being said and how it is said, in each of the two interlocutor's case, is *for* the other. It is not Jane's talk inde-pendently of the researcher's talk. There is one conversation with two voices, and what and how these voices speak is a function of the relation, the social situation rather than one voice making the other voice articulate what is in the mind behind it. This relation is produced simultaneously together with the talk about whatever the topic is. The text of the talk also produces the *con*text of the talk.

The talk is initiated by what chapter 4 discusses under the heading of formulat-ing. The researcher, in saying 'is that back to the drawing board for you' *formu-lates* the conversation that just has occurred. That is, it provides the 'gist' or 'es-sence' of a conversation in a conversation, which here, directly extends and is about the one preceding it. The point is not just that the researcher articulates this formulation but that it is formulated for Jane, the recipient. The formulation there-fore exists for both (it is in-the-telling and for-the-telling); and the nod that is pro-duced in reply is but the confirmation of an active reception of this formulation. Although the phrase comes from the researcher's vocal cords, from the perspective of this conversation, the formulation is a joint production as it involves an offer of a formulation and an acceptance. The formulation, from the perspective of the conversation as a *social* phenomenon exists only in and through the offer | acceptance pair and, therefore, is diastatically spread across and separated by that pair. Each part, offer and acceptance, is but a manifestation of the higher unit, which is the formulation as a social phenomenon.

Gloss 4: Transcriber's Comments

We actually find another type of gloss in the data: the transcriptions themselves. This begins with the original, raw transcript in the way that the graduate student employed on the project provided it. Even though the speakers do not employ commas, periods, and question marks, such forms of punctuation indicate just what the transcriber, apparently competent in the natural English language, hears (and sees) as going on. Thus, for example, at the end of the first speaking turn, we read 'Ok?' The question mark indicates that the transcriber has heard a question. Similarly, there are question marks in the third turn, which, following standard grammatical conventions of the written English language mark the presence of a question.

C: Ok, Oh, I better talk to Jane first. Ok change of plans Mmm to make the life easier, it has been decided that it is too difficult. Ok?
J: I just found out a way to do it.
C: Er … but so it might still work for the change of plan. It's on Moodle, the new statement but it is to do with having a lantern with hot air added to it by means other than using a flame, such as, can you think about anything? Hot air (pause), where do you get the hot air from?

We have to ask, just what is it in the talk itself that allows the transcriber to hear a question. Whereas this might be more obvious in the third turn, where the grammatical structure of two phrases ended by this punctuation form is that of a question (i.e., 'Can you think about anything?' 'Where do you get the hot air from?'), it is much less evident in the case of the first question mark: 'Ok?'. Competent speakers of natural language know that a rising intonation (pitch) tends to be heard as a question whereas falling intonation in the course of a phrase tends to be heard as a statement. The two ways of marking the phrase go together, because the intonation of a phrase such as 'Where do you get the hot air from?' often falls toward the end (Roth 2010). This means that the grammatical structure of the phrase is that of a question but the intonational structure is that of a constative statement. On the other hand, a constative statement that is offered as a replique to a question statement may be followed by a question mark indicating rising intonation. In this case, a statement is made all the while a question is raised: depending on the next turn, this may be heard as the student being uncertain about her response (see discussion of turn 012).

The glosses are also present in the transcriptions that I produced for the purposes of this book. These glosses appear in my transcripts literally bracketed: in double parenthesis and italicized or triangular brackets (chevrons), when there are markers as to the quality of voice. The transcriber, using everyday language, hereby provides descriptions of what the persons can be seen to be doing. There is very little to be doubted about these glosses, for these are of the nature that most or even any other observer would agree upon that this is what can be seen and heard. Such glosses pertain to facial expressions (e.g., gaze is averted, pensive) or ways of hearing a voice (e.g., assertive, subdued). Readers should take these descriptions for what they are: natural language glosses that mark a particular manifestation of the totality of the episode.

There were other markers of glosses, which have been changed in the production of the full transcript as presented here. For example, the transcriber of the initial, raw, word-for-word transcript used punctuation to structure the text. That is, a comma marked that something has been heard as a clause, a question mark is a gloss that something of questions, a period marks the end of a statement. All of these are glosses, because what we have in fact is an uninterrupted soundtrack; and, when there are voices, there are no punctuation marks. The transcript used here, on the other hand, marks what can be indisputably seen and heard because punctuation merely marks prosodic features (unless marked as a gloss).

Researcher's Formulations of Work and Glosses

In the preceding section, I present three glosses and a description of the glossing practices that transcribing embodies. But there is more to glossing practices, which are, in fact, the standard approach in social scientific research. For example, when ethnographers describe situations using a range of literary devices – which themselves change in the course of the history of ethnography – then they use glosses (Have 2004). The texts provided in Gloss 1 and Gloss 3 are of a specific form. They appear as narratives *as if* the participant herself had said these words and in this way, even though the researcher's questions are inserted in parentheses. The ethnographer may also write that a particular excerpt exhibits the 'opening of the bringing of "bad news"' or that in a particular segment of the videotape and transcript, the participants 'elaborate a change of plan'. These are perfectly legitimate ways in which standard ethnography reports is findings and denotes the phenomena it observes. Glosses and glossing practices, therefore, are integral parts of the resources available to ethnographers in their everyday work.

Ethnomethodological approach does not contest such practices or their validity. In fact, ethnomethodologists acknowledge the tremendous accomplishment of traditional social sciences in producing a corpus of studies that provide professional researchers glosses of the everyday world. Ethnomethodology is not interested in the function of glosses as resources. Rather, ethnomethodological inquiry makes these glosses its topic. In fact, such inquiry may mark some phrase as a gloss, by placing it in glossing marks '{…}', and then elaborate in just what the work consists that allows events to be seen and understood by means of the phrase. In chapter 1, I provide a tutorial example of {queuing}, where something in the everyday world recognized as an instant of 'queuing' is specified in terms of the mundane work that actually produces this order that we denote by the term 'queue'. Even though members of a queue may find it useless to describe the work (e.g., how they scan the counters in a bank to see whether there is an opening that would signal that it is their turn in the order of service), their very actions of competently queuing *exhibits* their practical understanding of how a queue works.

In chapter 3, where I exemplify an analysis of a brief classroom episode that participants had picked out and identified as something important. The teacher, Carrie, had glossed the event as one in which she 'had to tell Jane that they've changed her topic' and, in the event itself, she had announced in an anticipatory way as 'I better talk to Jane first. Okay. Change of plans'. She thereby announced that she would be talking to Jane and that a 'change of plans' was in the making. Taking into account a participant's own words, I render the event by the gloss {change of plans [in student-centered inquiry science]}. As such, this phrase is but a name or label for a complex event sequence. This gloss does not provide us with an account of the sympractical work by means of which the change of plans comes about. 'Sympractical' here denotes the fact that the change of plans *in this situation* is a collective achievement that arises from the mutual engagement of the participants. The adjective sympractical points to the fact that there is a joint orientation in the social situation, accomplished through their joint work rather than being instituted by one person (e.g., the teacher). This joint work does not arise from the addition of individual work, such as 'Carrie asks' and 'Jane responds'. Rather, the *sym*practical nature of the work is marked by the fact that the minimum unit of analysis irreducible includes both: '"Carrie asks" | "Jane responds"'. This unit constitutes the joint work, requires both parts to be realized.

In my presentation of the events, I use glosses in the way an ethnographer might do, but only to give a provisional descriptive label to what a stretch of transaction might look like to an observer. The analysis itself focuses on the *sym*practical work, which, consistent with the descriptions in chapter 1, exists in the 'doing' of the figure

'Doing {change of plans in student-centered inquiry science}'.

The question becomes, 'How do the members to the setting *together* achieve the change of plans?' 'By what means is the change of plans enacted?' 'What are potential obstacles to the change of plans?' Rather than saying that the participants 'negotiated' this or that we are interested in the work by means of which a stretch of talk comes to be recognized and produced as a {negotiation}.

For the purpose of the presentation of the classroom episode in chapter 3, I (rather than the participants) broke the episode into 9 sections:

– {opening the bringing of 'bad news'}
– {elaborating change of plans}
– {disallowing experiment with waxes}
– {arguing for and against maintaining the original plan}
– {pleading and closing out topic}
– {changing topic to talking theory}
– {reasserting plan and getting compliance}
– {changing topic for elaborating possibilities in changed plan}

– {ending a meeting}

Each of these ethnographic descriptions is marked as a gloss, which in itself is not very interesting. What *is* interesting is the work – denoted by the verb 'doing' that precedes each gloss – that produces something that we recognize as 'opening the bringing of "bad news"', 'elaborating change of plans', or 'ending a meeting'. Thus, the emphasis of the inquiries in the chapters that follow is in the *doing* of whatever is visible and recognizable as the 'opening of a meeting', 'closing of a meeting', and so on. Not only is there something visible and recognizable but also that we can teach it – the phenomena are *instructably* what they are. Just as we can teach a novice what is or should be a 'foul' in a game of soccer, and why it is so, we can teach, *and do so in and as part of everyday situations*, how to recognize that {pleading} is going on or that a {closing out [of] topic} has occurred.

Although these glosses are produced on the part of an ethnographically oriented researcher (me), they do so in ways that the participants themselves could have and even might have used when talking about the event to other people. For example, Jane might have told her mother explaining why she no longer needed all the materials that they had bought together that she 'begged the teacher' to let her go on she was not allowed to do so. She might also say that she really tried her best to argue for and convince the teacher to let her stick with the original plan. Thus, in choosing these glosses, I oriented towards descriptions that the actors themselves might use or would recognize as describing what they have done.

Traditional interests in science education include 'power', 'identity', 'third space', 'misconceptions', 'negotiation', or 'cognitive development'. In the research praxis described here all of these terms would be taken as glosses. What is the work by means of whatever these notions refer to is produced by the members to the setting? What is it in any particular situation that allows us to witness – see and hear – that there is a {power differential}? What is it in any particular situation that allows us to witness – see and hear – that there is a particular form of {identity} being played out, 'constructed', or performed? What is it in any particular situation that allows us to witness – see and hear – that there is a {third space}?

The Tutorial

In 2002, during a research stay with Ken Tobin at the University of Philadelphia, I told him about conversation analysis and the kinds of findings people report in that field. One day as we were going to his office, I was telling him about the work that the listener produces while attending to the speaker. As we entered the building, there was a work area for students. I asked Ken to take a look and observe the person listening to someone else, to note the head nods, to observe body orientations, to watch for rhythmic (beat gestures) and the like. He told me that he had never thought about or observed that this was happening – the listener was integral to the work of the conversation. Going further towards the office, we passed another place where students worked, and Ken pointed out that the students were doing the same. Over the next few days, he repeatedly remarked that he was seeing the transactional work being conducted in quite a variety of settings, restaurants, schools, and other places where we say people in conversation.

Whatever I had done on that first instant, it had been a tutorial. It allowed Ken to observe, for the first time, the contributions of listeners to the transactional work required to pull of a conversation. Moreover, whatever it was that I had said and done, it allowed him to identify the work in other places as well even though these differed from the first instance where the tutorial had taken place. He identified these behaviors in our own conversations in ways that became part of these conversations: he formulated these contributions to our transactional enterprise.

Notable about this situation is that Ken did not have to take a course on methods. Whatever he had brought to the situation and everyday explanations sufficed for him to notice and subsequently to find over and over again the contributions of listeners to the transactivonal work of talking. In this book, my reporting of phenomena should be thought of in the same way. Thus, for example, in chapter 3 I describe, among others, the work denoted by the glosses {opening the bringing of 'bad news'}, {elaborating change of plans}, and {disallowing experiment with waxes}. In each case readers should think of the text as a tutorial – not only for finding the work in the materials presented here but as a tutorial for finding the phenomena in every *this* place, that is, in any concrete (rather than imagined) science classroom situation.[8] We can conclude that 'from all this we have "a first observation" of tutorial problems. They are this-worldly settings wherein order productive parties so collaborate as to exhibit "just what a social fact is that makes it accountably just that"' (Garfinkel 2002: 250).

Ethnomethodological studies differ radically from those practicing formal analytic approaches. This is so because formal analytic approaches specify special research methods that are required to extract the structures from the data sources that the research reports. In ethnomethodology, the methods of interest are those that the members to the setting themselves employ in identifying, producing, or accounting for structure, that is, the work from which emerge the objectively available social facts of their everyday lives. In this research, therefore, any report is something like a tutorial. In the context of a study of the work of teaching undergraduate chemistry in lecture format, the purpose of the reporting text is this.

> The reader is urged to attend a lecture … In that setting read the article's descriptions of the lecture hall as doings as instructions with which to find them, locate, recognize, follow, further observe, and the rest.
>
> When the described doings of the article's text are read in this way they make the work of lecturing instructably observable as concerted and endogenously produced, naturally accountable ordinary activities. When the article is read in that way, the article is about {Lecturing's work}. The article then consists of a collection of tutorial problems. It reveals events of lecturing's work in the aspect of their achievedly coherent production just in any actual case. (Garfinkel 2002: 219)

---

[8] It is for this reason that ethnomethodologists, following Duns Scotus, use the term *haecceity* (Lat. *haecceitas,* thisness): social facts always exhibit themselves in concrete situations, as concrete '*this-es*'.

Readers will note that the author is describing an analogous situation to the tutorial I had given Ken Tobin and to how I understand my own descriptions of the work in/of science education. Just as Ken took my instructions 'to locate, recognize, follow, further observe and the rest' the listeners' contributions to the transactive conversational work, Garfinkel understands his article's descriptions as instructions 'to locate, recognize, follow, further observe, and the rest' of the work that he had observed, including {taking and holding places}, {paying attention}, {[being] late), and {interruption}'. Just as my tutorial has made the listeners' contributions to the conversational work instructably observable 'as concerted and endogenously produced, naturally accountable ordinary activities' to Ken Tobin, Garfinkel expects his descriptions to make the work of lecturing instructably observable and the descriptions provided in this book make instructably observable the *work* producing such social facts as {opening the bringing of 'bad news'}, {elaborating change of plans}, and {disallowing experiment with waxes}.

Formal analytic approaches operate in the same way in the sense that each research report constitutes a tutorial for finding particular orders when observing a segment of society at work. However, in contrast to ethnomethodology, formal analytic approaches require special methods for identifying what they gloss. These are specified in methods sections, which themselves are tutorials (for what to do to observe the social facts reported). These not only account for what the authors had done to identify and extract the orders they report on but also instruct the reader in what to do to reproduce the findings. Ethnomethodology has to do with procedures and has a *procedural* emphasis: 'By *procedural*, [ethnomethodology] does not mean *process*. Procedural means labor' (Garfinkel 1996: 6). At issue here is not the structure or an indifference to structure. Rather, ethnomethodology aims at providing *procedural* descriptions of – i.e., descriptions of the work producing – social structure *as an endogenously achieved, witnessable and witnessed phenomenon of order from within the event.*

3

The Work of Doing a Change of Plans

In this chapter, I develop an account of one classroom episode that both teacher (Carrie) and student (Jane) have marked as standing out. For the former, it stood out because she had to announce to the student a change in the task condition for the compulsory inquiry task that took up the term and would make up for the only grade. For the latter it stood out because the change of plans not only took away the experimental tests that she was really interested in conducting but also turned the purchased materials and equipment into a futile expense. In this chapter, I show that a change of plans is not merely some underlying ordered social phenomenon that requires special methods to extract from an otherwise unordered social life but that there is *sym*practical work in the production of this order, and both work and order are reflexively accountable to those who staff the social phenomenon (here, Carrie, Jane). Sympractical here means that we cannot separate the work into parts (elements) done by one and other parts by the second person. Rather, the adjective points to the fact that each relevant act (turn pair) involves contributions on the part of both. Moreover, the phenomenon is not something accessible only to researchers who have to use special methods for extracting the 'animal' (i.e., living work) 'from the foliage' (i.e., praxis). Indeed, the phenomenon is observable by those present and witnessing the situation (as shown in the researcher's opening question to Jane: 'is that back to the drawing board for you'). Specifically, this work occurs at the collective level and is not constituted by more basic elements such as individual actions. Accordingly, the minimal unit for a social phenomenon is a social (i.e., transactional) unit, inherently distributed across the setting; and, because of the Heraclitean flux of life, the analytic unit is diachronic (i.e., distributed over/across time). The following analyses provide us with an inside, from-with-the-conversation perspective on the unfolding event the end. This from-within perspective has two important consequences. First, the end of what is happening cannot be anticipated but is recognized only once it has been arisen as the joint accomplishment of the social actors. Second, because it is unfinished, the event as such has not yet presented itself entirely it also cannot be *re*presented (e.g., through a sign); and because it cannot be represented, it cannot be com*prehended.*

Doing {Opening the Bringing of 'Bad News'}

In the natural attitude, a teacher having a conversation with a student is something unremarkable. However, we may take from Carrie's gloss not only that she was the bringer of the bad news, but also that she was aware of the sensitive nature of the task. This is but another gloss that Carrie might have provided immediately preceding the conversation she will be having with Jane. In the approach taken here, one does not have to draw on such accounts, for it is accepted that conversations do not just begin but that there is joint work involved in opening and closing an exchange. In fact, this goes to the very heart of a standard question that reviewers ask, 'How were the episodes chosen?' and 'What makes an episode and episode?' In the present approach, episodes are defined and described by the members to the setting, who are part of the sympractical work that produces it, its beginning, its running, and its closing; and the members, with their glosses, also have their ways of describing what they are intending to do and what they have done and experienced. This is precisely what is denoted in chapter 2 in the three different glosses that those individuals present to the setting have provided.

In the conversation analytic and pragmatics literature, openings and closings as transactional work are well-known phenomena. In the materials selected for this book, one can observe opening labor at work. It begins as Carrie moves through the classroom and, in approaching Jane, begins to articulate her name, *formulating* what is to come: 'I better talk to Jane first' (turn 01). The speech intensity is high so that the locution is easily hearable from where Jane is sitting. There is pausing, then a constative statemment: 'change of plans'. With a natural attitude, one can hear disappointment and dejection; psychologists who use voice parameters to track emotion (e.g., Scherer 1989) would find correlates of disappointment and dejection in the sharply decreasing pitch, the increasing F_1, and decreasing speech intensity (351 $\rightarrow$ 199 Hz; 685 $\rightarrow$ 741 Hz, 74.0 $\rightarrow$ 67.8 dB). Jane also orients her gaze sidewards and downwards toward the floor with a facial expression that we might gloss as 'disappointment'. Here, I bracket both types of descriptions and focus on the work. There is pausing, and then a second turn completing the pair turns 003/005. The locution first reproduces part of the interjection of the earlier turn, then makes a constative statement that we can hear to be an explanation for the change of plans: 'to make life easier' (turn 005). There is a further constative statement, produced more slowly than normal speech, about a decision that 'it' is too difficult. (If analysts were to put in brackets behind the 'it' something like '[the experiment]', they would already use cultural competence to fill in, when the real question is about the role of this locution in the conversation rather than in the mind of the researcher.)

Fragment 3.1a

```
001    C:    okay. (0.24) OH; ((moves toward
             Jane)) i better talk to JAne first.
             (0.24) okAY:. (1.63) changef plA:Ns.
002          (0.26)
003    J:    U::M::: ((head sideward, gloss: dis-
             appointment on face))
004          (0.76)
```

The take up of turn 003 occurs in turn 005, with the reporting of 'uMM', then the explication of why the change. It is to make life easier. The change in plans is attributed to an unstated 'it', that might be used to refer to a higher power or collective, or to divert responsibility for an action. We do not know at this point, from the perspective of Jane, for example, who decided or how the decision has come about. But the work required for establishing the relation has been completed. We are now into the conversation. The opening work has been done and the topic, introduced simultaneously with the opening work, is developing. How it is developing is not in the hands of the individuals, who, respectively, are confronted with the locutions of the other. The conversation develops in excess of what the individuals might currently have in mind.

Fragment 3.1b

```
004          (0.76)
005    C:    uMM::tmake dlIfe EA:sier; (0.31) <<all>okay>; ..HHH
             UUm (0.42) <<len>it has (0.22) bin=decided that it is
             too dIFficult.> kAY:? ((187→300 Hz) ((head sideward,
             gaze down))
006    J:    <<plaintive>i=just=found=out=a=way=to='dO='it.>
             ((318Hz))
```

The constative stating that 'it' is too difficult is paired with another constative about 'having found a way to do it'. That is, in this turn pair there is an assertion about the difficulty of 'it' and a counter assertion about a way of doing 'it'. The voice quality is not neutral but might be glossed as 'plaintive' (turn 006).

Doing {Elaborating the Change of Plans}

There is a possible second part of an assertion/affirmation unit, which we may appear here in the gloss 'Yea, that may be', which is then immediately followed by a contrastive connective 'but' that receives a special intonational emphasis (turn 008). Even the 'but' is a chain in the link of a locution that begins with an affirmation or acknowledgment of what has been said and then anticipates some form of opposition or alternative form of action. There is pausing both preceding and following the oppositive conjunction, and then a second appearance of the conjunction preceding an assertion that whatever 'it' may be also 'might work for change of plans'. In fact, it is direct speech, a quotation of Jane's having found 'a way to do it', which is now taken up in the context of the reply, 'it [the way] might work for change of plans'. This would then be a case of '<u>doing *adequate reference*</u>'

(Sacks 1974), which is accomplished by maintaining the common referent, whatever this might be.

Fragment 3.2a
```
 007        (0.30)
 008    C:  ((200 Hz)) EE::: umm:::; (0.85) BUT (0.50) <<all>but
            it might still work for chAnge of plANs.> (0.22)
            .hhHH its (0.36) ↓'O::N:: (0.52) mOO:dl, the new
            stAtement, (0.24) but it is to dO with (0.21) .hhhhh
            <<len>hAVing a lANtern,> (0.50) with hOt AI::r (0.23)
            <<all>added to it> (0.26) by means other than using
            the flA:Me, (0.91) suchA:s;
            <<all>can=you=think=of=anything⁻>
```

There is a counter assertion that offers taking 'the way to do it' because it 'might
still work for change of plans'. That is, there is no take up and further development
what Jane has found out but using whatever it is within the changed plans. There is
an assertion concerning the new problem statement, and an elaboration that it is to
be made to work by means of a different way of heating the air, 'other than the
flame'. The final part of the turn is unfinished, leaving an opening for an alternative to be added: 'such as ...'. followed by a very rapidly produced 'can you think
of anything'. The unfinished statement is in fact an invitation to produce a completion. The 'new statement' is said to be found on 'Moodle', and, as it is formulated,
has to do with having the (Chinese) lantern with 'hot air added to it by means other
than using the flame'.

There is 'pausing', which, because anyone could speak, is a social unit. Every
speaker has an opportunity to take the speaking floor and both Jane and Carrie,
here, provide the other with an opportunity to continue. Although there has been an
invitation and offer to the other to speak, Carrie takes the next turn, saying 'hot
air', then offers another answer slot by means of a grammatically incomplete 'like
we get air from ...'. Another pause is developing, and then a locution that has the
grammatical structure of an assertion: 'breath into it'. It therefore would fulfill the
requirements of a second turn to a question | reply pair. But the intonation moves
upward towards the end of the speech unit, which characteristically tends to be
heard as a questioning part of a turn pair. That is, the locution both offers a reply
and, in articulating it in question form, also articulates uncertainty about the appro-
priateness of the said for the slot that it has (tentatively) filled.

Fragment 3.2b
```
 009        (1.11)
 010    C:  <<all>hotair> (1.88) <<p>like we get hot air from.>
 011        (0.75)
 012    J:  breath INto It?
 013        (1.25) (('yea' gesture))
 014    C:  EAsier=than=thA:t⁻
```

The next minimal unit actually stretches across three turns because in the pausing,
Carrie already produces gestural forms that can be seen as encouraging, an affirmation, 'yea but ...'. The second part of the reply arrives in turn 014, 'easier than
that'. It, too, contains affirmative value, which we may gloss in this way: 'where
we get the air from is easier than breathing into it [lantern]'. That is, the assertion-
question first turn is paired with a positive reception and an assertion that the
sought-after answer is easier. Moreover, we can hear an offer-invitation to try

again. This is so because whereas the reply has been accepted, there is an easier way to 'get hot air' than by breathing into the lantern; and this easier way is projected in the reply, which thereby opens up a slot for another try. Again, there is pausing (turn 015), while Carrie grins and laughs, as if saying, 'it is really easy'. But in not speaking, Carrie provides an opportunity for Jane to take a turn, who eventually does just that. The locution (turn 016) is the second part of a question–reply unit, articulating but also withholding a possible reply 'I would say fire', with an immediate evaluation following, 'but it's a flame'. Here, we actually find a dialogical form at the inside of the locution, where the shortcoming of a possible answer is immediately articulated. That is, the turn does not actually make an offer for a reply but states what would have been a reply had there been no constraint on the fire/flame.

Fragment 3.2c
```
015            (2.11) ((Carrie grins/laughs))
016    J:      i would say fIre but its a flame.
017            (0.30)
018    C:      yea::. (0.64) <<all>hairdryer, (0.77) somethI:Ng¯
               ((gesture as if wanting to 'draw something out'))
019            (0.54)
020    J:      that means i cant experiment with the wa[xes.  ]
021    C:                                              [wAX?   ]
               (0.93) NO. (.) <<assertive>you cA:nt experiment with
               different wA[xes.]>
```

The next turn pair (turns 016 | 18) constitutes an assertion | affirmation pair. The 'yea' (turn 018) is produced with falling intonation as in a constative. A pause is developing that is stopped by the word 'hairdryer'. It may be offered as the sought-for reply that would have completed the earlier answer slots. There is a new pause developing, then the word 'something' accompanied by a gesture that might be seen as inviting other possible second parts to complete a question | reply turn pair following the 'like we get hot air from ...?'

To understand the possible connection between hairdryer and the earlier turn containing statement-query about getting hot air, we may draw on existing findings conversation analysis. (Whether these findings apply remains a matter of empirical analysis.) If members to the setting (a staff) use a single category from a categorization device, 'then they can be recognized to be <u>doing</u> *adequate reference*' (Sacks 1974: 219, original emphasis, added underline). The current topic is hot air required for the Chinese lantern to rise. There is an open offer for a question about the sources given that the candles are not to be included. So far, breathing, fire, flame, and hairdryer have been offered as possible candidates for the answer slot opened up by the offer of a question. That these are all candidates for the source of hot air question because they all fall into the same category, hot/heated air. They can therefore be heard as doing their part in establishing adequate reference to the offered question. Even the 'something' may be heard as invitation for additional members that would fit the category of heat sources.

Doing {Disallowing Experiment with Waxes}

Turn 20 can be heard as the second part of a premise | conclusion pair. One may understand this if, following Vološinov (1930), one expands the reported speech that is only implicit rather than explicitly stated. Here, 'that means' gives a hint as to premise on which the second part of turn 20 is built.

```
Fragment 3.3a
    020    J:    that means i cant experiment with the wa[xes.    ]
    021    C:                                              [wAX?   ]
                 (0.93) NO. (.) <<assertive>you cA:nt experiment with
                 different wA[xes.]>
```

So far, the *con*versation (irreducible social fact!) has established that there is a change of plans, from the originally stated candles as source for heating the air inside the Chinese lantern to something else; possibilities for this something else include breathing (hot air) into the lantern or using a hairdryer. Fire and flame, as candle, are the excluded heat sources. The hairdryer or anything else fulfilling the 'change of plans', which is a change away from the candles, implies that Jane 'can't experiment with the waxes' (turn 020). The conclusion, as an assertion, is the first part of an assertion | affirmation pair, where 'Wax? No. You can't experiment with the waxes' affirms that the wax cannot be part of the investigation. In fact, it is because the candles are excluded that the implied experiment with the different waxes cannot be conducted. The 'can't' here is not about Jane's ability to experiment with waxes: there has already been an affirmation that there is a solution to whatever the problems might have included. The 'can't' can be heard as 'you are not allowed to' rather than 'you are not capable of'.

There is nothing that would prevent the student to learn to and about experimenting if the inquiry pertained to the waxes. But what the interdiction has as its unstated ground is the fact that there is a different purpose altogether. It is not just that students investigate something and, in the course, come to wrestle with a problem and its spin-off problems. Experimentation is to occur, but it cannot pertain to the different waxes.

The assertion about not being able/allowed to experiment with waxes is paired with an interjection, produced while Jane has her head and nose propped in her hand, gazing to the side (Fig. 3.1). Again, we may gloss it as 'expressing dejection'. In the situation, this turn is paired with a locution that begins with the oppositive conjunction 'but' produced much louder than normal, thereby standing out against everything else. There is pausing, and then an assertion about that something *can* be done, where the 'can' is clearly emphasized with respect to the remainder of the speech. An assertion follows, beginning what 'it' is going to be, which is, to investigate, 'a lantern that rises in the least amount of time for two meters with 20 grams on it' (turn 024). There is pausing, which gives space to Jane to take a turn. Then Carrie takes another turn that begins with a long drawing in of air, announcing the coming of speech, and then, with rising intonation, the latter part of the English word 'okay?' We can hear this as a question whether something is okay, where the preceding assertions are the objects of the query. The offered query – whether 'it' is okay – is paired with a subdued 'kay', produced with a con-

Fig. 3.1 Artistic rendering of the instant when Jane just hears the teacher say that she 'can't experiment with different waxes' as the student had originally planned (turn 022).

stative statement-denoting falling intonation. There is therefore an acceptance of the described situation, for which the first part of the locution seeks explicit agreement. The seeking and receiving of the agreement is the achievement of turn pair 026 | 027. In fact, we can hear the pausing (turn 025) as an invitation to reply; but there is no explicit next turn. We then have the specific invitation for commenting on or accepting the assertions as a description of the projected change in the plans for the experiment. Up to this point, therefore, there is not a negotiation but the announcement of a change of plans and an assertion for how the change is to be implemented with an explicit seeking of assent in turn 026. This assent to the change of plan, as articulated so far, is being obtained as part of the turn pair 026 | 027.

Fragment 3.3b
```
021   C:                                        [wAX?  ]
            (0.93) NO. (.) <<assertive>you cA:nt experiment with
            different wA[xes.]>
022   J:               [u:m:] ((nose, head as if propped up by
            hand, Fig. 3.1))
023         (0.44)
024   C:   BUT; (0.45) youcA:::n .hh and its going to bEE::
            (0.42) investiga:te (.) how you can hA:ve (0.60) a
            lANtern, (1.47) rI:::se (2.79) ((glances toward ceil-
            ing as if thinking)) <<all>in the lEAst amount of
            time for two meters> .hh with a:: (.)
            twen:ty:grammass=on=it.
025         (0.90)
026   C:   .hhhhkay?
027   J:   <<subdued, p>kay.
```

The next turn begins with an inhalation of air, announcing the coming of speech, an interjection ('so'), pausing, and then an assertion: 'Makes it easier for you' (turn 028). Whereas pair 026 | 027 has achieved the assent, there also is what might be glossed as disappointment co-articulated with the assent. Turn 028 can be heard as the second part of a disappointment | assuagement pair (pair 027 | 028). There is then the formulation of an explicit addition: 'and other thing is' followed by an

assertion about 'hold[ing] it until you finish up heating the air?' The intonation is
rising, as if a question had been posed. Pausing unfolds (turn 029), giving Jane
space to take a turn, but she does not, which gives Carrie space. 'Kay?', she says,
with rising intonation as she has done before. Again, we can hear it as a first turn in
the production of assent, which consists of a query seeking assent and a next turn
that gives the assent. There is more pausing, and then another assertion follows
about removing the heat source and then letting it go. At this point, Jane takes a
turn. She produces an almost inaudible (pianissimo) 'kay' with the falling intonation typical of an assertion. In the pausing that is unfolding, Jane nods, thereby
producing a second part in a statement | assent pair. The next locution begins with
the interjection 'kay', produced with rising pitch as in a question; but it is rapidly
followed by the drawing in of air, announcing that there is more to come. There is
the adverbial conjunction that introduces a conclusion or implication, 'so', which is
drawn out, thereby emphasizing it. An assertion that actually repeats an earlier one
about what the listener cannot do: 'You won't be able to test different types of
waxes' (turn 035).

```
Fragment 3.3c
   026   C:   .hhhhkay?
   027   J:   <<subdued, p>kay.
   028   C:   .hhh SO:; (0.50) makes it easy for you: and OTher
              thing is to (.17) un to: hOld ↑IT (0.30) untI::L:
              (0.81) you fINish up. (0.33) hEAting (0.22) the air?
   029        (0.75)
   030        kay?
   031        (0.46)
   032        remOVe the hEAt sOUurce (0.28) <<all>then let it go.>
   033   J:   <<pp>kay.>
   034        (0.94) ((Jane nods))
   035   C:   kAY? (0.23) .hhh (0.17) sO:::; (0.38) yes, you wONt
              be able to test different tYPes of WAxES=
```

Here, the assertion does not negate the possibility that waxes could be tested and
experimented with, but asserts that the recipient 'won't be able to test' them, within the context of the change of plans that have been announced and received assent.
   We might gloss what has happened so far as the announcement of a changed
assignment description. There has not been an attempt to jointly arrive at a new
experiment but there was explicit attempt to receive | give assent/compliance for
the new situation, even though there have been statements that can be heard as
attempts of assuaging the news, which had been recognizably (on the part of the
interlocutor) received with disappointment (on the part of the recipient).

Doing {Arguing for/against Maintaining the Original Plan}

So far, it appears as if assent has been achieved for the change of plans. The conversation has worked out the implication that the originally planned experiment
with waxes – the precise details are not made available here – cannot be done under the new conditions, which are specified in the Moodle environment. The next
turn, however, presents an assertion that 'heaps of stuff' had been bought for 'it'

(turn 036). The turn pair 035 | 036 confronts two assertions, one that disallows the testing of waxes and the second stating that 'heaps of stuff' had been bought for it. There is pausing, allowing the interlocutor (Carrie) to reply, but this does not happen. Jane takes another turn, stating what had been done the night before: she had 'bought all the candle bases' and 'ordered waxes and stuff' (turn 038). We therefore have two sets of assertions, one stating that a particular test cannot be done and another stating that much of what needs to be done for the tests has already been completed and the preparations have well advanced. In some everyday life situations, such a more advanced state of affair may actually suffice in getting a course of action done even though there had been statements that it was to be canceled. To see what the effect of these assertions is, however, we need to consider them in their pairing with the next turn.

Fragment 3.4a
```
035   C:   kAY? (0.23) .hhh (0.17) sO::::; (0.38) yes, ((facial
           expression of sorry)) you wONt be able to test dif-
           ferent tYPes of WAxES=
036   J:   =i just went out and bought heaps of stuff last night
           for it.
037        (1.95)
038   J:   went out and bought all the candle bASes and (?)
           things and i=ve gone and (0.35) ordered wAXes and
           stuff.
039        (0.30)
040   C:   yea. (0.15) but you can sEE thats (.) its been rEAlly
           difficult to actually get a lANtern [t go;]
041   J:                                       [yea, ]
042   C:   hAsnt [it.]
```

The next turn (040) begins with the articulation of an affirmative with constative intonation. It is immediately followed by the contrastive conjunction 'but', which, as such, introduces an oppositive form. Here, the assertion of the recognizability or intelligibility ('see') of something is made, which is followed by a statement of what is asserted to be intelligible: 'it's been difficult to actually get a lantern to go' (turn 040). That is, we have another assertion | assertion pair, where the contents of the second mitigate the contents of the first. We therefore have an assertion | counter-assertion pair. As the pair 040 | 041 shows, there is assent given even before the preceding locution has ended. Moreover, as turn 042 is produced with falling intonation, thereby constituting a constative, the pair 041 | 042, expresses joint recognition of the previously stated fact that 'it's been really difficult to actually get a lantern to go'.

Despite the joint recognition that there have been difficulties, the issue is not settled, for the next locution uses a contrastive conjunction 'but' to introduce a mitigating dimension. This mitigation, which states that something has been worked out, comes in the form of a description that unfolds over the turns 043–055. The locutions Carrie produces grammatically are interjections the functions of which, in the conversation, are to elicit further elaboration. The result of these turn sequences is a description of a new design: if you use a paper ring, and possibly use baking paper on top of the cup, with lightweight tinsel on the outside. As a result, there is something about the weight that will allow 'it' to go up easily, because it is full of air. In the course of articulating the design, Jane first shows a

paper ring already prepared and then shows a paper cup to which something like a
cutting gesture is applied at about 40% of its height. While the topic of talk is tinsel, she actually holds up tinsel.

Fragment 3.4b
```
041   J:                                          [yea, ]
042   C:   hAsnt [it.]
043   J:         [but] (0.25) i worked out that (0.77) if you
                 use a paper ring,
044        (0.46)
045   C:   u::::n?
046        (0.56)
047   J:   and possibly on top of the cup use baking paper;
           (0.58) and just use a lIGhtweight tINsel?
048        (0.56)
049   C:   [yEA::::?    ]
050   J:   [and put the] tINnsel OUtside, the inside of the tin-
           sel=
051   C:   =the wIre?
052        (0.31)
053   J:   that chANges make it prop up. and its only going to
           be at this weight and it will go up really EAsily.
054        (1.10)
055   J:   cause its [full of air. ]
056   C:             [will it bURn?]
```

Turn 056 is articulated with rising intonation, suggesting the possibility of a question about whether 'it' will burn, while the index finger simultaneously and repeatedly taps the bottom of the paper cup. The turn 056 is actualized as a question
when the next turn, following some pausing, provides an assertion to the contrary,
and then the adverb 'because' that introduces a reason. Here the reason comes in
the form of a statement about the nature of 'it' as being made from baking paper.
There is pausing, which then provides Jane with an opportunity to make another,
rapidly articulated assertion: 'baking paper doesn't burn' (turn 060). Pausing unfolds, and then Carrie produces a second turn to the assertion about the burning of
baking paper.

Fragment 3.4c
```
056   C:             [will it bURn?]
057        (0.75)
058   J:   <<all>oh=no cause i=m making it out of baking paper.>
059        (0.98)
060   J:   <<all>baking paper dOEsnt burn.>
061        (0.74)
062   C:   wE:ll: it can bURn but it chA:Rs and gets hOLes in
           it.
063        (0.96)
```

Turn 062 begins with the adverb 'well', which, in the combination with the oppositive conjunction 'but' accords agreement modified by what the conjunction introduces: rather than burning, baking paper will char and get holes. So it is true that it
does not really burn, but it does char and get holes. We therefore obtain an asser-
tion | counter-assertion pair (turn pair 060 | 062) that mitigates the use of baking
paper for the implied, but here-unstated purposes.

    There is pausing following the counter-assertion, which is brought to an end
when Jane begins to speak producing the adversative conjunction 'but' (turn 064).

Fig. 3.2 Artistic rendering of the instant after Carrie has just said, 'I know that you've put thought in what we were doing, but ...'

Another assertion about what can be experimented with: 'how tall it has to be. The smile on her face can be glossed as expressing both confidence and being pleased. There is an extended pausing, which, this time, Carrie brings to an end with the offering of a turn pair that has a question as its first part. It seeks to understand whether the 'same setup' could be used in the context of adding hot air, which is a restatement of the earlier articulated new task specification available on Moodle. The adversative conjunction that opens the next turn allows us to hear that a contrast is in the making, between what is stated, queried, or implied in first part of the turn pair (i.e., 066) and what is unfolding, which is wanting 'it' to be 'how tall it is to go up' (turn 067).

Fragment 3.4d

```
062  C:  wE:ll: it can bURn but it chA:Rs and gets hOLes in
         it.
063      (0.96)
064  J:  but i can experiment on how tall it has to be.
         ((Smiles at Carrie))
065      (2.08)
066  C:  can you use the sAMe setup (0.36) with (1.01) adding
         hotair?
067  J:  but i wanted <<all>it how tall it is to go UP.>
068      (0.61)
069  J:  <<all>it doesnt even matter if its a paper cUP it can
         go up. t can go up.> ((Smiles, as if she had made a
         'good play'))
070      (1.59)
071  C:  so have a think about (0.98) what you can do with
         that. (0.20) <<len>i kno:w that youve put thought in
         what we were doing;> but.
072      (1.67)
```

Before turn 069 there is pausing, which provides Jane with another opportunity for a turn at talk, which she does by rapidly producing two assertions, 'it doesn't matter if it is a paper cup, it can go up' and 'it can go up' (turn 069). Again there is pausing until Carrie asserts that Jane has to think about what she can do with that;

there is a further statement that acknowledges the thought that has gone into the work before the locution stops with what normally functions as a oppositive conjunctive ('but'), but here is not followed by further text. Whatever might have appeared following the conjunctive would be in opposition to having 'put thought into what we were doing', that is, in preceding actions, and, therefore, despite the actions that have already been completed. As the locution stops, there is little if anything to be gained wondering about what Carrie has 'meant' other than what she was saying, which is precisely what she would have made available to Jane.

Although the conversation in this subsection appears to open up the possibility of a negotiation of alternatives, one assertion for a design option has been opposed by a counter-assertion, and the oppositive but following a summary of the thought and actions done is a move toward closing any option other than compliance with the newly stated task condition.

Doing {Pleading and Closing Out Topic}

Further pausing follows, and then Carrie takes another turn at talk. The contents of the saying pertain to the variations in what is happening, the 'complications and difficulties in actually making it work' (turn 073). The next turn also is about getting something to work but here as part of a conditional statement, 'if I can get it to work'. This, then, is followed by an offer of a plea: 'can I do it, please'. Rather than responding to a plea, the next turn responds to a statement about doing the work, which it asserts to be taking time trying to make it work. That is, whereas the first part of the turn introduces the continuation if the conditional is met, the present statement asserts that time is spent *trying* to make it work – even though the initial assertion has not stated whether the 'getting it to work' would be done in class. Fulfilling the conditional itself would be taking time. The implications of this trying and spending time follow after Jane has uttered an oppositive conjunction 'but' and before there was time to elaborate what possibly could have followed the conjunction. Locution appears to be replying to the possibility that the trying may still not get it to work with the consequence that Jane 'will run out of time' (turn 078). That is, in this turn sequence, the conditional on which the plea is premised is confronted with the assertion of a failure and, as a consequence, the failure to complete the task in time. At precisely the same time, however, Jane, too, is speaking. She is producing another conditional, which, if true, would lead to a different course of action that is formulated as a promise to be followed: if it does not work this time, then Jane would do the hairdryer one. The locution restates the conditional following the oppositive conjunction, 'but, if it works', and follows it with a plea: can I do it please?

Fragment 3.5

```
071    C:    so have a think about (0.98) what you can do with
             that. (0.20) <<len>i kno:w that youve put thought in
             what we were doing;> but.
072          (1.67)
073    C:    the:::ee (0.79) variATions in whats hAPppening;
             <<all>and the complicATions and dIFficulties in ACtu-
```

Fig. 3.3 Artistic rendering of the instant when Jane says 'I promise I'll go back and do the hairdryer one'.

```
              ally> making it wO:::rk.
074   J:      <<all>if i get it to work can i do it> plEA::se.
075           (0.24)
076   C:      .hhhh but then youll be spending mORe time trying to
              make it wORk.
077   J:      but
078   C:      [and if doesnt youll run out of time.]
079   J:      [but if this time it doesnt work    ] (0.30) some
              (1.00) i promise i=ll: (0.17) go back (0.39) and
              (0.22) do: (0.44) <<all>the hairdryer one; but if
              this works (0.26) can i do it plEAse?
080           (0.75)
081   C:      so you:: (0.19) I:: wou:ld=suggest fr todA:Y: (0.48)
              you work on that (0.68) sort of (1.06) what ideas you
              can change for the other one .hhh and at hO:Me
              ((Jane's face changes to sad expression, averts gaze
              heretofore straight forwardly directed at Carrie's
              face)) (0.23) try:ing (0.41) <<all>try and get your
              wAX one to work.> ((Jane's face goes from smile to
              sadness))
082   J:      <<subdued, p>kay.>
083           (0.48)
084   C:      <<all>kay?>
085           (0.82)
```

There is pausing and then an assertion about a course of action. Although there is a formulation that the course of action is 'suggested', in the pairing with turn 082, the turn actually achieves compliance with the proposed action: 'work on that sort of what ideas you can change for the other one' relegating to the home 'trying to get your wax one to work' (turn 081). The course of action, therefore, states working under the new task condition during class time and pursing the other investigation, the one with the candle, at home. There is pausing, and then a rapidly articulated 'kay?' with rising intonation follows, as if a question was being offered up. More pausing is happening.

Fig. 3.4   Artistic rendering of the instant when Carrie says, 'How's your theory writing going' (turn 086); Jane: 's'alright' (turn 087).

Doing {Change of Topic in Order to Talk Theory}

In this subsection, we have a sudden change of topic. It is not to be explained by saying that a teacher has the power to change the topic when she wants and that the student, because of lesser power, is merely following. It should be clear by now that there is always sympractical work involved, which is inherently collective and irreducible to the individual. What we get in the first pair is the offering and de facto acceptance of the changed topic. Alternative possibilities always exist, and Jane could have made an offer to keep the preceding topic alive. In fact, in other instances, a student might have just said after the opening statement, 'Okay, thanks for telling me. I will check on Moodle and then redesign'. None of this conversation then would have been observed and the work of asking for and getting compliance for a change of plans would have been invisible.

Following the preceding locution of the questioning 'okay?', which can be expanded into the gloss, 'Is this way of proceeding okay with you?', there is no discernable reply in words or in other expressive modalities. Carrie takes the speaking floor producing a locution that is grammatically structured like a question but with an intonation characteristic of assertions: 'How's your theory writing going?' In the context of its pairing with turn 087 (Fig. 3.4), an adverb expressing the locution functions as a question, assent and satisfactory proceeding. An incomplete statement follows it: she has not done (possibly anymore on it?), and then another statement that she did not get a chance to do any more. The voice fades away and become inaudible. There is then an offer conditional on the existence of a theory about the 'wax bit': it can still be 'put in' (turn 089) (acknowledged in turn 091), pertaining to an experiment that she would not have done. The locution ends with the contrastive conjunction 'but', which may be heard as flagging that the change of plans has to be implemented. This first part, which constitutes an offer to include part of the work that has been done *if* a theory exists, comes to be paired with an opposing assertion: the experiment needs to be done (turn 081) to get the theory because nobody has an experiment like that' (turn 083). While the assertion is still unfolding, a modalizing statement is also unfolding: you *still* have the theory (turn 082). Here the adverb 'still' indicates the continuation of something, here it is the theory that can be put in even though the experiment with the wax cannot be part of the task under the new conditions. That is, the 'still' marks that something of the preceding work and thought can be retained in the new formulation; the statement thereby adds to the preceding turn that offers the possibility of keeping the wax-related theory if it in fact exists.

Fragment 3.6a
```
084   C:   <<all>kay?>
085        (0.82)
086   C:   'hows your thEOry wrIting gOing.
087   J:   <<unconvinced>s=alright.> ((gaze on to desk, averted,
           Fig. 3.4)) (0.18) avnt done (0.16) i didnt get a
           chance to do any more. <<pp>???>
088        (0.27)
089   C:   .hh if you hAve thE:ory for the wAX bit (0.17) you
           can stILl put it in
090        (0.32)
091   J:   un
092   C:   and it can be an experiment you didnt dO, but.
093   J:   no i need to [do the experiment                    ]
094   C:                [<<all>you still have theory on it.>]
095   J:   to get the theory because theres nobody whos dONe an
           expERiment like that. ((Fig. 3.5))
096        (0.40)
```

In a way, we could say that Jane is absolutely right. If there is no theory, an experiment can assist in producing results on the basis of which new theory may be developed. This in fact exhibits a form of understanding about different forms of realizing scientific inquiry, the one that is maintained by the teacher where theory is tested, and the one that Jane offers up, where theory is built through experimentation. At this point, and without reading further, we might ask, 'What will happen next?', or even speculate about what the course of action might be. But the type of approach to analysis offered up here is not concerned with speculating theoretically about unobservable things; the approach is concerned with describing the practical work that pulls of the conversation specifically and a part of a physics lesson more generally.[9]

The subsequent locution asserts that a reason for anticipated changes should exist; this locution is introduced by an agreeing 'yea', followed by the contrastive conjunction 'but' (turn 085). That is, the pairing of the preceding declarative statement (turns 081 & 083) and 085 yields an assertion/problem pair. The contrastive conjunction introduces the reason for a change *as if* the preceding assertion had not provided a reason. If a reason was stated, then the pair actually is an assertion | discounting of the presence of a reason. Pausing ensues; Jane's face features

---

[9] Of course, Jane and Carrie are not just talking about an experiment. In talking, in producing this relation, they are actually conducting the work of schooling. As such, the work we observe here is that of reproducing schooling as much as re/producing failure. If such conversation analytic research is conducted from a critical Marxist perspective, then issues of {power}, {ruling relations}, and {gender} come to the fore (e.g., Smith 1990).

Fig. 3.5   Artistic rendering of the instant when Jane says, 'Nobody whos done an experiment like that' (turn 095).

a pensive expression. Jane then breaks the pausing beginning with the adverb 'well' that introduces the continuation of something in the face of a change, but her voice fades and is drowned out by the other voice that articulates a conditional: 'If there is no reason, then there is not much point doing it' (turn 088). That is, the statement reasserts that there is no point doing an experiment in the absence of a theory or reason that would justify it. We therefore have the pairing of an assertion about doing an experiment to generate theory (081,083) with an assertion that there is no point doing an experiment unless there is a reason (085, 088).

Fragment 3.6b
```
095    J:    to get the theory because theres nobody whos dONe an
             expERiment like that. ((Fig. 3.5))
096          (0.40)
097    C:    yea but you should have a rEAson wHY: it chANges.
             ((Jane's face pensive))
098          (0.93)
099    J:    well it could [    (??)    ]
100    C:                   [because if] there is nO rEAson whY
             then theres nOT much point dOIng it.
101    J:    if gonna be (.) <<p>its gonna be hotter so it takes
             the little cup>
102          (0.83)
103    J:    and then the wax (0.46) or whether its going to be
             cool (0.38) cool and thirty minutes its cool wax and
             it burn faster. (0.28) or whether if its hotter it
             will rise mORe because of the hEAt.
104          (0.38)
105    C:    <<dubitative>n yea:h.> ((gloss: perhaps; or 'whatev-
             er.))
106          (3.25)
```

The conditional assertion is paired with several assertions of possible factors that might influence the experiment, involving 'small cups', whether the wax is cool, and the rate of burning, and a relationship between how hot 'it' is, 'the heat', and the rate or height of rising ('will rise more'). That is, we now have a pairing of not doing an experiment under certain conditions, the absence of theory or reasons, and a listing of a variety of reasons that affect the 'rising'. These assertions about possible factors are paired with an interjection and a drawn out affirmative 'n yeah'. Simultaneously, as the transcript shows, the quality of the voice is dubitative and may be glossed by a statement such as 'yea, perhaps' or 'whatever'. This subsection therefore ends with a constative | affirmative pair (though the affirmative was intonated in a way that may be glossed as dubitative). A long pausing develops, as if completion was achieved; it also provides an opportunity for something else to arise.

We may, then, gloss what has happened so far by saying that the student did in fact provide an argument for why there could not be a theory and she provides, when challenged, a list of possible reasons for testing something by means of an experiment. The teacher does not mount full counter-arguments so that we might in fact hear this part of the episode to be in favor of doing what the student proposes. A plausible alternative route for continuing with this assignment has been opened up in and by the exchange. But will it suffice for changing the task conditions in this case? What will come next?

Doing {Reasserting Plan and Getting Compliance}

Following a long, 3.25-second pause, Carrie then produces the adverb 'okay', which in constative form signals adequacy, agreement, or assent, but which, with rising intonation, is a move that requests assent. This possibility is actualized in the pairing with an affirmative 'yap' (turn 109). In what appears like an inversion of a constative description of what assent has been given to, turn 110 outlines a course of action: looking up on Moodle the new, edited statement; and paired with turn 112, assent is reasserted, though the voice is subdued and the eyes averted downward as if avoiding the gaze of the interlocutor. With turn pair 113 | 115, there is another actualization of a request for and giving of assent. Separated by pauses that each provides an opportunity for the other to take a turn, Carrie produces what might be heard as a description of the benefits arising from the agreed-upon course of actions (turns 116, 118, 120). These constatives pertain to (a) life being easier, (b) having data that can be analyzed, and (c) getting good marks for the analysis.

Fragment 3.7
```
 105   C:   <<dubitative>n yea:h.> ((gloss: perhaps; or 'whatev-
            er.))
 106        (3.25)
 107   C:   kAY?
 108        (0.22)
 109   J:   <<subdued, p>yap.=
 110   C:   =yup? (0.42) so look up (.) on::; (0.53) moodle the
            document has been edited (.) to have a new statement.
 111        (0.22)
 112   J:   <<subdued, p>yes.> ((Eyes avert-
            ed downward, Fig.))
 113        (0.29)
 114   C:   okAY?
 115   J:   (1.52) ((Jane nods slightly))
 116   C:   makes life way easier for you.
            ((Jane nods slightly))
 117        (0.75)
 118   C:   and youll get dA:ta and you can analyze it
 119        (0.62)
```

```
120    C:    and you can get a good mark for your analysis.
121          (0.68)
```

Although at the end of the preceding subsection there has been an elaboration of possible reasons for conducting alternative tests and experiments paired with an adverb of assent, the unfolding events in this subsection appear to constitute a radical break. This break in the nature of the conversation begins with a long pausing, then the requesting for consent to a course of action, which, in fact, seeks compliance with a changed task; this request is actualized and consent given with the repeated affirmative adverbs and gestures (nodding). However, the assent is modalized by intonations that weaken the assertive nature of the affirmative: the interlocutor speaks with low, subdued voice, does not see eye to eye with the other[10], and slightly rather than assertively nods. The locutions produced thereafter might be glossed as a description of why a course of action, though not preferred, is better for the person on whom it is imposed.

Although the effect of the conversation has different implications for the participating speakers, the achievement is a collective one. It is not that a student simply follows an instruction to change her experiment. There is considerable transactional work being done, including arguments for and against particular experiments, prior to the work that actualizes the assent. We must not be deceived by the fact that 109, 112, and 115 accept the changed course of action. It could have been otherwise, and further argumentative work would have been necessary. The conversation might have come to a point where the changeover to the new task condition be made contingent on one more attempt at getting the original experiment to work. Or, if the issue truly had been one of getting data, the candle experiment could have been accepted.

Doing {Changing Topic for Elaborating Possibilities in Changed Plan}

In elaborating the possibilities, there is therefore a de facto compliance explicitly enacted in the public sphere, observable to everyone, a compliance that has been sought earlier and, after a lengthy process, has been an achievement of the conversation. This achievement is a collective one, even though the effects are asymmetrically distributed across interlocutors. The next turn at talk shows that what has been described as the achievement of consent now is the de facto reality. Over the turns 122 and 126, Jane offers up the first part of a possible question | reply pair, which, in asking about a specific detail of it, takes the hairdryer experiment as given. The nature of the possible turn pair is actualized with the reply that the volume of the lantern determines the amount of air (turn 127).

We observe here a change of topic, which is that of the experiment under the new condition. Rather than continuing to argue for and against the original experi-

---

[10] On body orientation and seeing eye to eye see chapter 8. See also Fig. 3.7, which shows that the two are not seeing 'eye to eye' and a lot of work is required to get | give compliance.

ment, we therefore have a de facto acceptance of the new conditions, which are elaborated now in this part of the conversation. The change of topic is immediately accepted, constituted as an acceptable one, in the 'assistance' toward an articulation of a question (turn 124) and the production of a turn that actualizes what is being initiated as a possible question | reply ritual.

```
Fragment 3.8a
  120   C:   and you can get a good mark for your analysis.
  121        (0.68)
  122   J:   does it matter how much heat
  123        (0.31)
  124   C:   does that
  125        (0.28)
  126   J:   where you can measure how much AIr you put into it?
             (.) .hhh (0.24) because with the hairdryer you ca:nt
             blow.=
  127   C:   =well (0.24) itll have whatever volume your lANtern
             is.
  128        (1.09)
  129   J:   <<p>like> (0.30) no=like (0.63) well certain (0.75)
             like (.) the (0.82) spEEd.
  130        (1.86)
  131   J:   <<insistent>you=know like if you put more air in it
             it will go Up faster.>
  132        (1.40)
  133   C:   but it can only fIT the amount
             of AIr that fit inside the
             lA:Ntern.
  134   J:   but if you push it up with hot
             air it will move faster ((Fig.
             on the right)), it will go fast-
             er=
  135   C:   =you gonna hold it in its plACe
             if youre going to hold it in its
             place
  136   J:   un
  137   C:   until youve added (0.75) the air
             and then let it go.
  138        (1.51)
  139   J:   <<p>kay.>
  140   C:   kAY?
```

Turn pair 127 | 129 constitutes a constative | negation pair, as the second part of the pair marks the first part as inappropriate both in the 'no like' qualification and the articulation of an alternative topic (speed rather than volume). Pausing follows, giving Jane another opportunity of a turn at talk, which consists of a constative statement relating the amount of air in the lantern to the speed with which it will rise (turn 131). Combined with turn 133, we have an assertion | negation pair, as the second part begins with a contrastive conjunction 'but' followed by a constative about the maximum amount of air that fits inside the lantern. This turn then comes to be paired with another negation, which is introduced by the same contrastive conjunction 'but' followed by an assertion about the dependence of speed on the force from pushing the hot air into the lantern (turn 135). The next turn pair constitutes a constative | negation, as the state of affairs articulated in turn 135 (pushing air into the lantern will make it go faster) is negated by the statement that the lantern is held in place (turn 135) until the air has been added, and only then is the lantern released (turn 137). There is pausing, then a turn articulating the assent part completing the pair 135 | 137/139, followed by another articulation of the adverb 'okay' with questioning intonation.

In this part of the conversation, we therefore find repeated statements of relationships between different variables, negated by second turns that exhibit some reason why the relationship does not exist. The turn following the adverb of approval with questioning intonation (turn 140) does not consist in an articulation of explicit assent (e.g., 'yea' or 'okay'). Turns 141 and 143, as constatives that do not question the preceding content but that elaborates some aspect of it constitute assent. Intonated and grammatically formed as a question, it is actualized as such in the pairing with assent that is given twice (turns 142, 144), and acknowledged as such by an affirmation 'oo kay' (turn 146). There is pausing, which comes to an end with two aborted constative statements and then an articulation of how one can look at the relationship between hot air and the source: either the air in the Chinese lantern is heated, or the hot air is added from the outside (turn 148). This turn is the first part of a constative | affirmation pair, as Jane first nods (turn 149) and then produces an affirmative ('kay', turn 150).

Fragment 3.8b
```
140    C:    kAY?
141    J:    do I turn it off you turn it off
142    C:    yea.
143    J:    after you add the air?
144    C:    yea.
145          (0.40)
146    J:    oo kay.
147          (1.00)
148    C:    so you need to add it, you are not really (0.54) i
             guess you can look at ADding hot air or hEAting the
             AIr thats thEre.
149          (0.66) ((Jane nods))
150    J:    kay. but wouldnt that heat the air thats around the
             outside?=
151    C:    ^NN. thats an interesting pOINt you mIght lIke to (.)
             commENT on that.
152          (0.87)
153    J:    <<pp>kay.> ((Fig. 3.6))
```

The assent, however, is followed by the adversative conjunction 'but', used to introduce a fact that somehow stands in opposition of what has been stated so far. Here, the conjunction is followed by the auxiliary verb 'would' followed by a constative about the relationship between heating and the air 'around the outside' (turn 150). The auxiliary verb, among other possible uses, introduces an anticipation or expectation. As a whole, then, the turn offers up a question about an anticipated condition in the experiment: the hairdryer, with the lantern held in place, heats not only the air inside the lantern but also the air surrounding it. The next turn begins with an interjection 'nn' articulated with an intonation that might be heard as expressing a pleasant surprise, followed by a constative with positive evaluative quality: 'that's an interesting point' (turn 151). That is, rather than have a question | reply pair, the turn pair 150 | 151 comes out as a constative | affirmation pair. The second part of the turn pair treats the first as an affirmation that is interesting. As the locution unfolds, the positive aspect of the earlier part comes to be reasserted in

Fig. 3.6 Artistic rendering of the instant when Carrie says 'That's an interesting point you might like to comment on that' (turn 151).

the invitation that Jane 'might like to comment on that' (turn 151). There is pausing, followed by the articulation of assent (turn 153).

Doing {Ending a Meeting}

Meetings do not just end. There is collective (conversational, transactional) work that needs to be accomplished (Levinson 1983).

> Closings are a delicate matter both technically, in the sense that they must be so placed that no party is forced to exit while still having compelling things to say, and socially in the sense that both over-hasty and over-slow terminations can carry unwelcome inferences about the social relationships between participants. (p. 316)

Here, what will have been the closing part emerges from the constative | affirmation pair (150 | 151) followed by an affirmation | affirmation (turn pair 151 | 152). In turn 155, we find the same 'kay?' that already was articulated in turn 140. Here it is paired with 'yup', an adverb of assent, here articulated with very low speech volume in a manner that might be glossed as 'subdued'. Jane's gaze is averted, while Carrie squarely gazes at Jane. There is pausing (157), then Carrie turns 90° to her left, stands up and walks away.

Fragment 3.9
```
153    J:    <<pp>kay.>
154          (0.36)
155          kAY?
156    J:    <<subdued,p>yup.> ((Averted gaze toward paper cups on
             lab desk))
157          (2:06) ((Carrie gazes at Jane, who still has averted
             gaze))
158          ((Carrie turns, Fig. 3.7, gets up, and leaves Jane))
```

Fig. 3.7   Artistic rendering of the body orientations are part of the work that produces the end of the meeting. Carrie and Jane do not 'see eve to eve'.

Retrospectively, we may understand turn 140 as an invitation to close out the conversation. But, being followed by a question, the invitation is de facto declined and the conversation maintained. As this is a *con*versation, it is self-evident that it takes at least two voices for it to exist (as it takes two to tango): the conversation is an achievement of the two voices rather than that of one. Both interlocutors contribute to its maintenance in the preceding section. In the present, there is pausing following the subdued 'yup', and now exit has become possible. In the preceding instant, there still was something compelling to say, actualized in the question that eventually leads to an 'interesting point'. Turn 155 then can be heard as another offer for closing out the conversation, which is then in fact achieved in the sequence of turns that does not include an offer to continue it.

Here, the closing is of double nature. It not only achieves the ending of this conversation but also achieves closure to what had been, in part, an argument rather than acceptance of change of plans. The quality of the voice and of the gestural/bodily behavior contains signs that the consent has been given reluctantly. Moreover, Carrie articulates what can be heard as statements mitigating the acceptance of an unwanted course of action (e.g., 116, 118, 120).

Science Education Means Doing Sympractical Social Work

In this chapter, I provide a detailed analysis of the sympractical work that achieves a 'change of plans' in one project of an open-inquiry unit of physics. We do not know about all the other Chinese lantern projects that were subject to the same change of plans. In those other situations, the work of seeking | getting compliance with the change of plans may have been invisible. The work becomes visible here because of what Carrie subsequently glossed as 'Jane balking at it all'. That is, precisely because compliance was not given immediately, the work required became visible. It would not have been if Jane had turned around, consulted the new problem statement in the Moodle environment and designed an experiment in which she would have used a hairdryer.

In this chapter, I continuously emphasize the joint nature of the work. That this joint, sympractical work cannot be reduced to the individual is the result of taking the turn pair as the minimum unit of analysis. Thus, if, for example, 'question | reply' is the minimum unit of a transaction ritual, then this unit involves both speakers. We cannot say that one or the other speaker produces it. It takes both speakers to complete the turn pair. In this pair, each turn presupposes the other: A question is a question because there is a reply, and a reply is a reply because there is a question. Although the unit as a whole implies the two parts, it is neither the sum of two independent turns nor the interaction of two independent turns. The relation between the unit and its parts, question and reply, is that of a whole and its parts. It is a dialectical unit, each part presupposing and determining the other. The whole is a whole only because of the parts that constitute it; but these parts are parts only because there is a whole of which they are part.

The upshot of this approach is that the 'change of plans' is not something brought about by the teacher Carrie; nor is it brought about by Jane who from now on does something different. It is a sympractical achievement that only manifests itself in the contributions of different participants. Perhaps the following analogy may further deepen understanding of this point. To understand the functioning of a single-lens reflex (SLR) camera, we need to understand the wave and particle nature of light. First, to understand how the lens focuses the light we need to look at light as a wave that is refracted in the glass and projected onto the film or CCD[11] plate that records the image. Second, to understand the light meter that is used to determine the length of exposure, we need to look at light as a particle. Now we do not get at the nature of light by adding, abstracting from, or making interact wave and particle manifestations of light. Wave and particle are mere manifestations of a higher order unit: light. In the same way, the different turns taken by Carrie and Jane are manifestations of a higher unit: social relation or transaction ritual. In both ways of looking at a conversation, two sides are required and presuppose each other.

As a result of this approach, the analysis moves away from the individuals and investigates a *social* phenomenon consisting in the work of 'doing {a change of plans}'. This work, here, consists of a range of micro-practices that contribute to achieving the overall phenomenon including, for example, 'doing {beginning a meeting}', 'doing {ending a meeting}', and 'doing {a change of topic}'. Because this is social work, Carrie and Jane are but individuals staffing the phenomenon. If we were to look at other instances of 'doing {a change of plans}' we would be able to observe some of the same micro-features, such as 'doing {beginning a conversation}' and 'doing {ending a conversation}', whereas other micro-features may differ. For example, a person in an institutionally inferior position might request a change of plans and assent then would be requested from the person located higher

---

[11] CCD is the acronym for a 'charge-coupled device', the technology used, for example, in digital imaging. It consists of an array of tubes within which electrical 'avalanches' are produced when a photon enters. Each charge corresponding to such an avalanche is converted into a digital code.

in the institution. The work involved in 'doing {talking business}' would still be required (e.g., Boden 1994).

4

Endogenous Production of Order in Science Lessons

> The interests of ethnomethodological research are directed to provide, through detailed analyses, that account-able phenomena are through and through practical accomplishments. (Garfinkel and Sacks 1986: 163)

Science lessons do not just constitute boxes into which teachers and students step so that their actions can be shaped by the context – though it is true that when students enter special rooms denoted by the term 'science laboratory', particular events are anticipated to happen, associated with some behaviors but not with others. Still, science lessons are the result of societal relations that entirely produced endogenously, that is, from the inside. Students and teachers make available to each other whatever it takes to make science lessons for what they recognizably are; and this is the case whether the lessons are those characteristic of single-sex private schools, such as those presented here, or those of inner-city schools in metropolitan areas predominantly attended by students from poor families and often from particular groups or classes, races, ethnicities of society (e.g., working class, under class, homeless, welfare recipients). Thus, as the researcher collecting the data in chapter 3 stated prior to our viewing of the videotapes would be characteristic of one of the 'best schools in city'. Even when things go awry, such as when a chemistry teacher and his student have an altercation over a low grade that the former just has received (Roth et al. 2004), researchers and others still tend to recognize a chemistry lesson, but one that is more 'typical' for in a most difficult inner-city neighborhood school in a metropolitan area of the eastern US, represents 'poor teaching', or 'was not so much of a success'.

Better understanding the endogenous production of science lessons as irreducible societal events should be of interest to science educators because, for example, there currently is little understanding and theory why a teacher successfully teaching in one setting (e.g., inner-city Miami) should be failing in a similar inner-city setting in another setting (e.g., inner-city Philadelphia) even though he is African American just as his students are (Carambo 2005). Elsewhere I suggest that the problem is one of reducing a complex unit of analysis to the person (Roth and Barton 2004). In the situation of a teacher successful in one context but unsuccessful in what is an apparently equivalent context, these units might be something such as Carambo-teaching-in-an-urban-school-in-Miami-to-Cuban-African-American-students and Carambo-teaching-in-an-urban-school-in-Philadelphia-to-Afro-African-American-students.[12] However, even such inclusive units of analysis still highlight the *individual*, though now it is the individual in relation to the setting; it further underlines the individual by using a verb associated with the subjected co-articulated in the unit. These units, therefore, are the ethnographer's glosses of complex social/material relations reduced to one person rather than being concerned with the actual, *sym*practical work students and teacher do together such that the glosses 'successful teacher' and 'unsuccessful teacher' are justifiable accounts for what has happened.

In the present book, I suggest and exemplify a different tack. Rather than working with glosses, which always require some method different than what people actually do, I suggest focusing on the work that makes situations accountably what they are *within* the situation. This changes our interest from the descriptive glosses – which, because of the underlying 'interpretive work' on the part of the researcher, require the specification of method to ascertain the reasonable nature of the gloss – to the sympractical, situated work that itself exhibits the structures of the social situation to which the members to a setting orient, which they produce, and to which they are subject and subjected.

Primacy of the Societal Relation: Openings and Closings

> The original function of speaking is communication. Speaking is first a means of social intercourse, a means of utterance and understanding. (Vygotskij 2005: 675)

Vygotsky, as other practice theorists and philosophers, recognizes – in part on cultural-historical grounds – that the first function of speaking is not to be *about* something but that its function is *in order to* accomplish whatever needs to be or is in the process of being accomplished. Speaking is the foundation of language, which, as a grammatical and semantic system, emerges as the result of speaking (e.g., Leont'ev 1969).[13] The analysis of everyday language shows – and the analy-

---

[12] Carambo is the name of the teacher who writes about himself and this situation in the cited chapter.

[13] Here is not the place to elaborate on the dialectic of the genesis of language. There are two aspects to this. First, speaking emerges because hearing is already possible. That is, there is a primacy of hearing, that is, of the recipient, rather than that of speaking. Second, without speaking activity subordinated to life-sustaining activity more generally, there would be no language. Language is produced, reproduced, and transformed in real acts of speaking. Language, as a formal system, is the result of speech activity rather than the reverse (Leont'ev 1969).

sis of speaking in scientific laboratories is no different in this respect – that in 'most cases, speaking does not have the character of a theme of a definite statement' (Heidegger 19297/1977: 161–162). That is, first there is speaking, then there is grammar. Neither early humans nor children begin with grammar and then learn a language – only those who already know a language and grammar learn another in this manner. Immigrants with little schooling and little or no knowledge of formal grammar still tend to learn the new language through participation in everyday speech activity that occurs as part of society-sustaining productive or consumptive activity.

Early humans and young children, too, learned and developed language in speech activity, which is associated with existing social relations. Even before humans had language and even before children speak a word, they participate(d) in social relations. Sounds, as other signs, were part of the production and maintenance of the social relations: threaten another, give an order, organize a hunting party into, or showing the way. When language comes into play, there always already is an attunement (*Befindlichkeit*) and practical understanding of how the world works. Existentially seen, speaking is at the same primordial level: 'Attuned intelligibility *expresses itself as speech*' (Heidegger 1927/1977: 161). Thus, it is in speaking that the totality of practical understanding and intelligibility '*has its say*' (ibid: 161). We know that words do not initially exist for children apart from the situation in which they find themselves. Thus, objects and sound-words are tied into a whole. Without the thing that deserves the sound-word /tʃɛə(r)/ ('chair'), the sound-word makes no sense to the child. The sound does not 'represent' the thing: it cannot make the thing present again when it is absent. When the thing is present, then articulating the sound-word may lead to or be associated with a range of actions in the parent-child relation. New words accrue to always already existing significations rather than that word-things receive 'meanings' that science students somehow 'construct'. As a result, statements *about* things, phenomena, and states of affair are derivative of this original function of speaking. Genetically (developmentally), the soci(et)al relation exists prior to speaking.

Although speaking specifically and language generally are late-comers to societal relations, relations and communication belong together: We relate to others by communicating, and we communicate in societal relations. This is also the case when children develop competencies in natural language to the extent that they can talk *about* things and events not currently present, that is, that they *represent* things and events. All the while talking *about* something, they participate in making a societal situation whatever it recognizably is. Thus, while talking about the classroom episode, the researcher and teacher (Carrie) also make the interview situation. Speech itself is the articulation of intelligibility, both of the situation and the stuff (content, topic) that speech is about. In speaking, we make available to others just what kind of situation is taking place. Sometimes this goes without particular words that *formulate* the event; at other times, explicit formulations of precisely what is happening at the instants are integral part of the situation. In this case, the *about* and *in-order-to* functions of speaking are copresent. This is clearly the case in turn 151 of Fragment 4.1. Jane and Carrie are in the process of discussing possibilities that arise within the new task conditions. Rather than using candles to heat the air in the Chinese lantern she was designing, Jane was to use a hairdryer to heat the air while holding the lantern and, once the air was heated, let the lantern go. In the conversation, there is a statement | question sequence (turn pairs 148 | 150). The next turn pair 150 | 151 shows that it is not a question that has been heard but an interesting point that the student 'might like to comment on'.

Fragment 4.1
```
  148   C:   so you need to add it, you are not really (0.54) i
             guess you can look at ADding hot air or hEAting the
             AIr thats thEre.
  149        (0.66) ((Jane nods))
  150   J:   kay. but wouldnt that heat the air thats around the
             outside?=
→ 151   C:   ^NN. thats an interesting pOINt you mIght lIke to (.)
             commENT on that.
```

Here, turn 151 *formulates* what has been done in the preceding locution: 'an interesting point' has been stated. That is, the turn does not merely state something like 'Why don't you comment on that', 'How could we control for that?', or 'How will or might affect this the rising of the lantern?', which would have been *about* the experiment. The turn also formulates in just what the preceding turn existed: an interesting point.

In formulating what has happened, the conversation also contributes to managing the societal relation that is both produced in and through the talk and that gave rise to this very talk (see next section). The turn describes what someone else has done and then *invites* this other to do something else. That is, we witness relational work where one turn also produces an evaluative description of the quality of another turn; and it articulates an invitation.

Relations do not just exist out there; nor are relations boxes into which we step. Relations are made in and through relation-building (conversational) work. It is in and through the joint work that a relation comes into being. It cannot be otherwise, for both relation and conversation are irreducibly social in nature. Thus, if a *conversation* comes about and starts, then it as the result of the required conversation-opening work that gets the event going. That work is required we can easily when a 'pick-up line' remains without rejoinder. Thus, in an urban school, the following might be an intelligible second turn to the turn that opened the episode with a possible outcome that also might have constituted an end.

Fragment 4.2
```
  001   C:   okay. (0.24) OH; ((moves toward Jane)) i better talk
             to JAne first. (0.24) okAY:. (1.63) change of plA:Ns.
  002        (0.26)
  003   J:   dont disrespect me mam.
```

In this situation, the conversation produced and identified a 'disrespect'. Such an identification has consequences, for insisting on a 'change of plans' might be articulated as showing further disrespect, if in fact the change of plans is the issue responded to in turn 003. This is clearly apparent from a description concerning the refusal to comply that Ken Tobin provides from the classroom where he relearned to teach

One thing I learned from Tyrone is never to ask these students to do something if you cannot deal with the consequences of their refusing to do what is requested. What could I have done with Dante? Students like him are not afraid of the law and do not respect authority. Hence, threatening detention is no deterrent as most refuse to attend. In fact, if a student fails to attend a detention, s/he is suspended for 5 days. These students are not only unafraid of being suspended; many relish the thought of having a reason not to come to school and to stay at home or in the streets. (Roth and Tobin 2002: 56)

At this point in Fragment 4.2, just at the end of turn 003, the disrespect is the subject of the talk. Only further conversation and analysis by the participants themselves would show what precisely is going on. Most importantly, however, 'disrespect' is not something one person shows to another person. 'Disrespect' is a relation that involves at least two, one doing something and the other one *naming* the sign of disrespect that affects him. But words hurt only if they are let to hurt. Even a raised middle finger is a sign of disrespect (insult) only if it is taken to be as such. Something is a sign only when, being produced by one social actor, it affects or changes the behavior of another (Vygotsky 1978). That is, only on the condition that something – sound-word, middle finger, a whistle blow – affects or changes the behavior of others that it is a sign. In the words of the baseball umpire Klem, it is nothing until an action is called – in his situation, as a ball or a strike – that something comes to exist in and for a real social relation.[14]

In the present episode, Jane replies in a manner that permits further turns; and she does so in a manner that warrants the next turn to begin with the statement 'to make life easier' (turn 005). The statement explicates and provides a reason for 'change of plans' as an apparent replique to turn 003. Why might an explication of an announcement be necessary? Why might an explication be given? In any event, at that point we are already in the conversation. It has been opened. This opening arises from an offering to have a conversation with Jane that the speaker announces and the interjection with an intonation that makes disappointment hearable. 'Um' is an interjection that marks acknowledgment and assent but also hesitation. Even though heard in this way the interjection already would make sense, it may not be the ordinary sense that matters. It may just be a suitable sound carrier to make available an intonation that contains the real relational work (cf. Vološinov 1930; Vygotskij 2005) – in this case, the expression of disappointment over what the preceding utterance announces as something to come. The main point here is that in this case the *work* required to get the conversation off the ground is (almost) invisible. But the fact that something is invisible or that we tend to fail noticing it should not mean that it is nevertheless present and literally *at work*. Thus, for example, few people think about the shoes they are wearing while wearing them – unless there is trouble with these. So even though we do not normally attend to the shoes, they are still part of the unnoticed ground. Moreover, this example also

---

[14] It is useless to talk and speculate about ideal cases, such as whether a middle finger up in the air is or is not a sign. Here we are concerned with understanding real, concrete praxis. If a middle finger does not pair with a replique, if it is not 'called', then it is nothing *in the here and now of this situation*. This is the only thing that matters for our analysis concerned as it is with the endogenous production of concrete life in society.

shows that phenomena become apparent precisely when there is trouble, when a breakdown occurs.

We see another example of an opening in the subsection I glossed by the term {pleading}. The plea is introduced in reply to a statement that articulates variations in events, complications, and difficulties. In fact, the interjection 'please' *formulates* what the immediately preceding phrase, 'If I get it to work can I do it?' is intended to do: Make a plea for doing the original investigation rather than another one proposed in the course of the events. By adding 'please', Jane not only makes a plea but also explicitly states that she is doing so. The dictionary senses of 'to plead' include 'to contend in debate', 'to argue with or against', 'to make an appeal', 'to beg', and 'to implore'. But for the debate or argument to exist, it has to get off the ground. An invitation to a plea ('I>') – debate, argument – has to be paired with an acceptance ('A>') precisely as we find it in Fragment 4.3. The conditional statement 'If I get it to work can I do it' comes to be paired with the evaluating commentary 'but then you'll be spending more time trying to make it work' (turn 076).

Fragment 4.3
```
   073    C:   the:::ee (0.79) variATions in whats hAPppening;
                <<all>and the complicATions and dIFficulties in ACtu-
                ally> making it wO:::rk.
I>074    J:   <<all>if i get it to work can i do it> plEA::se.
   075         (0.24)
A>076    C:   .hhhh but then youll be spending mORe time trying to
                make it wORk.
```

Although the phrase neither accepts nor rejects what can be heard as a request ('can I do it?'), it does constitute a replique articulating a problem that already has been articulated in different ways: the difficulty of getting the investigation to work in the way that the teachers and curriculum want it to work. There is a replique and it is precisely in the replique that the plea is opened and can unfold. Only a few turns later, the plea is brought to a (sudden) end. Again, this is a form of event that does not just happen. It is brought about in and by the sympractical work of the members to the setting. Although the ending of turn 079 *could* be heard as an invitation to continue the plea, the next turn does not constitute the required acceptance that would bring about the continuation. Rather, turn 081 constitutes a 'suggestion' to work, 'for today', on the ideas arising from 'the other one' and 'trying to get the wax one to work' 'at home'. The suggestion is paired with an acceptance by means of assent expressing interjection 'kay'.

Fragment 4.4
```
   079    J:    [but if this time it doesnt work     ] (0.30) some
                (1.00) i promise i=ll: (0.17) go back (0.39) and
                (0.22) do: (0.44) <<all>the hairdryer one; but if
I>              this works (0.26) can i do it plEAse?
   080          (0.75)
→081    C:    so you:: (0.19) I:: wou:ld=suggest fr todA:Y: (0.48)
                you work on that (0.68) sort of (1.06) what ideas you
                can change for the other one .hhh and at hO:Me
                ((Jane's face changes to sad expression, averts gaze
                heretofore straight forwardly directed at Carrie's
                face)) (0.23) try:ing (0.41) <<all>try and get your
```

```
        wAX one to work.> ((Jane's face goes from smile to
        sadness))
082   J:   <<subdued, p>kay.>
```

In stating a suggestion for what to do on this day in the physics lesson, which is opposite to what has been pleaded for (i.e., a continuation with the original experiment), turn 091 also constitutes a rejection of the invitation to continue with the plea. Because of the suggestion | acceptance pairing, the conversation has ended the plea and simultaneously has established what is to occur next. There is more at issue here regarding the student–teacher relation and the question of power, which I attend to in chapter 6.

While organizing what to do next and how to do it, this stretch of classroom talk also is about a topic (the content of the talk); and it is providing the resources for conducting the relation, by opening particular forms of exchanges, like pleading, and closing them. These other forms of talk, though integral to the lessons, tend to be abstracted in the literature on learning science, as if students and teachers were attending to and talked about concepts first and foremost. As a result, it appears as if the thoughts were thinking themselves rather than mobilized by real people in real setting in the pursuit of needs, interests, and emotions – when in fact emotions are integral to the practical and intellectual dimensions at work (Roth 2007).

A most important aspect of the present section is that social relations and societal events – queuing for cinema tickets or lunch in a school cafeteria and bringing about science lessons as wholes and in each part – are *endogenously produced,* from the inside. Social relations are not fixed phenomena with roles into which social actors step. Rather, social actors – students and teachers in chemistry classrooms – observably and accountably together produce the structures that characterize the phenomenon. Although they may orient towards such phenomena in their conduct, these phenomena exist only in and through the joint (sympractical) work. The initial orientation *never* can guarantee that what is intended, on the parts of individuals, will actually happen. Thus, science teachers do not come to school to teach 'bad' or 'unsuccessful' lessons. Rather, such lessons emerge *despite* the intentions of the teacher and students. These lessons are the results of their sympractical engagement; these results have an *emergent, un-anticipated* quality much like any conversation involving two or more voices will lead to the emergence of ideas that no single individual participant has had or has thought about before.

Social relations, precisely because they are *social,* are phenomena that need to be studied as social phenomena sui generis. That is, we cannot describe, think about, and theorize them departing from the individual social actor who somehow throws something into a shared forum where others pick it up. In this latter way, we would lose our phenomenon of interest: the *social* in the social phenomenon. Rather, our unit of analysis needs to be framed such that it irreducibly encompasses the two or more participants (interlocutors) involved. The model in Fig. 4.1 shows how, if we take two turns as the minimum unit, then there are both synchronic and diachronic relations embodied in our unit. That is, framed in this way, we immediately have another theoretical pay-off: movement, (historical) change, and development are integral to the way *social* phenomena are framed.

When someone speaks, the other is actively listening. We cannot understand *any* conversation unless we attend to the simultaneous processes of speaking and

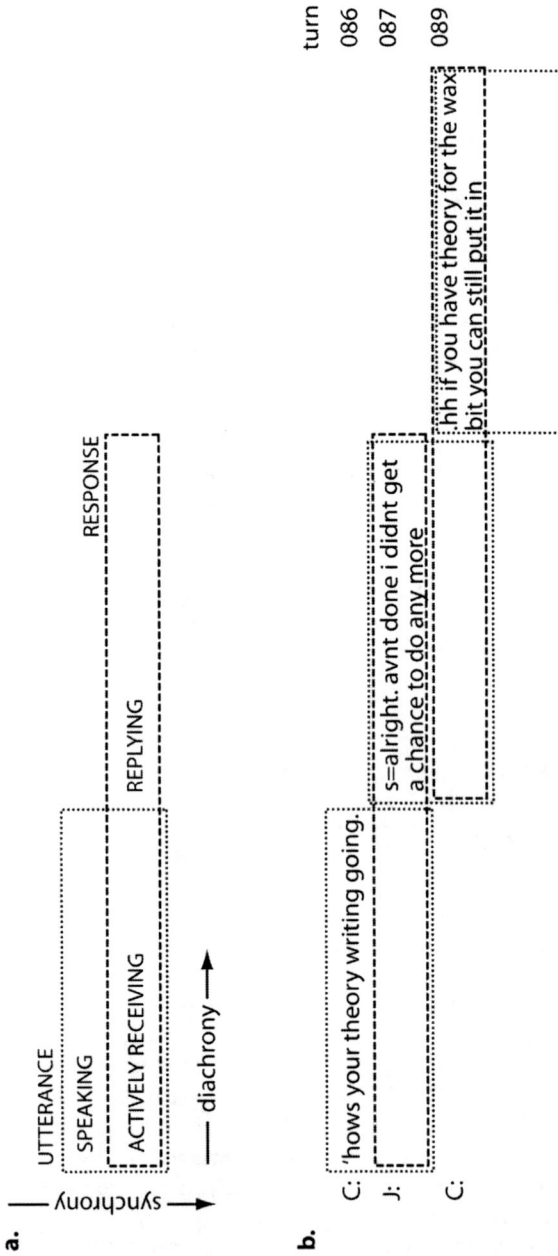

Fig. 4.1   a. A conversation, as irreducible social relation, involves synchronic (vertical) and diachronic (horizontal) dimensions: utterance and response, respectively. b. An example from the transcript (turns 086–089).

actively receiving (Vološinov 1930). That is, any word *immediately* is theorized as belonging to two or more interlocutors participating in the conversation. The fact that hearing occurs while speaking goes on is hardly ever theorized and brought to bear on the analysis of classroom talk. Words, therefore, tend to be attributed to the speaker rather than to speaker and recipient in the way a dialogical approach requires (Bakhtin 1979). Words tend to be expression of whatever is on the inside of the person, the person's mind. But in the present approach, the word belongs to both, so that the unit of analysis in fact constitutes a *social* rather than a individual psychological phenomenon. At the same time, the same word or phrase is not the same for speaker and listener: the word is one but not the same. There is an inner difference. This inner difference expresses itself as movement. In fact, to get movement into our theories, we need to think difference-in-itself rather than in terms of difference between concepts (Deleuze 1968; Roth 2008a). We can say that in a conversation each word, each phrase is *diastatic*, that is, spread across multiple, differing interlocutors.

As Fig. 4.1 shows, there is a second diastatic moment in conversations: the response. In the way articulated here, the response does not merely imply the reply but actually is stretched across active reception and replique (cf. Waldenfels 2006). The response, therefore is unfolding across time: it is inherently diachronous in nature. Therefore, not only speaking and hearing unfold in time, but the unit of responding, constituted by actively receiving and replying, also unfolds in time.

As a result of this framing, change is inherent in the model in a double and mutually constitutive way. First, difference and change is apparent in the word, which is both the same and not the same for speaker and recipient; second, difference and change is apparent in the temporal unfolding of speaking | hearing of the first moment of a turn pair and the hearing | speaking associated with the second moment of the turn pair.

A societal relation, therefore, inherently is something we need to think in dialectical terms, because it is the same (because it is *one*) and different (because it involves *two* or *more*) simultaneously. Moreover, a societal relation is something that changes in and over time. The very idea of exchange in and through which a societal relation is realized, if thought dialectically, leads us to history (Marx/Engels 1962). Thus, in a sociological approach to linguistics, the word, phrase, or statement,[15] lodged between interlocutors has precisely the same role as the commodity in a sociological approach to political economy, with its simultaneous manifestation as use-value and exchange-value. In fact, in the Russian language of Vološinov, Bakhtin, and Vygotsky, the word *značenie*, 'signification' (unfortunately often translated as 'meaning'), also is used as an equivalent of 'value'. The language theory that evolved from the work of the Bakhtin circle, therefore, is structurally equivalent to Marx's theory of the development of economic markets.

---

[15] In Russian, Vološinov uses the term *vyzkazyvanie* often translated as 'utterance'. However, there is confusion because Vološinov and Bakhtin emphasize not only the speaking but also the receiving dimension. In English, however, utterance tends to be tied to the act of speaking only disregarding the dimension of social evaluation that is bound up with. Thus, *vyzkazyvanie* is probably better translated by the English term 'statement'.

Endogenously Produced Objective Reality of Social Facts

> For ethnomethodology the objective reality of social facts, in that and just
> how it is every society's locally, endogenously produced, naturally orga-
> nized, reflexively accountable, ongoing, practical achievement, being every-
> where, always, only, exactly and entirely, members' work, with no time out,
> and with no possibility of evasion, hiding out, passing, postponement, or
> buy-outs, is *thereby* sociology's fundamental phenomenon. (Garfinkel 1988:
> 103).

Before taking a look at the endogenous nature of the work that brings about social
facts, I unpack this important statement concerning the ethnomethodological position. This quotation, especially the statement that there is an 'objective reality of
social facts' that is 'sociology's fundamental phenomenon' is likely to raise the ire
of avowed constructivists. My phenomenological stance *has* raised the ire of well-
known constructivists in mathematics education during a meeting where I also was
a plenary speaker talking about the difference between living and lived (constructed) aspects of mathematical work (Roth 2011b). 'There is no objective reality',
according to constructivists, 'there are only mental constructions'. Apart from the
fact that the present unit of analysis is not the individual who, alone or in collaboration with others merely constructs the world, saying that there is no objective
reality does not quite get (at) the point.

Take a look, for example, at the example of a queue. You may find yourself at
the end of a long line, and, after a while, having become annoyed by the fact that
there appears to be little movement, you decide to come back another day to see
the movie. You have attended to the queue not as a construction in your mind but
as something really and concretely there in the world. It made you upset – you did
not just construct being upset in your mind, you were really upset. You may have
cursed or said something to another person waiting next to you. You left, having
decided you would return another day. In these actions, the queue and the waiting
times are real things and they are objectively so for those who stand in line with
you. The phenomenon exists for you, with real implications for your emotions and
actions. If the queue had been a mere construction of your mind, a simple switch
could have made you see it differently.

Ethnomethodological studies take up and realize a program that has come to life
with phenomenological studies of the everyday world. The interest of such studies
lies in how we live, think, and act in our everyday world. In our mundane lives, we
take the objectivity of the world for granted (Husserl 2008). This taking the world
for granted pertains not only to the natural world but also to the social world,
which we experience as constituted by social facts. Queues, institutions, greetings,
or offenses all are real things with real consequences to what we do, think, and talk
about. The point of ethnomethodology is that what we do and say produces the
world as it presents itself to us – not individually but collectively. A queue is not
just some thing out there; real people acting in specific, recognizable and teachable
('instructable') ways make a queue for what it is. We not only contribute to making
a queue for what it is, we can recognize a queue in many different places, realized
in many different ways: in the bank, in front of a movie theater, on the ramp to a

freeway (motorway, autobahn), soup kitchen, school cafeteria, supermarket fish counter, and so on. Even young students, such as second graders, contribute to the production of lessons such that an accidental visitor would recognize that there is a geometry lesson rather than something else in progress (Roth 2011a; Roth and Thom 2009).

Social situations are not boxes or schemas that exist out there so that we only take a place. When the first people arrive in what will later be recognized to be a queue, there is nothing that they (could) step into. There is no line into which they could get themselves in. Someone wants a ticket but finds the window closed or has to wait because someone else is already at the ticket window. Another person arrives, then another, and another. Almost without realizing, we all of a sudden find ourselves in a queue. The others, as we, are real people doing what they might do in such a situation. It is from their sympractical work that the queue is forming in the *particular* way that we experience it; and, despite its particularity, and despite sometimes-large variation from what a queue normally looks like, we do recognize it – even though there might be scholars arguing that a queue is 'just a social construct'. It is not a construct – it is a real product of sympractical work. Thus, as pointed out in the introductory quotation to this section, the social facts are ongoing practical achievements. They are accountably so, as we know from those instances when a person does not act in accordance with the local customs of queuing.[16] Someone may butt in rather extending the queue at its end or the next person in line may not move even though an opportunity has arisen for being served. That they have done so might be the content of a remark, which makes available to everybody else present that a 'butt-in' has been noticed: 'Get in line as everybody else!'. And this remark might be a sufficient constituent for a compliance | acceptance pair, realized if the addressee turns around and goes to {the end of line}. Accountable also means that we can provide an account of the phenomenon, which we do when we return home to talk about the terribly long time we had to wait until being served.

In that work that produces social phenomena, there is no time out, no way of escaping when we are within. Even non-action is taken to be an action. For example, when there is no immediate student reply, teachers tend to provide some such themselves, ask another student, or rephrase a question until some reply that suffices the situation has been furnished. In the case of rephrasing a question, the non-response has de facto been taken as an inability to reply or a difficulty to understand the original question. There is therefore no time out in social affairs because every behavior, even inaction, is or can be taken as a form of action.

When the episode in the physics classroom begins, with the announcement of a talk with Jane and the change of plans, nobody has or could have an inkling about what is going to happen next, how long it would take, and when it would be completed. Let us take another look at how it all began (Fragment 4.5). We may gloss the fragment by saying that Carrie hearably announces what is to come, a talk and a change of plan. But just by looking at the opening four turns, there is nothing that would allow us to predict the next 154 turns, the more than 5 minutes that this

---

[16] The person would be performing the work of 'doing {not acting in accordance with the local customs of queuing}'.

would, or the specific course that the stretch of classroom talk would take. The organization, from the opening to the ending of the episode is entirely produced from within, as replique gives rise to replique gives rise to replique until the end of the entire exchange has been achieved and marked as such in the actions of the participants who attend to something other than the exchange: Carrie gets up, literally turns her back on Jane (and the episode), and talks to other students. Jane picks up some materials, diddles around with them, and works on her project.

```
Fragment 4.5
  001   C:  okay. (0.24) OH; ((moves toward
            Jane)) i better talk to JAne first.
            (0.24) okAY:. (1.63) changef plA:Ns.
  002       (0.26)
  003   J:  U::M::: ((head sideward, gloss: dis-
            appointment on face))
  004       (0.76)
```

The list of ethnographer's glosses that together constitute the main gloss of 'change of plans' shows that there aspects to this conversations that do not need to be there. In other circumstances, we might not have had a plea to continue with the same investigation. The presence of the plea – the beginning, unfolding, and ending of this happening – are completely produced and organized from within the conversation. There is no schema for a conversation to have such a part included. There is no schema for the two interlocutors to jump into an transaction of the type called 'plea' and then enact it. A better way of looking at, understanding, and theorizing what was happening and the turns that the conversation was taking is to think about it as organized on the fly, with the resources at hand – most notably language – without time out and 'with no possibility of evasion, passing, postponement, or buy-outs'. The actions of one interlocutor would not bring about happenings that could have been ethnographically glossed in the way I did (e.g., 'pleading to be able to continue with original plan'). The hardest part in making the switch from thinking about social events from the psychological to the sociological perspective lies in overcoming our own (naïve) epistemologies, which arise from the fact that we appear to be stuck in bodies and see the world through a lens that always is *mine* (Husserl 2008). But this lens is itself a *result* of societal relations and it is only when we conceive it as such that we come to better understand the sociality of societal phenomena, including issues such as consciousness, language, queues, and science lessons.

Changes in conversational topics are not just happening; these are not just events or schemas into which interlocutors step. Topics are not merely changed because one participant wants to change topic – though this may *also* be the case. Changes of topic are conversational phenomena and therefore require a *social* approach, that is, we have to look at, understand, and theorize them as irreducible social phenomena sui generis, the results of coordinated, *sym*practical *social* (rather than individual) action. The topic changes repeatedly in the conversation analyzed here, but the *work* aspects may be more difficult to see because the invitations to change topic are immediately and unproblematically accepted. Thus, for example, when turn 086 articulates and therefore proposes theory writing as the new topic and turn 087, by taking up this topic also accepts it as new topic, the real work completed is easily overlooked.

```
Fragment 4.6
I>086   C:   'hows your thEOry wrIting gOing.
A>087   J:   <<unconvinced>s=alright.> ((gaze on to desk, averted,
             Fig. 3.4)) (0.18) avnt done (0.16) i didnt get a
             chance to do any more. <<pp>???>
```

Here, the invitation ('I>') to talk theory writing is accepted ('A>') in the next turn. The *joint* work, however, exists in the relation of inviting | accepting. That a change of topic was offered would have been made explicit if the second turn had taken a different form – perhaps in a different school or with a 'difficult' or 'reticent' student. In a self-reported event, Ken Tobin writes about such an instant: 'I was speaking to Dante about his annoying habit of speaking loudly to a peer whenever I spoke to the class. I believed that Dante was testing me and I was aggravated by his increasing tendency to be disruptive. However, my making his behavior an issue gave him a public forum in which to impress his peers. Dante looked at me with disdain and commenced a rebuttal: "You speaking so loud I have to ..."' (Roth and Tobin 2002: 55–56). Leaving aside the typical psychological tendency of researchers to attribute intentions and motives, the narrative shows that invitations offered by teachers, here to be quiet or talk less loudly, are not always accepted by students. In fact, the student did commence providing an intelligible reason for having to speak loudly: the teacher was speaking so loud that the student has to ... do something that remains unstated here as a school-employed guard intervened. The following two fragments provide alternative second turns that would have practically changed this situation.[17]

```
Fragment 4.7
I>086   C:   'hows your thEOry wrIting gOing.
R>087   J:   but i dont want to change i want to do my experiment
             with the waxes.
```

```
Fragment 4.8
I>086   C:   'hows your thEOry wrIting gOing.
R>087   J:   you are trying to change topic but we are not done
             yet talking about change of plans.
```

In both fragments, the invitation would have been (implicitly) rejected as the second turn returns to the preceding topic. In Fragment 4.8, this change of topic would have been explicitly named – i.e., formulated – *in* the conversation and *for* the conversation. My own formulation {change of topic in order to talk theory} would then be an instant of a witness hearing the talk about a change of topics. That is, turn 087 in Fragment 4.8 would have exhibited the formulating '*for* the telling' (see next section).

Science lessons are not just 'enacted', as some scholars intimated already around the end of the 1980s (see chapter 8). Enactment is enactment of things or

---

[17] These fragments constitute phenomenological variations generated to explore to totality of possibilities of a situation for the purpose of investigating the underlying work required for producing a particular phenomenon (e.g., Husserl 1976).

plans – which, in the Piagetian, embodiment, and enactivist traditions have come to be schemas. But schemas would not explain the sudden and not so sudden changes in social transactions and conversations. Whatever happens and whenever it happens is organized from within so that there is both a problem when things and plans change and not a problem when they change, because next steps are again arising from the symplpractical work itself without requiring the presence of any individual or shared schemas. These, I would understand as but glosses of complex events, phenomena, and happenings and, therefore, as precisely not explaining the *work* that brings events, phenomena, and happenings *to life*.

Managing Social Relation – Formulating

Science educators interested in the role of language in science classroom will be familiar with the notion of *IRE*, an acronym standing for a sequentially ordered turn-taking routine or transaction ritual with three parts: an *i*nitiation, a *r*eply, and an *e*valuation. The *IRE* transaction ritual has come to be much maligned because of the way in which the participants in lessons occupy the three positions: the teacher tends to take and have the first and third position, students take the second position. In the sociological approach, evaluation of a preceding utterance is *inherent* in the transaction ritual (Vološinov 1930), though not quite in the way it functions here – even the middle term, the reply, would be an evaluation, here of the preceding initiation. The third position, in the way it is employed in school-based transaction rituals, has a particular function: it leads to the historical reproduction of the sciences, including mathematics, because the evaluative turn provides a judgment as to the degree to which a student reply matches with a historical precedent (Roth and Gardner 2012). On an historical scale, mathematics and the sciences come to be reproduced in and through the singular actions of individuals because of the particular nature of the turn-taking rituals in which children and students partake in the course of their development. In this section, I develop a further dimension concerning the evaluative turn specifically and all forms of classroom talk that pertain to, and are integral features of, the classroom talk itself.

I begin with the observation that 'among conversationalists it is an immensely commonplace feature of conversations that a conversation exhibits *for its parties* its own familiar features of a "sef-explicating colloquy"' (Garfinkel and Sacks 1986: 170). That is, as I state above, the conversation, by talking about itself, exhibits features of the conversation *for* the participants; the conversation thereby comes to explicate itself, it is a 'self-explicating colloquy'. The purpose, I suggest, is to manage the conversation and, thereby, the social relation that it produces and that itself gives rise to the conversation. Thus, a member of the conversational setting 'may treat some part of the conversation as an occasion *to describe that conversation, to explain it, or characterize it, or explicate, or translate, or summarize, or furnish the gist of it, or take note of its accordance with rules, or remark on its departure from rules*' (ibid: 170–171, emphasis added). Doing something with an aspect of a conversation as part of the conversation – naming, identifying, defining, describing, explaining, and so on – has come to be known as *formulating* the conversation. Formulating has important functions in science lessons as well. Take the following example, which in fact constitutes an instance of an *IRE*-type transaction ritual.

Fragment 4.9

```
  008    C:    ((200 Hz)) EE::: umm::::; (0.85) BUT (0.50) <<all>but
               it might still work for chAnge of plANs.> (0.22)
               .hhHH its (0.36) ↓'O::N:: (0.52) mOO:dl, the new
               stAtement, (0.24) but it is to dO with (0.21) .hhhhh
               <<len>hAVing a lANtern,> (0.50) with hOt AI::r (0.23)
               <<all>added to it> (0.26) by means other than using
               the flA:Me, (0.91) suchA:s;
  I>           <<all>can=you=think=of=anything>
  009          (1.11)
  I>010  C:    <<all>hotair> (1.88) <<p>like we get hot air from.>
  011          (0.75)
  R>012  J:    breath INto It?
  013          (1.25) (('yea' gesture))
  E>014  C:    EAsier=than=thA:ī
```

At the end of turn 008, Carrie is offering an opportunity to Jane to provide something, as a reply, which would put hot air into the (Chinese) lantern 'by means other than using the flame'. There is no response, which gives Carrie another opportunity to frame an invitation to reply by what we can hear as reframing or elaborating the question (turn 010). In other words, the pause in turn 009 is treated here as an instance that whatever has been said before is not understood, was unintelligible, or in other ways interfered with soliciting some intended reply. There then is a reply, articulated not in the form of a statement but, as there is a rising intonation towards the end, as a question: the statement is a tentative one, involving also the possibility to hear it as a question about whether the statement is a correct one. Jane thereby does two things at once. The evaluative turn 014 then is about the preceding turn, evaluates it all the while contributing to the conversation: whatever the intended reply, it is easier than breathing into the lantern.

In the present situation, therefore, turn 014 comments on and evaluates a preceding turn. It *characterizes* the turn as stating something more difficult than what the initiation was intended to solicit. In this way, turn 014 manages the conversation in that it seeks to bring forth, as a matter of the conversation, a particular feature. But the student is to produce this feature for the teacher; by the very fact that the teacher provides the evaluative turn, she also comes to be in the know about what the preceding turn really should have been. In turn 151, we observe another evaluative statement, where 'that's an interesting point' comments on the preceding student-generated statement that using a hairdryer to blow hot air into the Chinese lantern also would heat up the air surrounding the lantern. The conversation, again, turns upon itself by commenting upon an aspect of itself that has immediately preceded it. This commentary is as much an integral part as any other statement about the real topic of talk.

Another instance of a 'self-explicating colloquy' immediately follows in the episode. Here the function is to offer both a candidate response together with a critique. That is, the same turn 016 provides a candidate answer and possible evaluation of it. The turn begins with 'I would say fire'. It thereby states what would have been said. But this reply would have not been in accordance with the rule that is to regulate replies: 'hot air added to it *by means other than using the flame*'. That is, turn 008 states the rules of engagement, the nature of candidate replies, and turn 016 explicitly makes reference to this rule by using it to delimit what would have been said. I return below this point under the perspective of formulating practices as being '"exhibited *in* the speaking"' and as '"exhibitable *for* the telling"' (Garfinkel and Sacks 1986: 172, original emphases).

Fragment 4.10
```
→ 016     J:   i would say fIre but its a flame.
  017          (0.30)
  018     C:   yea::. (0.64) <<all>hairdryer, (0.77) somethI:Ng⁻
               ((gesture as if wanting to 'draw something out'))
```

In using the conditional, turn 016 both states and at the same time withholds an answer and *re*states the rule for why the answer should be withheld. By restating the rule, the turn not only exhibits the rule, *again*, but also shows that in its initial form, it was exhibited so that it subsequently could be talked about or referenced in further talk.

The verb 'shall' or more frequently its past tense 'should' also is used to articulate something that has *not* been said without actually stating the situation as such. Followed by an infinitive, such as 'should have', the verb states what is right or what is becoming. When it appears as a second turn, then the phrase 'you should have ...' states what would have been the right thing to do when it *actually* has not been done. Take the following example. The instance takes place when the conversation orients to the theory that Jane is to write for her investigation. Carrie says that if Jane were to have a theory about the effects of different waxes, she could state it but without doing the investigation. In Fragment 4.11, Jane states that she 'needs to do the experiment ... to get the theory because nobody has done an experiment like that'. The next turn then uses the expression 'should have' to *formulate* what is missing from the preceding statement: 'a reason why it changes' (turn 097).

Fragment 4.11
```
  093     J:   no i need to [do the experiment               ]
  094     C:                [<<all>you still have theory on it.>]
  095     J:   to get the theory because theres nobody whos dONe an
               expERiment like that.
  096          (0.40)
F> 097    C:   yea but you should have a rEAson wHY: it chANges.
               ((Jane's face pensive))
  098          (0.93)
  099     J:   well it could [    (??)    ]
  100     C:                 [because if] there is nO rEAson whY
               then theres nOT much point dOIng it.
  101     J:   if gonna be (.) <<p>its gonna be hotter so it takes
               the little cup>
```

Turn 097, therefore, states what ought to have been stated before, a reason, and the phrase 'should have' allows us that has not been stated. The exchange that follows shows that the interlocutors are oriented precisely to this hearing. Turn 099, which cannot be discerned in its entirety, clearly uses a conditional 'could' that might have introduced a possible cause. There is an overlapping turn stating that there would be no reason why changes are expected, there is no reason for doing an investigation in the first place. Turn 101 then states the condition of an hypothesis, 'it's gonna be hotter' followed by the beginning of an implication, 'so it takes the little cup ...'.

We already observe another feature of self-explicating colloquy in the very opening of the conversation where Carrie offers up an invitation to start a conversation. In Fragment 4.5, the first locution states 'I better talk to Jane first', which is said within hearing range of Jane. Because it comes to constitute the beginning of the conversation, an offering to start it, it is also a statement that talks about itself. It addresses and speaks to Jane by stating just that very fact. Under normal situations, this would be odd, if, when we are talking to someone (e.g., Jane) we were to say 'I better talk to Jane'. The latter part of the turn, too, makes a statement about the conversation, not backwards about what has been said so far but forwards, about what is to come: 'change of plans'. Whatever it turns out to be, the conversation will be taken, from the perspective of Carrie, as producing a 'change of plans'. This is her plan. We do see that in the present case, the change of plans comes to be realized. But this does not mean that this will be the actual course of the events. There are always opportunities for events to be different than anticipated, for example, if Carrie had been open to the Jane's plea and, as a result, if Jane had had another opportunity to try her wax experiment.

We also take note of the fact that Jane not only says 'if I get it to work can I do it?' (turn 073) and 'but if this works can I do it?' (turn 079) but, in both instances, follows the statement by saying 'please'. She thereby explicitly describes the function of the preceding locution as attenuated pleas. In that same context, there is another formulation when Jane not only articulates 'going back and doing the hairdryer one' 'if this time it doesn't work', but she also formulates the former as a promise. She does not merely make a statement of what a current course of action will be when the planned investigation fails but, in stating the intended course of action as a promise, offers a form of a social contract. The implications of not following the stated course of actions are very different when articulated in the form of a social contract that can subsequently be said to have been broken.

Fragment 4.12
```
   079   J:    [but if this time it doesnt work      ] (0.30) some
   F>           (1.00) i promise i=ll: (0.17) go back (0.39) and
                (0.22) do: (0.44) <<all>the hairdryer one; but if
   F>           this works (0.26) can i do it plEAse?
```

There are further instances of this conversation as self-explicating colloquy, which exemplify further functions that may be of interest to science educators. One occurs immediately following the preceding fragment and the statement of the hairdryer as the sought-for means to supply 'hot air by means other than a flame'. (In the subsequent conversation with the researcher, Carrie articulates the hairdryer as the only alternative she could think of.) The offer of the hairdryer as an alternative for supplying hot air to the Chinese lantern is followed by an explication of what the preceding turn 'means' without actually stating so: Jane 'can't experiment with the waxes'.

Fragment 4.13
```
  018    C:    yea::. (0.64) <<all>hairdryer, (0.77) somethI:Ng⁻
                ((gesture as if wanting to 'draw something out'))
  019           (0.54)
F>020    J:    that means i cant experiment with the wa[xes.  ]
  021    C:                                              [wAX?  ]
                (0.93) NO. (.) <<assertive>you cA:nt experiment with
                different wA[xes.]>
```

Here, turn 019 states what turn 018 is telling without actually saying it in so many words. To elaborate, we may gloss what is happening in this way. We may hear Jane to be saying 'You are telling me to use the hairdryer, but you are really saying that I can't do the experiment with the waxes'. The next turn, which takes the form of a constative statement that repeats the preceding one and therefore reifies it as being the case: 'You can't experiment with different waxes'. That is, Jane can be heard as offering a candidate hearing of what Carrie is really saying and Carrie affirms this is what she is saying without actually having articulated it. This excerpt therefore illustrates 'the point that along with whatever else may be happening in conversation it may be a feature of the conversation for the conversationalists that they are doing something else, namely, what they are doing is saying-in-so-many-words-what-we-are-doing (or what we are talking about, or who is talking, or who we are, or where we are, etc.)' (Garfinkel and Sacks 1986: 171).

What is happening in Fragment 4.12 can also be thought about in terms of the notion of *euphemism*. This is a rhetorical figure whereby a word or expression with less unpleasant implications and associations is used to replace an intended expression that is harsher but more accurately articulates what is intended. The conversation already has announced a change of plans; but it is here that Jane articulates for the first time what the 'change of plan' describes: she cannot do the investigation that she has designed and instead she is to heat the air by means of a 'hairdryer, something'. We have seen that Jane's disappointment is written all over the situation (turn 022) and addressed in the subsequent turn that states what she can really do instead. In this case, therefore, formulating was used to say what a statement has meant without stating it and, here, has uncovered a euphemism. The emotional expression that follows makes available the harsher and more offensive nature of the *real* message that has been provided as compared to the original form of speech that appeared to be more favorable. Chapter 3 also shows that the correct nature of the hearing provided in turn 020 is reiterated in turn 035, which states 'yes, you won't be able to test different types of waxes'.

Another case of what can be heard as a euphemism occurs when teachers somehow 'suggest' a course of action all the while it may be apparent that there would be sanctions of the suggestions were not followed. A suggestion *proposes* a course of action as one among possibly many possible courses of action. In Fragment 4.14, the verb 'suggest' is articulated as part of a conditional, 'I would suggest'. Here, rather than simply stating 'today you work on that', which could be heard as an order, and, therefore, as something more unpleasant, coercive, or harsher, a euphemistic 'I suggest' is further attenuated by a conditional construction. This is quite in contrast to the earlier, unattenuated statement 'you can't experiment with different waxes'.

Fragment 4.14
```
F>081   C:   so you:: (0.19) I:: wou:ld=suggest fr todA:Y: (0.48)
             you work on that (0.68) sort of (1.06) what ideas you
             can change for the other one .hhh and at hO:Me
             ((Jane's face changes to sad expression, averts gaze
             heretofore straight forwardly directed at Carrie's
             face)) (0.23) try:ing (0.41) <<all>try and get your
             wAX one to work.> ((Jane's face goes from smile to
             sadness))
   082  J:   <<subdued, p>kay.>
   083       (0.48)
   084  C:   <<all>kay?>
```

The function of the formulation in these examples is to place an intended course of action into a better light, to make the intended action appear less harsh than it really is. In this analysis, I emphasize what the actors, here Carrie and Jane make available *to* and *for* each other. Later, in her explanations to the researcher interviewing her about the event, Carrie says, among others 'I sort of knew that she wouldn't be particularly happy with it and I guess I approached her with the idea that I wanted her to feel that it was a good thing rather than meaning she'd done all this work and it was wasted' (see chapter 2, Gloss 1, p. 31). We return to these issues in the context of knowledge/power, a particular form of relation that tends to be taken as if it existed out there but that really requires work from which the unequal status of the participants emerges as the result. In the present context, we simply note that formulating in the way observed has a function of managing the social relation. Formulations such as 'I guess' (turn 148) also constitute mitigations of a conversation of which they are integral part. Thus, in turn 148, the verb precedes the phrase 'you can look at adding hot air or heating the air that's there'. This phrase states two ways of looking at the same situation: the hairdryer adds hot air to the Chinese lantern or heats the air that is there. But the statement is changed because 'I guess' introduces uncertainty. Such uncertainty places speakers in positions where they can easily back off a statement without losing face (Roth and Middleton 2006). Turn 150 evaluates the statement by stating that 'that' 'would heat the air that's around the outside'. This could be heard as a critique of using a hairdryer, at least when it is used to 'heating the air that's there'.

Fragment 4.15
```
   148  C:   so you need to add it, you are not really (0.54) i
             guess you can look at ADding hot air or hEAting the
             AIr thats thEre.
   149       (0.66) ((Jane nods))
E>150  J:   kay. but wouldnt that heat the air thats around the
             outside?=
   151  C:   ^NN. thats an interesting pOINt you mIght lIke to (.)
             commENT on that.
```

But, the fact that the two possibilities have been offered together with a statement that makes them more tentative provides an easy way out. We see this occuring in turn 151, which evaluates 150 to constitute 'an interesting point', that is, a point of sufficient interest to warrant a comment about it (possibly in the write-up).

Endogenous Production is Joint, Sympractical Work

This chapter chiefly is concerned with the *endogenous* production of societal situations in conversations. That is, social situations and individual actions are not taken to be routine *enactments* of individual or social schemas that actors have acquired at some other stage of their lives. If this were the case, social life would be quite boring as actions always could be anticipated because they would always be based on a perhaps large but limited number of schemas. This approach would also not address the disjunction between plans and situated actions that are such that even highly experienced scientists may not know what they have *actually* done until much later when they realize that they have done something else than intended (e.g. Roth 2009a). The analyses provided in this chapter, by focusing on the *conversation*, take emphasis away from the particular speakers. This is consistent with the emphasis on the conversation as a social phenomenon rather than as a phenomenon composed of simpler elements. Phenomena such as *openings, closings,* and *change of topic* always are conversational, that is, irreducible to individual actors and therefore have to be theorized as the result of joint, sympractical work. The minimum unit of work always includes multiple actors, who realize the work but whose contributions can be understood only through their relation to the whole, joint work. There is a true whole–part relation, where the parts cannot be understood without reference to the whole, and the whole exists only in and through its parts. Moreover, because it is understood in and through its contribution to the whole, each part requires and presupposes all other parts. We cannot therefore attribute statements to individual speakers, because *within* the conversation, the statement inherently relates (or does so in negating a previous turn, such as in change of topic) to the preceding statement and to the subsequent statement. In each case, a statement is produced *in* and *as* replique to what has happened before and sets up – but does not complete – the next turn pair. Each statement, therefore, only makes sense in this double relation to preceding and succeeding turns. Fig. 4.1 makes explicit how each turn does linking work, producing the conversation as an unfolding phenomenon that organizes itself from *within*.

This has immediate implications for the way in which we think about science lessons. It is not that the teacher has sole responsibility for what happens generally and for students' achievements specifically. If science lessons are endogenously produced, then there are relations that we need to focus on. Once administrators think about relations as the sources for what happens in the classrooms of their jurisdiction (school, school board), then they need to address more than individual teachers – who might be required to take additional training, or who might be 'let go' – or individual students – who are suspended and expelled for their behavior – and focus on the real, *societal* determinants of events in *societal* institutions such as schools and their constituents, the classrooms that are of interest to science educators.

In their paper on the formal structures of practical action, Garfinkel and Sacks (1986) use square brackets to set apart text within a conversation where a speaker engages in formulating. In the present chapter, typical examples of this would include '[but if this one works can I do it please?]' (turn 079) and '[I would suggest for today you work on that]' (turn 081). The authors then elaborate just what we are to understand when seeing these square brackets making three main points, which I elaborate and unpack referring to specific examples from the present setting. First, 'formulating is an account-able phenomenon' (ibid: 172), which involves the following six points. (a) Formulating 'is a phenomenon that members make happen: that members *perform*' (ibid: 172). Thus, for example, pleading is not just some fact but something that is performed; moreover, it is not the work of one but is a social phenomenon, involving someone who pleads and something to whom the plea is addressed. (b) The phenomenon 'is observable *by its members*' (ibid: 172). That is, in contrast to constructive and constructivist approaches, where, for example, the 'misconceptions' are not recognized as social facts by those who are said to express them, in the approach articulated here the social fact (formulating) is observable by the members themselves. (c) 'In that members can do the phenomenon and observe it, it is *reportable*' (ibid: 172), which means that both participants and vicarious observers can report that this is what members have said to be going on. For example, when Jane talked to the researcher, she reported to him an earlier formulation on the part of Carrie the teacher: she had to [come up with a good reason] (Gloss 3, chap. 2). Researchers, too, are among those who, after watching a videotape or after having participated directly in a conversation, what a participant has said was going on. After having watched the videotapes, I was able to report that Jane pleaded her case, as indicated by the fact that she said 'please' repeatedly. (d) 'The phenomenon is done and reportable by members with texts such as those that are bracketed. It is done as well with script, utterances, or graphics, i.e., with circumstantially particular, notational displays' (ibid: 172). In the present case, I used precisely the members' own words to state what they have formulated and how they have formulated it. (e) 'The bracketed text is a phase of an interactional enterprise' (ibid: 172), which we can see because it is part of the transcription that has been prepared on the basis of the videotapes recording the event. Finally, (f) 'the text is meaning differently than the speaker can say in so many words' (ibid: 172), a point that is immediately clear when we think about the relationship between the bracketed phrase and what it refers to. These two are not the same so that the phrase *inherently* means differently than it can say. A particularly striking instance occurred when Jane says '[that means I can't experiment with waxes]', which refers to a very different phrase, which is about using a hairdryer.

A second major point to be articulated in using the square brackets is that 'all of the foregoing features are *practical* accomplishments over the *exigencies* of *actual* interaction' (ibid: 172, emphases added). In the learning sciences literature, use is frequently made of the notion of practice, a term that refers to patterned actions. In saying that we participate in practices, theorists emphasize the commonalities across singular performances. These commonalities underlie what have been known as communities of practice[18], that is, groupings that are defined by series or sets of actions that share a high degree of commonality. There are some core prac-

---

[18] Although the term still tends to be used unproblematically, there are considerable internal contradictions in its use (e.g., Roth and Lee 2006). I know from personal conversations with J. Lave about her ambivalence with respect to the ways in which the term 'communities of practice' is used.

titioners that more typically stand for the community in and with their performances and 'newcomers', who are only beginning and whose performances, therefore, are not yet of the precise nature of the core practitioners, though already recognizable to the extent that the newcomer is a newcomer in and to a whole. This framing, however, does insufficiently justice to the fact that there is a wide variation of actions and happenings or that it is precisely in those variations that the usefulness of a generalizing concept exists. The idea of documentary evidence, here, is much more powerful because it plays on whole-part relations. Although every member part in a whole is different in its outer manifestations as are the living members of a family, the family is what it is *because* of the variation. The same idea is at work in the ethnomethodological framing, where, for example, the queue in front of the cinema ticket window and the line-up of cars trying to get onto a motorway (freeway, Autobahn, autostrada, autoroute) is part of the same family of phenomena. These phenomena are always practical accomplishments in the face of the exigencies of every actual situation and transaction. In this framing, therefore, we have a radical departure of the commonly used schemas and practices, which focus on similarity and self-identity, whereas the approach championed here focuses on diversity and the situated, always differing accomplishment of social structure. Heterogeneity and difference-in-itself rather than self-identity underlies how we know, experience, and learn (Roth 2008a).

The dimension of social structure as *accomplishment* is highlighted by the third dimension that comes with the use of square brackets. This 'expression, [ ], is prefaced with "doing" in order to emphasize that accountable-conversation-as-a-practical-accomplishment consists only and entirely in and of its work' (ibid: 172). Because the work of producing some social structure is always subject to contingencies, whether it is a queue or a science lesson, it is always singular and never repeats itself in a self-identical way. Thus, although extended experiences readies science teachers for every next lesson they teach, they cannot ever be certain what they will come to face when they are actually in the classroom. Thus, although Carrie will repeatedly experience students who "balk" at what she asks them to do, in each case, the particular way in which a transaction with a balking student will unfold cannot be predicted and anticipated. Even though each instant is singular, there are aspects that a member to the setting can report, aspects that precisely because of their reportability have a general and situation-spanning quality. Thus, 'the prefix "doing" is also used to emphasize about this work of accountable conversation that it is members' work. That is to say, this work has essential ties to mastery of natural language' (ibid: 172). The very fact that members to the setting use and, at their level, master natural language, aspects of the singular, once-occurrent event are and become repeatable.

The contents of the last paragraph also sheds light on method. Formal analytic approaches, whether quantitative or qualitative, create concepts that refer to situations. But, as concepts, they are abstracted from situations. Their relation to the concrete instances they gather – concept, from Lat. *con-*, together + *capēre*, to take – is one of abstract and concrete in the epistemology of Kant. The relation of ethnomethodological descriptions of sympractical work to concrete instances of social life is different: The work produces structure in any concrete case. Knowing the work allows us to understand what happens in every concrete case, whereas know-

doing [pleading and closing out topic]

doing [elaborating change of plans]

'Doing' designates the work for which the formulation/gloss
is the accountable text

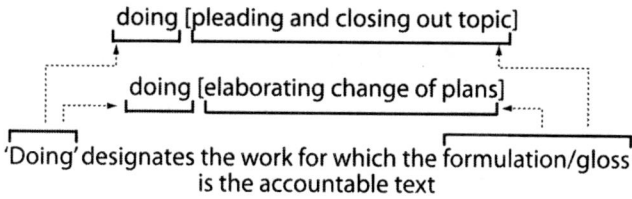

Fig. 4.2   Relationship between actual social structure-producing sympractical work and the formulation/gloss of the result.

ing the concept (formulation, gloss) still leaves us confronted with its application to a concrete case (because of the often-bemoaned theory-practice gap).

Formulating as Science Education Research Enterprise

In chapter 1, I point out the decided orientation ethnomethodological researchers take on social facts. Thus, in Fig. 1.3 we observe a distinction between what people do, what their doing produces (e.g., social fact), and what researchers do in researching and describing those facts. There is a disjunction between the methods actually used to make social facts and phenomena observable from within societal events and the methods researchers use to extract these facts and phenomena from everyday life. The concept of formulating affords us another take on this issue and to the different orientation that ethnomethodological research takes when compared with formal analytic approaches. Fig. 4.2 shows the relation between the structure-producing, endogenous, sympractical work and the text that accounts for what has been done and produced. The figure uses two glosses from this study that appear in chapters 2 and 3 as example. That is, I segmented and denoted a particular stretch of talk as 'pleading and closing out topic'. This is but a gloss. To make this event thereby named stand out, the researcher – here I – has to have the same particular social competencies that are required for seeing *this* event. The text of the gloss or formulation is *accountable*, that is, it is a text that one can be held to. But this text does not produce the phenomenon, in the way (social) constructivist might be tempted to say. Embodied work is being conducted that produces whatever the text formulates, glosses, and accountably describes. As shown in this and the preceding chapter, pleading, closing out a topic, or elaborating a change of plans, as observable social phenomena, are the result of irreducible *social* and collective work.

The difference between ethnomethodology and other approaches in the social sciences is their orientation toward the structure depicted in Fig. 4.2. Thus, quantitative and qualitative researchers produce glosses; they do so using their own methods that they are accountable for. These methods are other than those that the people use *within* the situation to produce whatever becomes observable both on the part of the members to the setting and to the researcher. Ethnomethodology, on the other hand, as its name suggests, is interested in the methods that members to the setting themselves draw upon for producing, recognizing, and critiquing social structure and phenomena. It is a truly *methodological* enterprise because it is a study of methods rather than a description of one method, such as the one a particular qualitative or quantitative study uses. A second major issue pointed out in ethnomethodology is the fact that the special methods that professional researchers employ presuppose ethnomethods. For example, the Australian study in chapter 1 (Belocchi and Ritchie 2011) included the following glosses of the actual research work they conducted: {conducting interviews}, {recording lessons}, {conducting fine-grained analysis focusing on content of classroom talk}, {marking transcripts}, {omitting and replacing turns with missing turn numbers}, {identifying hybridization of everyday discourse and chemical discourse}, {listening and reviewing of audio and video materials}, {identifying insight-yielding audio and video data}, {coding data sources}, {making themes emerge}, {refining coding categories}, and {recoding transcripts and artifacts based on new themes}. These glosses only gesture towards but do not describe the actual work, the doing, that produces what the authors present in their study. All of these glosses point us to the practices of 'constructive analysis'. Ethnomethodologists point out that 'irreconcilable interests exist between constructive analysis and ethnomethodology in the phenomena of the rational accountability of everyday activities and its accompanying practical technology of practical sociological reasoning' (Garfinkel and Sacks 1986: 162). Throughout this book I show that the ethnomethodological alternate offers new opportunities to science education research and a virtually unexplored terrain of possible investigations.

5

In the Midst of the Thickets

The event arrives, or rather it happens to *me* [*m*'arrive], by surprising me, and by befalling me unexpectedly .... Such an incident affects me more than I constitute it; first of all because it gazes at me more than I gaze at it from my perspective; then because it imposes itself on me like a fact that gives itself, decides itself and withdraws at its will. (Marion 2010: 286, original emphasis, underline added)

Educators have become familiar with the distinction between science-as-a-ready-made-fact – the result of philosophical and social science inquiries prior to the now-epic ethnographic studies of scientists at work – and science-in-the-making. Time and again science education research articles denounce the classical perspective on science, which depicts it approached and known through its published results versus when seen through the eyes of the ethnographer who spends time in the scientific laboratory. The classical perspective (science-as-a-ready-made-fact) gives an inappropriate account of science as a process. Those educators interested in allowing students to understand the nature of science are adamant about presenting science students with opportunities to come to understand what happens when scientists actually engage in their daily work, in their laboratories, during meetings with team members, or at the desk while writing research articles. Interestingly, however, science educators do not use, in their own work, approaches that would allow us to understand what happens in science classrooms *in the making, from a first-time-through* perspective, through the eyes of a witness who does not know whether a lesson will have been successful or unsuccessful, in fact, who does not know whether a lesson will have come to an orderly conclusion at all. In this chapter, I suggest taking an approach that takes us in the midst of the thickets, that is, I advocate an approach that emphasizes science-education-in-the-making. The perspective on events then provides us with a view through the lens of the unfinished event itself, an event-in-the-making, where we never quite know what the event will have been once everything has been said and done.

To understand how lessons become what they are – as 'enacted curriculum' – we need to take the actors' perspectives, who are witnesses to the event without knowing *what* kind of event they will ultimately be referring to (see chapter 8). A striking rationale for taking such a perspective was reported from one study in which an undergraduate physics students, working as my research assistant, did interview/think-aloud protocols with experienced physicists (experts) concerning graphs and graphing (Roth and Middleton 2006). Although most sessions more or less went 'according to plan', one particular protocol turned into a {tutoring session}, where the undergraduate student taught the professor how to read a simple correlational graph displaying birthrates and death rates as function of population size that biology students during their first or second semester find in their textbooks.

In this situation we have a clear example of a dramatic change: a planned think-aloud/interview protocol changed into a tutoring session. Nobody told the two members to the setting to engage in tutoring. There are no schemas for tutoring that the two invoked. Entirely organized and managed from the inside of their relation *at this point in time*, the overall event evolved such that what begins as thinking aloud turns into tutoring. Following the contents of chapter 4, we understand this change as the result of sympractical work. But this work was not planned by one or the other member. They suddenly found themselves in a situation where the undergraduate student told the physics professor that she might be looking at this graph inappropriately and where, following some back and forth over the request for 'hints', the former provided first one, then another one, until there is a full-scale tutoring session in which he teaches the latter on how to read the graph at hand. To understand these events, it does not help if we begin our (constructive) analysis with the final result in which quite innocent beginnings, which are not even recognized as such, all of a sudden make the actors find themselves in a situation that was not planned, anticipated, or at some horizon in any other manner.

Agential perspectives on social phenomena – whether realized in the constructivist agent or sociological agency/structure form – inherently presuppose a cause–effect figure. This figure grammatically is realized in the structure of the sentence where some agent (subject) does something (verb) often *on* something (transitive object) to achieve a result. Researchers take phrases or actions on the part of research participants and attribute to these not only the status (e.g., 'she asks a question') but also future results of the actions. For example, in the Australian study presented in chapter 1, the authors write: 'Trev intervenes … to correct Mal's spelling. This led to a brief exchange with a play on the word whether as also meaning a sheep' (Bellocchi and Ritchie 2011: 779). Trev is the agential subject and his intervention is to 'correct Mal's spelling', the object of the action. The authors do not tell their readers whether Mal actually adds the letter 'h' to the word 'wether' right after the 'w'. Had Mal changed the spelling, Trev would have been attributed the agency that led to the change. It is also common to attribute responsibility for lessons to teachers. Moreover, 'excellent teachers' will lead to exemplary lessons, whereas 'poor teachers' tend to produce 'unsuccessful lessons'. With respect to the present study, how well or poorly Jane is doing comes to be attributed to particulars that characterize her agency. For example, Carrie says about Jane: 'I don't think she is as interested in physics as she is in singing, music'. This is

then used to describe why Jane is doing what she is doing. As a result, *social* phenomena are considered to be the result of actions of individuals, who intend this or
that to happen.

Ever since Heraclitus stated that we could not place a foot into the same waters
twice, philosophers have been interested in understanding *process* and *events*. Process philosophers, however, note that our language gets into the way of truly understanding process because of the way in which causes and effects are linked to
actions and their outcomes: *'There are neither causes nor effects.* Linguistically we
cannot get away from this. But this does not change matters. When I think the
muscle separately from its 'effects', then I have negated it ... *In summa: an* <u>*event*</u>
is neither caused nor *causing. Causa* is a potential to bring something about, invented and added to events' (Nietzsche 1954: 768, original emphasis, underline
added). This quotation is taken from a text in which the philosopher is concerned
with understanding *events* – not as things or completed phenomena but as unfinished happenings.

The different perspective gained when we look at events from within, when we
do not yet know where they lead to and what the outcomes will be are perhaps
more easily grasped in historical case examples. For example, when the first
demonstrations began in Tahrir Square (Cairo, Egypt) in the Spring of 2011, the
media were not even there. Nobody aware of the demonstrations at this point – the
participants, the Egyptian police and army, the government – could anticipate that
this would eventually be the beginning of an event now referred to as the 'Egyptian
Revolution', a part of the 'Arab Spring'. Although subsequently becoming part of
what now is denoted by the term revolution, these initial and initiating demonstrations came to be an aspect of a revolution only with hindsight, after the president
stepped down and the government was replaced. But 'as soon as it has begun to
appear, the event had ended to begin and had begun to end' (Marion 2010: 286): in
its very nature, the event can be grasped only when it has already ended. As Nietzsche points out, causes are added to events afterwards, once specific outcomes
are said to be the effects of whatever happened before. The happening as a whole
can be grasped only after the fact when something has come to the end and then
exists in its entirety to be named, to be made present again (i.e., *re*presented), and
reasoned about. *While* things are happening, however, we most often do not know
what event is occurring until after some closure has been achieved. Although a
teacher may have prepared a lesson plan, whether a particular lesson will achieve
anything is completely unknown at its beginning – both within and outside happenings may contribute to the complete abandonment of a class. To approach an event
as event means 'admitting its irreducibly originary spontaneity, sovereignty in
short' (Marion 2010: 281).

In ethnomethodology, the interest in social phenomena that are not yet completed underlies the notion of a 'first time through'. It means following social actors in
their structure constituting work *before* they know the product that this work will
have produced and, therefore, *before* they can attribute causes and effects. For example, one study follows astronomers before they know that as a result of their
work on a particular night they will have in their hands evidence for a pulsar (Garfinkel et al. 1981). Treating a videotape recording from this perspective means
engaging in an analysis where the researcher does not know or take the end results

as resources for explaining just what is going on at an instant. This is important because in an ever-changing 'once-occurrent' world, every event is contingent, never repeating itself (Bakhtin 1993); no word, phrase, or work has the same signification[19] (Vološinov 1930) and therefore requires investigation of the word in its situated use. In the mentioned study of astronomers, this first-time-through approach allowed a description and understanding of the discovery process of what now is known as pulsar. That is, the astronomers, while conducting their work did not know that they were discovering this object while they were doing the work, especially when they were first observing some graphical features that ultimately turned out to be the signature of a pulsar (Garfinkel et al. 1981). Responding to the question why the audiotapes recorded during part of the night of the astronomers' conversation does not document the received empirical and theoretical provisions for the optical pulsar, the authors note:

> Our reasoning was that to do so construes the work of their discovery to be no more than a strategic solution to 'the coroner's problem'. The evil thereof is that the 'coroner's problem' abandons the relevance of first time through. The coroner begins with the remains in hand. With what the corpse looks like as his point of departure he imagines alternative ways the deceased could have lived so that as a phase of the way he lived he came to look the way he does. The corpse's actual appearances are problematic as events-to-start-with. They take on their demonstrable facticity in the course of his inquiries (e .g., the open throat was done with an assailant's slash, not with a suicide's cut). Further, his inquiry is conducted toward an end to it when he must select one of four possible theoretically pre-decided causes of death – natural death, accidental death, suicidal death, or murder – as the legal-professional-name for his reasoning. His problem of deciding manner and cause of death is solved under a combined constraint and resource of his inquiries: that just what, to start with, it came to, is what it has to come to. Obviously, the entire matter can be held in the air undecided until beginnings and in-course-ness are available for their demonstrable coherence. (Garfinkel et al. 1981: 136)

Readers will immediately note that the authors state, in different words, the problem that Nietzsche articulated in his critique of the cause–effect figure that reigns in the descriptions and explanations of science learning that our field produces. The authors note that the coroner gives up the first-time-through perspective that social actors have on what is happening at the moment. The coroner begins with the end result and then imagines alternative courses of actions and happenings that would have caused and led to the end results that he has in his hands. Semioticians refer to form of reasoning as abductive, because the coroner takes a concrete result, hypothesizes or speculates about beginnings, and derives from these hypotheses and speculations courses of events. Whereas the resulting 'just-so' story provides an account of possible events, it does not actually reproduce the way in which the world presented itself to those social actors involved, who acted before they knew

---

[19] Instead of signification, many translators into English use 'meaning' to render the Russian *značenie*. For Vološinov (1930), the theme [*tema*] is the upper limit of the signifying power of a word, and this theme never repeats itself identically.

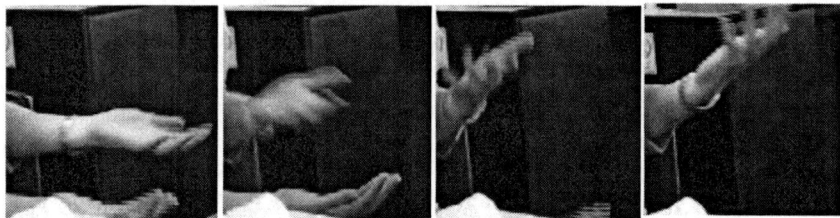

Fig. 5.1   Carrie's left hand moves through ¾ of a circle in a gestures that together with 'can you think of anything' 'invites' an item for the preceding designedly incomplete phrase.

what eventually would be in the coroner's hands. As the authors of the article on the astronomers emphatically note, 'this does nothing for the first time through' (ibid: 136). My focus in this chapter is to articulate a way of working with videotape and understanding science lessons and the learning therein from a first-time-through perspective.

First Time Through – A Demonstration

Down in our hearts, we, researchers, know that events unfold on their own, unpredictably, and always present something new even when it is of the most routine type: the world never is precisely the same. To get a deep sense of the nature of events, it is useful to watch some classroom video that one has never seen before and that one does not have background information about (which would only lead us to mobilize prejudice of all sorts). Then we might stop the videotape at any one instant and attempt to predict or hypothesize about what will or could possibly happen next based only on what we have seen so far. In any concrete case, these possibilities are virtually limitless. We can do the same exercise with any single instant in the data presented throughout this book, such as just after turn 008 when Carrie has announced that there is a new problem statement on Moodle, which specifies that the air in the Chinese lantern should receive hot air other than by using a flame. Following a pause there is then a designedly incomplete phrase, 'such as', which invites to be filled with a response; a further invitation follows in rapid, single-breathed 'can you think of anything' that is accompanied by a hand gesture (Fig. 5.1) that also can be seen as inviting a reply. We stop the videotape at this precise instant such as after turn 008 (Fragment 5.1). Will what has happened so far become an invitation? Or will it be reified as some other social action? We can already understand the phrase 'can you think of anything' as a reiteration of what is a potentially ambiguous 'such as'. There might be a firm reply, such as if Jane were to say 'a heat lamp', or a tentative reply, where the word supplied is pronounced with rising intonation, or she might not reply at all. In each of these situations, a different next turn might be required. But until the reply occurs, Carrie has no way of designing her own next move because she does not know what is coming at and hitting her in and with the student reply.

Fragment 5.1
```
   008   C:   its (0.36) ↓'O::N:: (0.52) mOO:dl, the new stAtement,
              (0.24) but it is to dO with (0.21) .hhhhh
              <<len>hAVing a lANtern,> (0.50) with hOt AI::r (0.23)
              <<all>added to it> (0.26) by means other than using
I>    a       the flA:Me, (0.91) suchA:s;
I>    b       <<all>can=you=think=of=anything⁻> ((Left hand moves
              in circle, 'inviting' response, Fig. 5.1))
```

When we turn on the videotape again, there is a pause developing (turn 009). It extends, and eventually becomes longer than the time teachers normally wait to allow a student reply to come forth. The pause actually provides both members to the setting an opportunity to speak: Jane might speak and produce a reply, or Carrie might speak and continue in one or another way. In the present situation, as the videotape inches along, we see and hear Carrie take the next turn, rapidly repeating a word she has said before 'hot air' (turn 010). Looking 'sheepishly' a bit to the side, she produces a wink with her eyes. It is as if she were again inviting a reply. But another pause develops: this one being even longer than the preceding one. Jane does not offer a reply (turn 010a). There is no reply, but, as the pause also gives Carrie an opportunity to take the next turn, she does. 'Like we get hot air from' (turn 010b), she says in a more piano voice. Again the phrase is designedly incomplete, offering the opportunity to be treates as an invition to produce a word such that the phrase achieves a completed grammatical form.

Fragment 5.2
```
    009          (1.11)
I>010   C:       <<all>hotair>
    a            (1.88)
I>    b          <<p>like we get hot air from.>
    011          (0.75)
```

So far we now have had four turns that *could* be heard as initiating questions. However, we do not yet know whether they in fact – from the level of the conversation – actually will have been such. The nature of these turns *will have been* invitations only when the next turn in the turn-taking sequence that constitutes the present transaction ritual is reifying them as such. Rather than hearing a reply, we observe another pause unfolding (turn 011). Again, the conversation offers Jane the next position in the turn-taking ritual, though this does not exclude the possibility that Carrie will be having another one or will have to have another one in the case that there would be no reply. And then, just as it nears the standard wait-time length of about 0.7 seconds, Jane articulates with rising, that is, questioning intonation: 'Breath into it?' (turn 012). Again, we might want to stop the videotape precisely at this point and hypothesize about what might come next. Again, there are many different ways in which the conversation could unfold and continue. Jane might articulate another means of adding hot air, Carrie perhaps suggests a method that she might already think of, or, following the *IRE* transaction ritual, she might produce an evaluative turn. The possibility for the IRE ritual to take place would be opened precisely if Jane had produced something that could be heard as constituting a reply rather than something else. But whether her locution functions as a reply has to await the next turn.

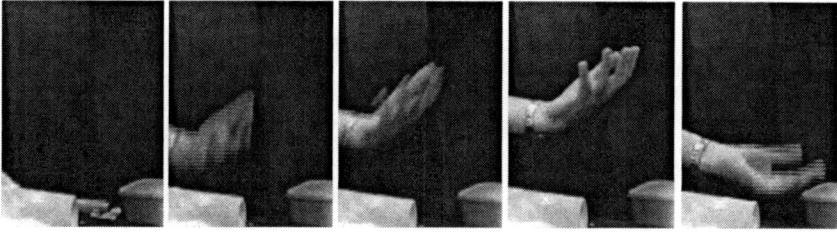

Fig. 5.2   Carrie's left hand moves through a full circle in a gestures that together with 'something' 'invites' an item for the preceding designedly incomplete phrase.

Turning the videotape on again, we first notice a pause that exceeds the standard waiting time teachers tend to allow for students to take the next turn (0.7 s) or the standard maximum silence typical of conversations (1 s). A hand gesture with a churning motion as in Fig. 5.1 is produced during the pause; it can be seen as symbolizing motion, as if it were continuing to invite the production also glossed by the phrase 'come on, give me a word' or 'go on'. Then we hear a turn that does many things simultaneously: it is multi-functional: 'easier than that' (turn 014).

```
Fragment 5.3
R 012    J:    breath INto It?
I>013          (1.25) ((churning gesture as in Fig. 5.1))
I>014    C:    EAsier=than=thA:t⁻
   015          (2.11) ((Carrie grins/laughs))
```

The phrase first indicates an acceptance of the preceding turn as a reply; second, it also constitutes an evaluation; and third, it invites an alternative and, therefore, the production of another term that would (also) complete the incomplete phrase. First, the phrase 'easier than that' accepts 'breathing into [the lantern] as a possibility but also marks that 'we get hot air' from a source that is easier than the solution offered ('that'). The phrase also is an evaluation. While it accepts the solution offered, it also marks it as more difficult to achieve than the one implied in the sequence – if it in fact contributes to realizing an IRE ritual, which, as non-genuine question, already presupposes the existence of a correct answer. Finally, it can also be heard as inviting another attempt at a reply that would provide a solution to the problem of adding air easier than breathing into the lantern.

Following Carrie's turn, there is a pause developing. As Carrie just has had a turn, it would be up to Jane to take the next one. The pause would then function as a space for her to think about and evolve another reply. But unlike what the wait-time research literature in the 1980s suggests, the pause is not something that the teacher is responsible for. The pause is a feature of the conversation and, therefore, a *social* phenomenon that cannot be reduced to the individuals. Jane, as much as Carrie, is responsible for the unfolding pause. It belongs to both. Eventually, it is Jane who takes the next turn at talk. This turn, in providing a possible answer that it itself excludes because it does not fit the condition, does in fact constitute a reply, as marked by the adverbial 'yea' (turn 018). This adverb both accepts the turn as a reply and evaluates the conditional and the implication that the phrase articulates.

Fragment 5.4
```
  015          (2.11) ((Carrie grins/laughs))
R> 016   J:    i would say fIre but its a flame.
  017          (0.30)
A> 018   C:    yea::.
      a        (0.64)
R>    b        <<all>hairdryer,
      c        (0.77)
I>    d        somethI:Ng⁻ ((churning gesture, as in Fig. 5.2,  as
               if wanting to 'draw something out'))
  019          (0.54)
```

At this point (turn 018), we still do not know what kind of happening we are witnessing. We do not know whether it will have been an IRE sequence, for despite
what is possible to be heard as repeated initiation for the production of an alternate
means of filling the Chinese lantern with hot air, it apparently has not yet been
named: there is a continued provision of opportunities for the production of alternative sources. The evaluative dimension of the 'yea' in turn 018 concerns the implication rather than the source for hot air offered, as can be seen from the pause
that is unfolding next (turn 018a). The pause again provides opportunities to both
for taking a turn; it invites the two parties to take a turn: for Jane to produce another alternative, for Carrie to articulate further invitations or, perhaps, to articulate a
solution (i.e., the intended one) that would complete the phrases in turns 008a and
010b or responded to any of the six turns possibly functioning as initia-
tions/invitations (turns 008a, 008b, 010, 010b, 013, 014).

We then hear the word 'hairdryer', produced with a slightly rising intonation
(see comma following the word in the transcription), which could be heard as a
question glossed as 'what do you think of using a hairdryer?' Another pause follows, providing yet another possibility to produce an alternative source of hot air.
Then another term that potentially invites another turn on the part of Jane.

When she finally provides the apparently intended word herself (turn 018b),
Carrie cannot know what comes next. As there are more pauses and another incomplete phrase 'something [like that] …' that could be followed by a term that
would provide a reasonable alternative to flame and other than the hairdryer
(though 'easier than' blowing into it), closure has not yet been achieved. There is
again the churning gesture, as if Carrie continued to invite the production of alternatives (Fig. 5.2). There is a pause, which provides opportunities for her to continue or for Jane to take a turn at talk. Which will it be? Here, Jane comes to word.
But what is she going to say? Will she have an alternative heat source? Will she
change topics? Will she be talking about the materials for her investigation of the
different waxes that she has already purchased on the night before together with
her mom?

Fragment 5.5
```
  019          (0.54)
E> 020   J:    that means i cant experiment with the wa[xes.   ]
  021    C:                                            [wAX?    ]
A>             (0.93) NO. (.) <<assertive>you cA:nt experiment with
               different wA[xes.]>
```

We hear Jane say 'that means I can't experiment with the waxes', which, as seen in chapter 4, is a formulation of what Carrie can be heard to have said or implied by offering the hairdryer as the alternative source of hot air. We also see in chapter 4 that turn 021 confirms this hearing. In fact, this turn 020 may actually be heard as a gloss of the entire exchange between turns 008 and 019. The hairdryer, the production of which unfolded between the the designedly incomplete phrase in turn 008a until its appearance in the public forum of the conversation, as a suggested means for supplying hot air, also means that Jane cannot investigate the effect of different waxes on the rising motion of her Chinese lantern.

When we look back at what has happened so far, in its entirety, and as something (tentatively) completed, it has not been an IRE sequence at all. Carrie, the institutionally designated teacher has provided a (or the) sought-after reply and, therefore, the whole sequence has come to be upset. There has been one alternative source of hot air articulated on the part of Jane, but the means to be chosen were marked as being easier than breathing (air) into the lantern. As the turn-taking ritual unfolds, there is no room for the evaluative turn, as it is the teacher who takes what would have been the middle position in the IRE sequence, therefore eliminating the need for an evaluative turn. Jane would later comment on the proposed solution – which in fact eliminated her planned investigation – that 'it sucks'. It is not too far-fetched to say that a comment such as 'in turn 020, the "message" of having to change her investigation has finally sunk in for Jane' would be understood as a possible gloss for what is happening at that point.

The point of this brief analysis is that from the perspective of the event-in-the-making, we do not know what something will be called until after it has ended and until after 'a call has been made'. An analogy to sports may assist in bringing to the foreground just what we can learn from this about the nature of events – to be available only as entities that can be denoted as such only after they have come to completion and, therefore, no longer exist as such. In baseball, for example, we do not know whether a pitch is a 'ball' or a 'strike' until the umpire has made a call. That is, if we were to play a recording of a pitch in slow motion or step through the video in an image-by-image fashion that places us *within* the event-in-the-making – later called a 'ball' or a 'strike', as in 'the pitcher has thrown a strike' – we would be unable to say just what kind of event we are in, a ball or a strike. It does not help knowing whether the pitcher *intends* to throw a ball or a strike (e.g., to let the hitter walk to first base). In a straight analogy to the conversation, we do not know what a pitch is even though the baseball has passed the batter until the subsequent turn is completed. This turn consists in the umpire's call. In soccer, we are unable to say *in the present tense* that someone is shooting a goal; from the perspective of the game as a whole we can only ever say *in the past tense* that someone has shot a goal. It does not even matter what physically has been the case, whether a camera shot later will reveal that a ball has crossed the goal line fully as required for a goal. What matters to the game is the actual call on the part of the referee. In conversations, too, the fact that someone has been speaking, the words subsequently attributed to him/her, cannot be evaluated as to their function in the unfolding event until after their active reception and the reply. It is only in the past tense that we can say what has been said and done (e.g., hurt, insult, or comfort). But to understand the logic of the sports or language game, we need to be situated within, because none of the actors individually or as a group has access to what will be present in the future. The future perfect only states a possibility among other alternative possibilities.

Accounting of events after the fact, we can only construe phrases such as 'this pitch will have been [called] a strike' or, pertinent to science education, 'this lesson will have been [called] a successful intervention' or 'this lesson will have led to conceptual change by means of analogical transfer'. From within the lesson, we do not know *what* kind of event we witness. The proposal to use a first-time-through perspective on science lessons means taking the actors' view, in which the future is inherently open and the nature of the current happening remains unfinalized and in the making.

Of Causes and Effects

> An event as unitary and self-equivalent is something that could be read *post factum* by a non-particiapting [bezučastnoe] consciousness that is not interested in the event; yet even in this case there still would have been something inaccessible: the very eventfulness [sobytijnost'] of the event. (Bakhtin 1993: 46)

In the introductory part to this chapter, I quote Nietzsche who notes that '*There are neither causes nor effects*'. In the preceding section, I walk readers through a short piece of videotape and transcript to exemplify that at any one chosen point, we do not know what is being done until after some form of social evaluation has occurred. From the perspective of the conversation, to understand its unfolding and the directions it will have taken, we cannot ever say looking at a phrase what it has done and how it has functioned within the conversation as a whole: Is it an invitation, a question, an interdiction, an order, an observational statement, and so on? As Bakhtin suggests in the quotation that opens this section, an event as unitary and self-equivalent something is the result of a reading constituted post factum. It is a reading by a non-participating and therefore detached consciousness that has no contribution to the making of the event, i.e., a consciousness that is 'not interested' or, rather, not invested in the event as such.

The problem to properly understand an event in its eventfulness, therefore, is the consciousness that has no stake in what is happening, a consciousness that looks at events after the fact. Whereas this consciousness arrives at a form of understanding, what it misses is precisely the *eventfulness*. It misses to render what is particular about being in the midst of the thickets, 'with no time out, and with no possibility of evasion, hiding out, passing, postponement, or buy-outs' (Garfinkel 1988: 103). This description is especially salient when there are pauses, which arise when a projected next speaker does not take a turn for whatever reason this might be. There are consequences precisely because there is no possibility of evasion, passing, or postponement, for whatever next thing happens has consequences on how to understand what is currently in the making. We see this across Fragments 5.1 and 5.2, here reproduced in part in Fragment 5.6. Turn 010, which involves the same speaker as turn 008, treats the silence as a failure of a reply to come forth; similarly, turn 010b treats the preceding silence as an absent reply so that there is a reiteration of a designedly incomplete phrase. We know that these are invitations not because of their appearances in themselves but through the evaluation and re-opening of the invitation that occurs in turn 014, itself a next-turn with respect to the reply that completes the fourfold delivered initiation (turns 008a, 008b, 010, 010b).

Fragment 5.6
```
I>  8a   C:    the flA:Me, (0.91) suchA:s;
I>   b          <<all>can=you=think=of=anything¯> ((Left hand moves
                in circle, 'inviting' response, Fig. 5.1))
    009          (1.11)
I> 010   C:    <<all>hotair>
     a          (1.88)
I>   b          <<p>like we get hot air from.>
    011          (0.75)
R  012   J:    breath INto It?
I> 013          (1.25) ((churning gesture as in Fig. 5.1))
I> 014   C:    EAsier=than=thA:t¯
```

These pauses cannot go on forever or, rather, a very strange situation would present itself where there are initiations without rejoinders. As there are situations when a person does not reply to an initiation, or rather, replies by not responding, there always is the possibility that Carrie might say something like 'Okay, you don't want me to help you and make things easier, go ahead and find out for yourself' or 'I will attend to the needs of other students; let me know when you are ready to talk to me'. But this too, might entail consequences for the teacher deriving from subsequent actions on the part of the school administration or parents.

In its contribution to the conversation as a whole, any phrase has to be seen in its relation to what precedes it and what follows it. In relation to the preceding turn, a phrase constitutes the effect and conclusion of a unit such as question | reply, invitation | acceptance, invitation | rejection, instruction | following, and order | disobeyal. When we are in the first part of the unit, we cannot say what type of event is occurring until the unit has been completed, that is, until we know the effect. At this point, once we know the nature of the turn pair, we can attribute cause to the first part and effect to the second part just as this is done within speech act theory, where a locution comes to be paired with the perlocution (effect). Just as Nietzsche suggests in the quotation above, the cause is added after the event as a whole is completed and we can grasp it as such. Before completion, the event as a specific thing does not exist as such. Within the conversation, we do not know whether we are in the middle of an IRE transaction ritual until it exist as a whole, at which point we may attribute what has been said to individual turns and positions that the members to the setting play. It is precisely for that reason that the mentioned physics professor and an undergraduate student from her own department all of a sudden find themselves in a tutoring session with the undergraduate student in the tutor and the professor in the student role.

Actions are what bring about effects: they are causes; and actions are produced by agents. But the perspective developed here, on both empirical and philosophical grounds, suggests that this figure of reasoning in terms of causes and effects is problematic. In fact, it does not describe what is actually happening when we take a first-time-through perspective. Tape recordings – which can be stopped at any time and therefore situate us like the actors themselves with respect to what will have come to be known as a specific event – should encourage us to ask the question 'What is happening in the here and now of the situation?' This attitude, realized in the stopping of the tape and questioning prior to knowing the final result or type of event enacts a first-time-through perspective.

Taking a first-time-through perspective appears to be a must when we attempt to understand phenomena such as discovery, insight, and learning. Inherently, those involved – the subjects who will have discovered, had an insight, or have learned something after the fact – do not know what it is they do until after they have recognized it in the results of their work. Christopher Columbus did not go out to 'discover' the Americas. He was looking for a shorter route to India, a subcontinent that had already been discovered by and for Europeans (e.g., Alexander the Great). It is *after* it had been realized that he had landed on a continent heretofore unknown to Europeans that his actions have been consistent with a discovery story. Similarly, we do not know which action leads to student learning or whether any learning of interest to science educators will have occurred at all (e.g., which is not the case when students 'resist' conceptual change, which itself is a result of sympractical work, the identification of the phenomenon and the lack of achieving it). That something will have been an insight cannot be ascertained until *after* such a phenomenon has actually occurred and been recognized as such. The phenomenon comes to exist precisely when it no longer exists. The cause–effect figure, which attributes a specific characteristic to an action – i.e., its intention – leads to a poor and impoverished account of the eventfulness of science lessons generally and of those phenomena occurring in them specifically.

Eventfulness: Being-in-the-Midst with No Time Out

In the quotation that opens this chapter, the philosopher Jean-Luc Marion suggests that events arrive and happen to the persons that these include. In this, events always surprise and befall the subject unexpectedly. Even though the classroom talk involving Carrie and Jane may be said to be ordinary, we cannot deny the fact that once we take a position within the conversation, whatever comes arrives rather than is intentionally produced. In the event, intuition always exceeds intention. This is so not in the least because intuition is related to the situated participation in concrete, inherently once-occurrent societal life whereas intention exists in and as a generalized form of action. Plans are separated from situated action by ontological gaps; and so are intentions from situated actions. There is no determinate cause–effect relationship between intentions or plans and situated actions. Whether a plan is being followed or whether an intention is being implemented always can be assessed only after the fact – and even scientists might find out only hours or days afterwards what they have really done by engaging in one or a series of actions (Roth 2009a).

Etymologically, the term *event* derives from the Latin *ēventus*, occurrence, issue, itself the perfect participle of *ēvenīre*, to come out, from *ē-*, out + *venīre*, to come, go, arrive, arise, come to pass, proceed. In their eventfulness, events are happenings that come out 'from nowhere' and come at us. The associated verb, to event, in its intransitive form, signifies 'to happen', 'to take place'. Like the verb 'to be', to event transports us in the midst of things where some*thing* is happening the specific nature of which we can establish only after the fact. But that which comes at us also *advenes* (from Lat. *advenīre*, to arrive, from *ad-*, at, to, + *venīre*, to come, to pass), that is, the process of the event-in-the-making and the process of arriving completed in the *advent* go together. But what arrives cannot be known until the arrival has completed. That which arrives comes to be seen *as such* only after it has arrived. Prior to that it is the unseen and therefore unforeseen. Once grasped as something completed, an event also supervenes: it comes on and occurs as something additional, an addition that cannot be seen foreseen and therefore, as noted, always remains unforeseen. The slow reading of the videotape and transcript enacted in the preceding sections reveals precisely this nature of the future aspects of the conversation as something unforeseen. For if it were otherwise, if Carrie had foreseen what was to come, she would not have needed repeated attempts to 'coax' Jane into and 'wrench from' her a reply. From the within-the-event, first-time-through perspective, Carrie cannot know what will happen only seconds hence so that whatever she says it will always fall short of remediating the contingencies that come with her saying. The same of course is true for Jane. She cannot anticipate what Carrie will be saying, or she might not say what she is saying at any one point in time. Both can find out only after the fact what will have been happening to them at some prior instant in time.

In the fragments, we can say after the fact that Carrie is finding a way of asking questions so that Jane *eventually* replies. She can only set up opportunities for this to happen without having certainty that on any *this* occasion the reply will in fact arrive. The replies come in, with, and as constitutive part of the event-in-the-making.

The need to use a perspective from within the event became quite clear to me when I wanted to understand more about learning to teach by (observing) teaching, especially by coteaching. Having continued to teach in real classrooms once I started at the university, I practically knew that in teaching science, we are caught up in the events. We lose the overview. It is only afterwards that we reflect and play through certain episodes again. At that point, it appeared so easy to deal with situations, play them over and over again to think about alternative actions. I sometimes thought, 'I should have done this or that'. But in the class I had not done this or that precisely because I did not have the benefit of hindsight. I was dealing with issues *while being in the midst of the thickets*. I used the German term 'Spielraum', room to maneuver, to articulate a phenomenological perspective that captures our experience when we are in the midst of things, in the thicket of action, and with no time out or reprieve (e.g., Roth 2002; Roth et al. 2001). Then I came to work with Ken Tobin, who, while new at the University of Pennsylvania, observed science teacher aspirants during their practicum. In one instance, after Tobin had watched a lesson from the back, he told his supervisee what this aspiring teacher had done wrong and what he might want to try. The supervisee challenged Tobin to try himself. Lo and behold, despite his 35-year experience as a science teacher and science teacher educator, Tobin failed according to his own account (Roth and Tobin 2002). It was precisely at that point that we began to think more deeply about the difference between the perspective from the back of the classroom or as the proverbial 'fly on the wall', on the one hand, and from within the lesson event where there is no time out, on the other hand.

The inside perspective developed and taken throughout this book better than the reflective perspective from the outside accounts for the position and view of the social actors involved in the endogenous production of social situations. Whatever actors do has consequences and even not doing something has consequences. But there is never space to step back from social life, for even a stepping back would be integral part of social life – e.g., a student who has been asked to stay in the corner or who has been sent out of the classroom for misbehavior. Because events continuously 'come at us', happen to us despite of us, any ethnographic account that aspires to be adequate to the situation needs to address the pernicious disunity and non-interpenetration of the theoretical approach and real social life (Bakhtin 1993). Formal analytic approaches to understanding classroom events, of both quantitative and qualitative kind, identify order of social life *from the outside*, requiring special and specified methods for extracting the order from the data sources. Ethnomethodology's enterprise is different in the sense that it aims at procedural specification of the endogenous work that produces the orderly properties of social events from the inside, without time out, reprieve, escape, time to reflect, and so on.

Researching Science Lessons as Events-in-the-Making

To study science lessons from the perspective of the insiders, that is, from the perspective of the event-in-the-making, an ethnomethodological stance is the position of choice. This stance is that taken by ethnographers interested in providing *adequate* descriptions of concerted activities and their contexts (McDermott et al. 1978). That stance presupposes that social actors do in fact speak authoritatively on their own behalves and make their relevant knowledgeability available to each other competently rather than deficiently. Social actors speak the way they do precisely because they can take what they say and how they say it as accountably shared – they can always provide a *reason* for explaining why they have done what they have done. If actors note that such assumptions are violated, they generally engage in organized repair sequences to recover from the situation. Within this perspective, there is no place or use for deficit models. From this perspective on the event-in-the-making, researchers therefore attend to the way in which members to the setting *formulate* contexts for each other, act out context in form and content (often by pointing), behaviorally orient to patterns at significant times, and hold each other accountable for acting and speaking in particular ways. This requires us turning to a topic that I already began to elaborate in chapter 1: research policies. Here I articulate further research policies to take into account the perspective from within the event-in-the-making to produce an ethnographically adequate account, that is, an account that retains the inherent uncertainty of the future that is an integral part of human experience. We must not talk about being in a certain kind of event while the happening is still ongoing and prior to knowing a namable event crystallizes as such.

A first research policy consists in the refusal to assess, recognize, categorize, or describe a situation and the actions occurring therein in terms of rules or standards obtained outside – such as a researcher's academic theory – and to rely on the actively ordered and orderly properties that the participants (members) themselves draw on for constituting the nature of the setting in which they are part.

A second research policy consists in viewing any social setting in terms of its self-organization with respect to the intelligible character of its appearance to those present under the constraints of social life that never stops. The policy explicitly acknowledges detectable, countable, recordable, reportable, and analyzable features as properties of a naturally and endogenously organized environment. These are precisely those properties that the participants produce for each other as resources for organizing, managing, recognizing, and acting in the situation. To understand the emergence of a science lesson episode – such as the 'change of plans' in the student-directed inquiry that features throughout this book – differently than as spontaneous (immaculate) conception (in the double sense of the word), we have to make thematic the apodictic (i.e., clearly demonstrable) aspects of the world available to *these* actors (e.g., Carrie, Jane); these aspects are available to them in the situation and constitute the fertile ground (a) for science lessons to emerge and (b) that serves as material for any 'scientific knowledge' that arises as a consequence.

A third policy orients us to trouble, in the literature often referred to as 'breakdown', because it is precisely when members to the setting identify a situation as problematic that their usually hidden methods that bring about successful social actions come to the fore. In the case of trouble, members articulate on a one-for-the-other basis what they have said (done) or meant to say (do). It is precisely when trouble emerges in familiar scenes that members begin to produce ordered, organizationally designed repair sequences and articulate the normally hidden methods by means of which structured everyday activities ordinarily and routinely are produced, sustained, and maintained.

A fourth policy is to see in children and students full, constitutive members of society and their conduct therefore rational and legitimate peripheral practices. By peripheral I mean that – as any other (adult) work in the same cultural setting – children's and students' work is a constitutive aspect of the situation. Thus, researchers deviate from the constructive analyses that depicts children and students as being at a stage toward adult scientific rationality. This stage tends to be characterized by a lesser status of cognitive behavior that learners need to overcome toward the development of formal reasoning. From the stance chosen here, students are enacting and displaying forms of rationality that are necessary for, and constitutive of (a developing) school culture as researchers can witness it.

Given these policies, the categories and predicates students use all are held to be examples of indexical expressions, just like any other natural language phenomenon. The senses of words and other sign forms are situated, contextually embedded achievements rather than things that obtain to words independent of their context.

In this, the properties of indexical expressions are taken as ordered properties; and the fact that they are ordered is an ongoing, practical accomplishment of the transaction rituals that our constitute everyday praxis. As collective achievements, these properties are available to those who are co-present in a setting: these resources therefore are available to everyone participating and to those over-hearing and observing the situation. These therefore are also available to the analysts who directly or vicariously (i.e., on videotapes) witness the production of these resources – as long as they are culturally competent – and who use them as data for developing ethnographically adequate accounts of the events.

6

Knowledge and (Institutional) Power

> 'Power/knowledge relations' are to be analyzed, therefore, not on the basis of a [given] subject of knowledge who is or is not free in relation to the power system. But, on the contrary, one has to consider the subject who knows, the objects to be known and the modalities of knowledge as so many effects of these fundamental implications of power-knowledge and their historical transformations. (Foucault 1966: 36)

In the research literature, we can frequently find the term 'power-over', which may be associated with the relationship between science teachers and their students or between science education researchers and their research participants. If we take the stance advocated throughout this book, then power, as any other social fact, is not some thing out there, existing independently of what we do. Rather, it itself is an endogenously produced order. If it is endogenously produced, we should therefore be able to find that work which produces what insiders would recognize to be a situation where one person has power over another. There are many reasons for abstaining from the use of institutional designations, such as 'teacher', 'student', or 'principal', to explain what happens in any *this* social situation. Consider but the following two observations that I have made in my own research. Both show that taking institutional positions and relations as starting points for analyzing social situations would hide and obliterate the real work that social actors produce.

- An undergraduate student of physics doing a co-op internship with me sets up interview/think-aloud protocols with physics professors and postdoctoral fellows at the same university (i.e., his department). In one of these sessions, as noted in chapter 5, the interview/think-aloud protocol turned into a tutoring session. Here, according to the institution, the professor would have been said to be in a power-over situation with respect to the student; with respect to the research, the student would or might be said to be in a power-over situation with respect to the professor, especially if it were assumed that as the researcher he would know the authoritative, correct way of completing the task. Neither relation would allow us to understand that there was in fact a continual exchange over who is in the know over what (Roth and Middleton 2006). Moreover, when the professor initially asked for hints, the student exhibited resistance to acquiesce.

- In research using the theoretical concept of the *zone of proximal development*, the focus tends to be on the institutionally designated teacher, held to be in the know, who somehow 'scaffolds' the less knowledgeable, institutionally designated student. When we look closely at any recorded classroom talk, we observe instances where the institutionally designated student assists the institutionally designated teacher in learning to teach (Roth and Radford 2010). That is, when we just focus on using the labels 'teacher' and 'student', we miss (a) the *sym-practical* nature of the transactional work, (b) the fact that teachers learn by teaching, and (c) the fact that students, in the very orderly way that they participate in classroom interaction rituals, contribute to teacher learning.

In both these examples, using institutional positions as points of departure and as lenses for investigation social events such as classroom lessons obscure what is really at work and what is the real work underlying the endogenous production of the social order. I do so in the present data instances where Carrie apparently does not know from the outside how to elicit a reply from Carrie. I have already pointed out the sequence reproduced in Fragment 6.1, where Carrie {tries to solicit from Jane an alternative means to add hot air to the Chinese lantern}. One observes four initiations rather than one. If Carrie had been 'the perfect teacher', she would have required but one initiation to get Carrie to produce the item that would have filled the designedly incomplete phrase in turn 008a. There are three more initiations prior to the first reply (turn 012). In a way, one might gloss the micro-event as a seeking of an appropriate initiation that would lead to the production of the solicited second-turn completion.

```
Fragment 6.1
I>  8a   C:   the flA:Me, (0.91) suchA:s;
I>  b         <<all>can=you=think=of=anything¯> ((Left hand moves
              in circle, 'inviting' response, Fig. 5.1))
    009       (1.11)
I> 010   C:   <<all>hotair>
     a        (1.88)
I>   b        <<p>like we get hot air from.>
    011       (0.75)
R  012   J:   breath INto It?
```

If one were to follow Carrie over longer periods of time, one might indeed observe – as I have in other instances (Roth 1996) – that teacher's questioning changes over time, becoming increasingly adapted to the situation, producing first turns that contribute to elaborate second-turn student completions. That is, if one were to focus on Carrie as a teacher, one would miss all the learning that occurs in and through the classroom transaction rituals that she is part of.

Power has come to be associated with knowledge: power and knowledge imply one another. But both power and knowledge are not just things out there. Both terms need to be made thematic as glosses, {power} and {knowledge}, which then orients us to look at these orders in terms of the sympractical, endogenous work performed so that members to the setting and vicarious onlookers (e.g., researchers) can recognize these orders within the situation and orient to them.

> The study of this microphysics presupposes that the power exercised on the body is conceived not as a property, but as a strategy, that its effects of domination are attributed not to 'appropriation', but to dispositions, maneuvers, tactics, techniques, functionings; that one should decipher in it a network of relations, constantly in tension, in activity, rather than a privilege that one might possess; that one should take as its model a perpetual battle rather than a contract regulating a transaction or the conquest of a territory. In short this power is exercised rather than possessed; it is not the 'privilege', acquired or preserved, of the dominant class, but the overall effect of its strategic positions – an effect that is manifested and sometimes extended by the position of those who are dominated. (Foucault 1975: 35)

In this quotation, Foucault articulates a position on power/knowledge that is consistent with the stance advocated in this book. Power is not something people, including science teachers, have because of their institutional positions. Rather, power is a form of exercised relation. Foucault makes thematic action terms: maneuvers, tactics, techniques, and functionings. Power/knowledge exists in and as activity, to be understood as a 'perpetual battle' rather than a privilege. But power/knowledge does not come to life in the exercise of just one person. It is, as Foucault points out, manifested by the position of the dominated. We might want to articulate this even stronger: Power/knowledge is the effect of the sympractical work of a societal relation. In science classrooms, power/knowledge arises from the sympractical work of all participants. We are then in a position to study the work that leads us to asymmetrically assign power/knowledge even though, at the outside, the relation itself is symmetrical requiring the joint contributions of the members to the setting.

Foucault suggests that the way in which we have to analyze these power/knowledge relations is not by starting with some given subject of knowledge who may or may not be free in relation to the powers in the system. What we need to consider instead are the effects of power/knowledge and their historical transformation: the knowing subject, the objects to be known, and the modalities of knowledge. Knowledge, as a corpus, is not produced by the actions of the subject. Rather, the forms and possible domains of knowledge are determined by the processes and struggles that traverse and make up power/knowledge. Here, it is not only power that is at issue but knowledge as well. As my study of the undergraduate physics student and one of his professors shows, knowledgeability itself was up for grabs and the question 'Who is in the know over a given topic?' was itself an effect of the sympractical work that simultaneously gave rise to the endogenous recognition of asymmetrical power.

Power/Knowledge: Asymmetry in Symmetry

That power/knowledge is the result of sympractical *work* easily gets lost from sight in 'unproblematic' situations where students do {what they have been asked to do}. In the following hypothetical exchange the work involved in 'change of plans' would be entirely hidden if Jane then went on, looked up the new task definition, and proceeded on the basis of what she has been reading there. In chapter 5 I show how important it is to abandon a cause–effect figure of reasoning about social events. If one were to take such a figure, Carrie would be said to have brought about the change of plans. She would have been attributed the causal agency for the change to occur and, therefore, she would be said to have had power over Jane making the latter do what the teachers ('we') decided beforehand.

Fragment 6.2
```
    001    C:    we changed the task definition in all classes. we are
                 no longer experimenting with candles. you can see the
                 new definition on moodle.
    002    J:    okay. i=ll look it up and get started anew.
```

What such an analysis would not show is (a) the symmetrical condition of the conversation where each word and phrase belongs to speakers and listeners simultaneously. It would hide that there is an active reception that makes the preceding turn a request or instruction for following a revised task definition. It is immediately evident that if there is differential power, it arises from the sympractical work of giving | accepting an order or giving | following an instruction. Carrie would be giving an order only because Jane is accepting (or rejecting) it; and Carrie would be giving an instruction only because Jane would be following it.

But if power/knowledge is observable *from within* the social situation, then we will be able to exhibit it in all its concrete detail as an asymmetry arising in the fact of the symmetry that the very concept of a relation involves. There are necessarily two sides to a relation, as there are equal and opposing forces in physics, as lightness presupposes darkness, as sound presupposes silence. The question then is this: Just what do interlocutors do so that 'power', 'knowledge', or 'power/knowledge' becomes an apparent social fact so that those present can point to, talk about, gloss, report, or otherwise act upon it? That is, the apparent power, the exhibited existence of order of a relation of ruling is witnessable because shown 'in the identifying details of its orderliness' (Garfinkel 2002: 254). In just what does the sympractical work consist that allows educational researchers to identify in any *this* situation that there is a 'power relation' – or any associate concept such as {paternalism}, {deference}, {disrespect}, and {symbolic violence}. To elaborate on these issues, let us take a look at a fragment that we already considered under a different aspect.

In Fragment 6.3, the first thing that becomes apparent is the differential knowledge (rather than power). We see that there are four turns that can be heard as initiations requesting the production of something that the other interlocutor 'can think of'. There is then the production of a phrase such that it becomes the second part of an initiating-question | reply turn pair sequence. Then there is an

evaluative term, 'easier than that', which in fact is the second part of a statement |
evaluation pair.

Fragment 6.3
```
I>  8a   C:   the flA:Me, (0.91) suchA:s;
I>   b        <<all>can=you=think=of=anything⁻> ((Left hand moves
                 in circle, 'inviting' response, Fig. 5.1))
    009         (1.11)
I> 010   C:   <<all>hotair>
     a         (1.88)
I>   b        <<p>like we get hot air from.>
    011         (0.75)
R  012   J:   breath INto It?
I> 013         (1.25) ((churning gesture as in Fig. 5.1))
I> 014   C:   EAsier=than=thA:t⁻
```

This exchange shows that something is to be provided, here on the part of Jane,
that the questioner (here Carrie) already knows, which allows the person to evaluate the actually given reply against the hidden, already known normative answer.
That is, just from the way the turn taking is organized, we notice that one person
already appears to know what the other is asked about and the knower assesses the
replies of the person queried.[20] It is in the acceptance of the assessment that Carrie
comes to be recognized and reified as 'being in the know'. This transaction ritual is
not particular to schools. Little children playing 'Do you see what I see?' already
practice it, because one of them identifies some entity or phenomenon in the world
and asks the second to guess or find it. Whatever the second child's reply, the first
child will evaluate it. That is, even before children know about schooling and the
particular transaction rituals common in school classrooms, they are familiar with
this transaction rituals, which is based on differential knowledge and assessment.
Just as in the case of queues, the *IRE* transaction ritual exists across different settings and can be recognized as such. In this latter case, it is a game. In other imaginable situations, if someone were to initiate this kind of game, it would be considered to be extremely odd, and the person in the second position, as any witness,
would ask him/herself seriously about the one who initiated it. Consider this situation, where a passer-by asks you for the time.

Fragment 6.4
```
I>  001   X:   what time is it.
    002         (1.2) ((Y looks at watch.))
R>  003   Y:   fivefifteen.
E>  004   X:   no; its fivethirteen.
```

If this were to happen to you, the reader, then you would probably shake your head
and wonder what this was all about. But structurally, it is the same, as shown by
the I-R-E notation, as the one involving Carrie and Jane. It turns out that at school,
this transaction ritual is played out over and over again, and in most instances the

---

[20] In my graduate seminars on research methods, I ask students to bring anonymized transcriptions
without providing any further information. So that graduate students can experience an expert at work, I
analyze the transcriptions for the first time in their presence (often recording the session). Invariably, I
pick out what are real, genuine questions from those where the questioner already knows the answer,
that is, those that are part of an IRE transaction sequence.

institutionally designated student takes the middle position, whereas the institutionally designated teacher takes the first and third positions in the sequence that constitutes the ritual. The event is a ritual precisely because of this role distribution. It asymmetrically attributes knowledge, whereby the individual taking the third position in the ritual also comes to be reified and inherently constituted as the knowledgeable one. I return below to a situation where a contest over knowledgeability flares up. Even though the contest will not be sustained over a long period of time, it illustrates that what constitutes relevant knowledge is always up for grabs even if in educational institutions, instructors often tend to end up in position that is associated with greater knowledgeability.

Instructors do not have to end up in those positions. Pertinent to this case are episodes from my own biography, where I had been repeatedly involved in knowledge contests with professors during lectures but on the side of the institutionally designated student. In one lecture of solid state physics, the contest ended when the professor said that the lecture notes had been prepared by a post-doctoral fellow and could well contain the error that I had pointed out and that had led to the {interruption} of the (normal course of) the lecture. In another instance, an advanced, doctoral course on statistical thermodynamics, the professor recognized the error I pointed out and then adjourned the lecture because the remaining notes where based on and included the error. In both cases, there was a contest for knowledge involved before the lecture resumed or was abandoned. In both cases, it therefore was not just the presentation of the correct knowledge but also the simultaneous recognition – on the counterpart – of the differential value of the two forms of knowledge that were at issue. The second episode is, of course, also interesting from the perspective of the eventness of the event, for it is not likely that the professor intended to cancel the lecture when he started it. The cancellation evolved out of the issue over an error that the professor himself had not recognized before.

A different issue is at play in the following fragment, where the talk is about what the first speaker can, or rather cannot, do. There is an assertion | acceptance sequence that confirms the referent of the "I" and "you" in turns 020 and 021, who cannot do some experiment with (different) waxes. The statement *could be* heard as denoting the speaker's self-recognized ability for doing something, such as when a person says 'I can't run the 100 meters in less than 10 seconds'. It is possible to hear turn 021 in the same sense, this speaker confirming that the interlocutor indeed is not capable of doing some experiment – which would make sense if the experiment involved gas chromatography–mass spectrometry. But the same turn sequence can be heard as part of an interdiction, where the second speaker (here Carrie) does not allow the first speaker (here Jane) to do something (here the experiment with different waxes). In this case, the turn sequence would reveal an asymmetry with respect to the position of determining future actions: the second speaker can be said to be in a power-over relation with respect to the first speaker. This analysis, then, is consistent with the statement that 'this power is *exercised* rather than possessed; it is not the "privilege", acquired or preserved, of the dominant class, but the overall effect of its strategic positions' (Foucault 1966: 35, emphasis added).

Fragment 6.5
```
019          (0.54)
020   J:    that means i cant experiment with the wa[xes.  ]
021   C:                                              [wAX?  ]
            (0.93) NO. (.) <<assertive>you cA:nt experiment with
            different wA[xes.]>
```

It is important to retain, however, that the sequence or the content alone does not allow us to state that there is a relation of power or ruling. There are other aspects of the setting, for example, the recurrence of similar patterns of determining future actions that are distributed unequally and in the same way across the interlocutors.

In the present episode concerning the change of plan, there are repeated instances where the future courses of actions of one person are articulated by the other person (Carrie), associated with the search and provision of assent. Again, although there is transactional symmetry, arising from the fact that we are dealing with irreducible *social* facts, witnessable in this way by whoever cares to take a look, there is also an asymmetry in the positions different members to the setting take in the transaction ritual. The following fragment begins with a phrase that states what the interlocutor actually *can* do. At first, there is a pause developing, providing Jane with an opportunity for taking the next turn at talk (turn 025). Just as the pause extends beyond the length that teachers have been reported to wait for a reply, Carrie takes another turn producing a version of the interjection 'okay' with rising intonation, that is, what we can hear as the interrogative form, a request for assent (R>).

Fragment 6.6
```
024    C:    BUT; (0.45) youcA:::n .hh and its going to bEE::
             (0.42) investiga:te (.) how you can hA:ve (0.60) a
             lANtern, (1.47) rI:::se (2.79) ((glances toward ceil-
             ing as if thinking)) <<all>in the lEAst amount of
             time for two meters> .hh with a:: (.)
             twen:ty:grammass=on=it.
025          (0.90)
R> 026  C:    .hhhhkay?
P> 027  J:    <<subdued, p>kay.
```

The next turn consists of the same interjection but which, because of the strongly falling intonation, can be heard in constative form, the provision of assent (A>). That is, the turn pair constitutes a request | provision of consent to whatever has been stated as the course of action that 'can' unfold. Here, as in turn 021, the assertion of what can (cannot) be done is asymmetrically distributed over speakers. We observe precisely the same transaction ritual and position distribution in the next fragment. In turn 028, the statement describes a future action. As before, there is a pause that develops just past the maximum teacher wait time of 0.7 seconds (turn 029) when Carrie takes another turn, producing, with interrogative intonation, a form of the assent-denoting 'okay'. Following another brief pause and a statement that can be perceived as elaborating the preceding action description, we hear a version of the assent-denoting interjection 'okay' in constative form and at very low speech intensity, which one might gloss as 'subdued'. In the pause that follows, the giving of assent is further observable in the head nods (turn 034).

Fragment 6.7
```
  028   C:   .hhh SO:; (0.50) makes it easy for you: and OTher
             thing is to (.17) un to: hOld ↑IT (0.30) untI::L:
             (0.81) you fINish up. (0.33) hEAting (0.22) the air?
  029        (0.75)
R>030        kay?
  031        (0.46)
  032        remOVe the hEAt sOUurce (0.28) <<all>then let it go.>
P>033   J:   <<pp>kay.>
P>034        (0.94) ((Jane nods))
R>035   C:   kAY? (0.23) .hhh (0.17) sO:::; (0.38) yes, you wONt
             be able to test different tYPes of WAxES=
```

In this fragment, there is actually a third occurrence of a version of the assent-denoting 'okay'. In turn 035 it is produced with rising intonation, as if querying in a way glossed by the phrase 'is it really okay?' But, as Carrie continues, there is currently no room for taking a turn.

A final example of the same transaction ritual involving the repeated articulation of the assent-denoting 'okay' occurred near the end of the episode. The point about the air outside the lantern being heated if a hairdryer where to be used comes to be accepted as an 'interesting' one in turn 151. This turn also includes a possible ('might') course of action, which, paired with the assent-denoting 'okay' in affirmative intonation, comes to be accepted.

Fragment 6.8
```
  151   C:   ^NN. thats an interesting pOINt you mIght lIke to (.)
             commENT on that.
  152        (0.87)
  153   J:   <<pp>kay.>
  154        (0.36)
  155   C:   kAY?
  156   J:   <<subdued,p>yup.> ((Averted gaze toward paper cups on
             lab desk))
```

The sound-word is repeated but with rising intonation in the next turn, thereby constituting the pair unit: 'okay. | okay?' Again, we can hear the second part of the pair as both a confirmation and as the offering of a query concerning the assent. In the next turn pair, assent is produced again, this time involving the adverbial interjection 'yup' articulated as a constative (turn 156) leading to the formation of the pair 'okay? | yup'. We may gloss what the two pairs achieve in this way: 'It is okay', 'Is it really okay?', and 'yes it is okay'.

In these fragments, therefore, we observe asymmetry emerging from an inherently symmetrical relation as a *social* phenomenon. The asymmetry exists in the positions that the different speakers take within the transaction ritual producing turn sequence: proposal for a course of action of another member and seeking of assent for the proposed or disallowed course of action (Carrie) and the giving of assent on the part of the speaker (Jane) whose actions thereby come to be specified by the counterpart. Carrie would later gloss the proposals of actions by saying 'I'll try and give her more guidance to try and get her doing things so she can get to ...'. In their back and forth and in their taking the particular positions, these interlocutors *produce*, in and through their joint action, a situation that we may gloss as a {power relation}, where 'power' comes to be attributed to one and lack of power to the other party. But this effect is achieved in the seeking | provision of assent for a stated course of action, that is, in their sympractical work. To bring out the current issue even more, think about the following analogy. {Power} is something like a movement in tango. We cannot understand that movement by putting together the independent contributions of the dance partners – who do what they do because of the movement. We need to think the individual contributions through the lens of the collective movement.

Power/Knowledge and {Contestation}

In chapter 3, we see that the {change of plans} requires a lot of sympractical work before the teacher continues on her way visiting with different student groups. Later, Carrie would gloss the situation by saying that 'Jane balked at it all'. After Carrie has proposed an alternative course of action involving a hairdryer to add hot air to the Chinese lantern, Jane talks about what she had done and thought about to address the problems that was experienced trying to get the lantern to rise by means of candles. She talks about a paper ring attached by means of light-weight tinsel and that these changes will make the entire setup have 'this weight and it will go up really easy, 'cause it is full of air'. But before Jane could complete her turn, Carrie is taking the speaking floor simultaneously with her: 'Will it burn?' (turn 056). There is an assertion that it will not, because 'it' is made of baking paper, followed, as Carrie does not use the opportunity to take a turn during the developing pause, by the statement that baking paper does not burn. This assertion is paired with a counter-assertion, according to which the referent of 'it' 'chars and gets holes' (turn 062).

```
Fragment 6.9
    056    C:                [will it bURn?]
    057           (0.75)
    058    J:     <<all>oh=no cause i=m making it out of baking paper.>
    059           (0.98)
A> 060    J:     <<all>baking paper dOEsnt burn.>
A> 061           (0.74)
C> 062    C:     wE:ll: it can bURn but it chA:Rs and gets hOLes in
                  it.
    063           (0.96)
```

At this point, then, we find an assertion | counter-assertion pair. Because the two assertions state different, mutually exclusive events to be happening, both cannot be true simultaneously. This sets up a contestation, a contradiction, or conflict that requires some form of resolution to continue. Or something else that avoids addressing the contestation might follow, thereby avoiding *this* conflict. What we observe here, therefore, is a contest over knowledge, who is in the know about what baking paper will do when it comes into contact with a candle flame. If there was an avoidance of conflict, it could be heard as an acknowledgment of the truth of the counter-assertion or of a certain degree of uncertainty about what actually would happen in the case the candle flame reaches the baking paper. In both cases, an asymmetry with respect to knowledge would be enacted. This does not mean that the other interlocutor, here Carrie, is somehow right. It means that in this conversation and at this point, the counter-assertion has been attributed a higher value and, therefore, greater knowledgeability about the issue might be attributed to the speaker who has made the statement.

After a pause, Jane takes a turn, which in fact is the second part of the pair including that turn 062 has initiated. It consists of an assertion about the ability to do an experiment 'how tall it has to be', where we can hear 'it' as referring to the candle(s), which come(s) or can be cut to different lengths. It is possible to gloss Jane's smile that follows as 'triumphant'. There is an extraordinarily long pause – the 2.08 s (turn 065) are more than twice the standard maximum silence in (telephone) conversations (Jefferson 1989). Has Carrie lost her words? Is she beginning to give into the argument? But then the second part to the turn is produced: 'Can you use the same set up with adding hot air?' (turn 066).

Fragment 6.10
```
  064   J:   but i can experiment on how tall it has to be.
             ((Smiles at Carrie))
  065        (2.08)
  066   C:   can you use the sAMe setup (0.36) with (1.01) adding
             hotair?
  067   J:   but i wanted <<all>it how tall it is to go UP.>
  068        (0.61)
  069   J:   <<all>it doesnt even matter if its a paper cUP it can
             go up. t can go up.> ((Smiles, as if she had made a
             'good play'))
  070        (1.59)
  071   C:   so have a think about (0.98) what you can do with
             that. (0.20) <<len>i kno:w that youve put thought in
             what we were doing;> but.
```

Again, as before, an assertion about doing an experiment with different candle lengths comes to be paired with an assertion that states an experimental condition in which the candles inherently do not appear because hot air is 'added' to the lantern. We have a pair of statements with incompatible content: either the experiment is done with candles that heat the air in the lantern directly or hot air is added to the lantern, for example, by using a hairdryer. The subsequent turn shows that the second statement is heard as a contrast just as the analysis reveals: 'But I wanted it it how tall it is to go up' (turn 067). That is, we have a second turn pair in which the hairdryer experiment comes to be confronted with a restatement of the experiment involving the length ('how tall') of the candles. There is a developing pause, which allows Jane takes the floor again: 'It doesn't matter if it's a paper cup, it can go up'. As before, if we stopped the videotape at precisely this point during a first-time-through analysis, we may hypothesize about possible future actions. There is nothing, however, that would allow us to specify with absolute certainty what actually will happen. There is a conflict that needs resolution or a strategic move that avoids it or some other move that puts away with the conflict.

At first, there is a pause about twice the length of the standard maximum wait time teachers allow and then Carrie takes a turn – though the pause, because it is also her pause is, in a way, both part and not part of her turn. It makes an assertion about the next action, inviting the interlocutor to 'have a think about what you can do with that'. Here it is open whether 'that' refers to the candle or hairdryer experiment, though a tendency would be to hear it as referring to the statement the speaker herself has previously articulated. There is then a statement about knowing how much thought the interlocutor has put into their collective doings, followed by the contrastive conjunction 'but'. This is in fact an incomplete phrase, where whatever is to come is to be in contradiction with the alternative proposal. We know from chapter 3 that there are further articulations of future actions, which follow the same pattern as that analyzed in the preceding section.

To provide another example of a contest in the making consider the following fragment. It begins with the articulation of an assertion ('A>') that there are two ways in which using the hairdryer to have hot air in the lantern can be looked at: as 'adding air' or 'heating the air that's there' (turn 148). This assertion comes to be paired with a modalized counter-assertion that this also would heat the air around the lantern. Because of the modalization, turn 150 does not constitute a pure counter-assertion. The modalization derives from the use of the 'would not'.

Fragment 6.11
```
   148    C:    so you need to add it, you are not really (0.54) i
   A>            guess you can look at ADding hot air or hEAting the
   A>            AIr thats thEre.
   149          (0.66) ((Jane nods))
C> 150    J:    kay. but wouldnt that heat the air thats around the
                outside?=
   151    C:    ^NN. thats an interesting pOINt you mIght lIke to (.)
                commENT on that.
```

The modalizing verb can be heard here as function in one of two ways. First, it can be heard as introducing the opinion that the air surrounding the lantern is heated together with the air inside it. It can also be heard as a conditional with the condition understood but unstated: 'if the air that's there is heated then would that not heat the air that's around the outside'. In both cases, a contrast is set up that something also happens which potentially – without being stated as such – could lead to a problem. The counter-assertion in the opinion / conditional is then acknowledged to constitute an 'interesting point'. That is, it is not only accepted but accepted as something of sufficient interest to be addressed by commenting on (in the final [lab] report). In this case, then, knowledgeability in the contest comes to fall on Jane's, the student's side rather than that of the teacher.

The turn sequence in fact reaffirms that the next steps to be taken would be those that the teacher has articulated: the experiment using the hairdryer. As we see in the preceding section, Jane articulates the assent-constituting 'okay' so that sequence in fact constitutes a move away from the experiment with the candle, exploring ways of thinking about and possible problems arising from the use of a hairdryer as a source of hot air. It therefore also asserts asymmetrically the positions taken for and against the two ways to proceed: doing the experiment investigating the minimum length of a candle required to make the lantern rise versus making the lantern rise using hot air supplied by means of the hairdryer.

Power/Knowledge and {Pleas}

Cultural-historically, pleas are associated with court cases, and, thereby linking to the preceding section, especially to conflicts. It also denotes an urgent and emotional request. Although of etymological different origin, the partially homonymic adverb 'please' – from the verb 'to please', to be pleasing or agreeable – is used to formulate and insist upon a kind request. In both situations, whether in a case of law or in a request, something is asked from someone else. That is, the requester does not have what is being asked for, but the interlocutor, the one to whom the plea is directed, is in a situation to dispense whatever is being requested. What we recognize as a plea or as a kind request underscored by the use of the interjection 'please', therefore, is a joint achievement in which the position in the transaction ritual comes to be associated with the discretionary power over what is requested. The person or organization may or may not respond favorably to the request. In the approach here, as shown in chapter 3, the social fact of pleading / requesting (a favor) is jointly achieved. But in the transaction ritual, an asymmetry comes to be asserted on the part of both requester and respondent.

The fragment begins with a statement about what the interlocutor has to do: to think about what she can do with that, which is, as we see above, followed by the contrastive conjunction 'but'. A long pause follows. It comes to an end when Carrie takes another turn articulating statements about variations, complications, and difficulties making it work (turn 073). The second part to this turn pair is a conditional with the grammatical structure of a request, 'If I get it to work, can I do it?' (turn 074). This turn pair, therefore, includes a statement of mitigating circumstances to get it (the experiment) to work and a conditional involving the getting it to work as the premise for the permission-requesting plea 'can I do it'. The same plea structure is repeated some time later: 'but if this works, can I do it?' (turn 079b,c). In both instances, what is already sufficient for constituting the first turn of a {plea} is followed by the pleading and politely urging interjection 'please'.

```
Fragment 6.12
    071    C:    so have a think about (0.98) what you can do with
                 that. (0.20) <<len>i kno:w that youve put thought in
                 what we were doing;> but.
    072          (1.67)
    073    C:    the:::ee (0.79) variATions in whats hAPppening;
                 <<all>and the complicATions and dIFficulties in
→                ACtually> making it wO:::rk.
P>074    J:    <<all>if i get it to work can i do it> plEA::se.
    075          (0.24)
C>076    C:    .hhhh but then youll be spending mORe time trying to
→                make it wORk.
    077    J:    but
C>078    C:    [and if doesnt youll run out of time.]
→ 079    J:    [but if this time it doesnt work       ] (0.30) some
p>   a         (1.00) i promise i=ll: (0.17) go back (0.39) and
P>   b         (0.22) do: (0.44) <<all>the hairdryer one; but if
P>   c         this works (0.26) can i do it plEAse?
    080          (0.75)
    081    C:    so you:: (0.19) I:: wou:ld=suggest fr todA:Y: (0.48)
→                you work on that (0.68) sort of (1.06) what ideas you
                 can change for the other one .hhh and at hO:Me
```

```
                    ((Jane's face changes to sad expression, averts gaze
                    heretofore straight forwardly directed at Carrie's
                    face)) (0.23) try:ing (0.41) <<all>try and get your
    →               wAX one to work.> ((Jane's face goes from smile to
                    sadness))
    082     J:      <<subdued, p>kay.>
    083             (0.48)
    084     C:      <<all>kay?>
    085             (0.82)
```

A {plea} can be realized by direct acceptance or rejection, that is, realized in a turn
pair of the type 'articulating | accepting the plea' or 'articulating | rejecting the
plea' – e.g., if the second member of the turn pair would be 'okay, try, but if it
doesn't work you do the hairdryer one' or 'no, you do the hairdryer one' (Fragments 6.13a, 6.13b).

Fragment 6.13a
```
P>074    J:    <<all>if i get it to work can i do it> plEA::se.
A>076    C:    okay; try and if it doesnt work you do the hairdryer
               one.
```

Fragment 6.13b
```
P>074    J:    <<all>if i get it to work can i do it> plEA::se.
R>076    C:    no. you do thehairdryer one.
```

In the actual case of the first plea offer, the second member of the turn pair articulates statements of possible negative consequences ('C>', turns 076, 078). statements constitute the first part of a pair, in which a bargain is offered that takes into
account both the possibility that the experiment does and does not work. In the
latter case, the course of action would implement the hairdryer experiment. This
part of the bargain, which involves the change of plan from the perspective of the
pleading agent, is supported by offering a promise ('p>', turn 079a).

In the second case where a first turn in the direction of a {plea} is made, the
second turn does not directly reject it by means of a statement such as 'no'. But in
this pair, the offer for {plea} is confronted with a constative statement of what the
course of action for the pleader is suggested to be. The fragment ends with an exchange of versions of the assent-related interjection 'okay'. The assent seeking
'okay' is not present here here, but the fragment ends with the same sequence as
Fragment 6.7, where the assent-giving version of 'okay' (turn 082) is followed by
an assent-seeking 'okay' on the part of the speaker who had just stated assertively,
though with a mitigating 'I would suggest', that the course of action will be of a
specific type: working on the change in the here and now of the situation and trying at home to get the wax experiment to work.

The entire plea is about the working and not working (see turns marked '→' in
Fragment 6.12) of the experiment with the candles and the alternative experiment
with the hairdryer (turn 079b). The plea concerns the permission to do the candle
experiment. But like in a court case, the 'judge' throws out the case (turn 81), having already cited that this requires 'spending more time trying to make it work' and
running out of time if it does not work. The entire sequence then is something like
an offer to a plea bargain on the part of the 'accused' (turn 079), where the different outcomes of an effort on the part of the person pleading lead to different cours-

es of actions: submitting what the authority decided and following the original, alternative course of action.

As all instances of social talk, there is turn taking, which realizes a relation. Each word and phrase inherently exists *for* the two parties to the setting. At the outset, therefore, there is symmetry simply based on the fact that both relation and exchange are social phenomena that require multiple parties to be constituted. However, we observe asymmetry to emerge in how the different actors take particular positions in a consistent manner. The opening turn of the two {plea} offers fall to Jane, just as the offer of a {promise}. The second turn in the {plea} always falls to Carrie, to whom the plea is directed. Although symmetrical in requiring initiation and reply, the structure of the {plea} is asymmetrical, for the person pleading is requesting something from the institution (here the teacher) who can accept or reject it. In the same way, the {promise}, though requiring the person making and the one receiving it, is asymmetrical in the sense that the speaker stating the promises also commits to a course of action. An asymmetry is offered between promiser and promisee. In the present instance, the opening position that offers the promise falls to the same person who also pleads.

Power/Knowledge: The Cumulative Effect of Strategic Positions

In the introduction to this chapter, I present a quotation in which Foucault explicitly states that power is exercised rather than possessed. He further makes the point that power is not an acquired or preserved privilege, which, in the present case, would be that of the institutionally designated teacher. The teachers would be something like the representatives of 'the dominant class' in the hierarchically structured system of schooling. Rather, Foucault states that power is the overall effect of strategic positions. In the preceding analysis, the 'strategic positions' are those that fall – taken and being given – differentially to the parties present to the setting. Across the different phenomena treated in the preceding sections, that is, *cumulatively*, the position associated with the possibility of deciding what happens next are taken by the same person: Carrie, the institutionally designated teacher. It is not that she somehow is imbued with power or that she *has* power in the way she may have coins in her pockets or purse.

The strategic positions that come to be associated with and produces power effects are not just taken by one person but they are also given. For power we may make the same kind of statement that has been made for experience: 'Experiencing like breathing is a rhythm of intakings and outgivings' (Dewey 2008: 62). In the same way, power is the result of taking and giving, giving and taking, on the part of all those who staff the phenomenon. This can be seen, for example, in the pauses, which provide opportunities for both speakers to take the next turn even to the person who has just had one. Moreover, for *social* phenomena such as {pleas}, {promises}, or {decisions} to come to life we require multiple social actors acting *in concert*, like those who offer and those who accept or reject a plea, those who offer and those who accept or reject a promise, those who state courses of social actions and those who follow or reject them. Thus, in the examples given, as all the other examples that occurred throughout the entire episode without being mobilized here, Jane takes particular positions in the turn taking rituals as much as she is given these positions; Carrie takes particular positions as much as she is given these positions. In fact, thinking the transaction rituals requires us to begin the analysis with the social dimension of the phenomenon before proceeding to identify recurrences in the taking/being given of particular positions in unitary but inherently asymmetrical social phenomena. That is, in the approach presented here, the strategic positions are not just taken – as one may read in the current literature, including those studies that focus on 'the presentation of self in everyday life' – but also are given. This, then, allows us to understand power/knowledge as continuously produced in and through transaction rituals without a prior attribution of it to one or the other member to the setting. Thus, even in the case where a particular individual comes to be in a specific strategic position, this position cannot ever be taken for granted, for it is continuously up for grabs. In this approach, then, we would understand any situation to be in flux so that it can and does change. There is no time-out, no reprieve, no possibility for a cop-out. Only continued processes that attribute strategic positions to the participants in social affairs. This then allows us to understand that even 'the best teachers' may have a 'bad hair day', and even 'the best teachers' may be attributed to have done 'something stupid' in class. Even the best teachers may find themselves in situation, where a lesson 'gets out of hand' over the challenge an 'A student' makes concerning a chemistry test where he has been attributed a low grade (e.g., Roth et al. 2004).

In the introduction to chapter 4, I point to a study investigating a science teacher, who, having been successful in inner-city schools of Miami, Florida, moved to Philadelphia, Pennsylvania, where he, also teaching in an inner-city school, by and large failed according to his own account. Observers suggested, however, that he again became a successful teacher over the course of a few years. This assessment can be seen to be validated by the fact that he was made director of one of the schools within that school where he initially experienced problems. We can understand these historical changes in terms of the approach presented here. That is, over time, and as he became familiar with the setting, he ended up, cumulatively, in the strategic position that attributes to him control and therefore power. But it is not just him. Throughout the present chapter I emphasize the need to understand power/knowledge as a *social* phenomenon that requires the sympractical action of all parties involved.

In the position on power/knowledge articulated in this chapter, persons neither have nor are imbued with power. The ethnomethodological approach leads us to investigate the actual work by means something like {power} or {power/knowledge} comes to be a *demonstrable* and *instructable* social fact. This points us to the sympractical nature of {power}, that is, the collaboration of those coming to be invested or divested of it as a result. Some readers may balk at such a framing. However it has been noted that '[t]he fact that persons may be required to reproduce the very social forms that oppress them is a much more powerful and frightening vision of tension and inequality than the idea that independent individuals exist in some sort of primeval struggle against society' (Rawls, in Garfinkel 2002: 56). Our orientation, therefore, continues to be towards the social in its sociality.

7

The Actor's Point of View

> A population is constituted not by a set of individuals with something in common but a by a set of practices common to particular situations or events: the crowd at the coffee machine, the line at the supermarket, the 'gang' at the science lab, and so on. (Rawls, in Garfinkel 2002: 60)

In this book, I am concerned with the endogenous production of soci(et)al order that we recognize and denote as 'science lessons'. The approach advocated and promoted here radically differs from other approaches to science education research in that it does not focus on reporting the social facts, which are the results of constructive formal analysis; rather, I emphasize the embodied character of the social actors' joint and coordinated, sympractical *work* that produces the social order to which the actors themselves orient, make available to each other, hold each other accountable to, and so on.[21] The phenomena of interest *are* social, which means, the individuals who appear in these *social* phenomena are understood as the staff or population that concretely realize them. We do not need to study the motives, thoughts, or concepts of individual actors to study and understand queues, especially in the extreme variety that this phenomenon exists. Independent of the particular psychological states that we might want to ascribe to those who line up in front of a cinema ticket window, before a company store to purchase its latest branded gadget or product, at the bus stop, or on the freeway ramp, the phenomenon plays itself out independent of the specific actors staffing

---

[21] Theorists may be interested in taking multiple perspectives that play internal-subjective versus external-objective – e.g., semiotic versus phenomenological perspectives (Roth and Bowen 1999a) or a cognitive phenomenological approach to learning science (Roth 2006). However, objective methods need to explain rather than brush aside the experience of the human beings who produce and experience the phenomena of interest. Such theorists therefore would strive to find a framework in which any differences between theoretical-scientific and practical-phenomenological can be explained.

the phenomenon. This is so even though the phenomenon only exists in and through the concrete, situated action of the members to the setting.

Throughout the foregoing chapters, I insist on reading and hearing the tape-recorded materials from the perspective of the social phenomenon. The lens on the event, therefore, is through that of the sympractical work in and through which the social actors involved produce accountable social facts. They do so not because their individual acts somehow add up or synthesize into a social practice but because each act is a manifestation of an irreducible *social* act that involves two or more actors. This approach decenters the analysis in that I 'approach linguistic behavior, not by referring it to private states in individuals, but by observing its social function of coordinating diverse actions' (Mills 1940: 904). That is, the social action no longer is theorized from the perspective of the individual. Instead, intelligibility is theorized as being 'achieved in and through the enactment of recognizable practices, not through interpretive processes in the minds of individual actors' (Rawls, in Garfinkel 2002: 60). Thus, language is not taken to be 'expressing something which is prior and in the person'; rather, 'language is taken by other persons as an indicator of future actions' (Mills 1940: 904).

In an exchange with a colleague over such an approach to the analysis, he noted his impression or 'complaint' that I am 'disinterested in the specific individuals and the statements that they make. These are only sources of text, material for the analyses. He added: 'I have the feeling that it could be any student, any interviewer, and any topics, completely exchangeable'. Rather than seeing in this comment a critique, I see it as evidence that my text and analyses achieved precisely what I intended: a description of *social* phenomena that are independent of the particular staff or population that concretely realizes it in any *this* instance. This is consistent with the ethnomethodological approach according to which, in an important sense, the actor's point of view and the significance of social action no longer has to be thought of as belonging to individual actors (Rawls, in Garfinkel 2002). The empirical study of observable practices does in fact articulate and reveal the actor's viewpoint, that is, a viewpoint *from within* the unfolding event.

Although I present the actors' point of view here, my account of social events 'through the lens of the actors' is not characterized by the intentions, plans, or motives that are ascribed to individual actors, whether such ascription occurs on the part of others or on the part of the actors themselves. Rather, I pursue a *sociological* approach to linguistics and psychology. In such an approach, '[r]ather than fixed elements "in" an individual, motives are the terms with which interpretation of conduct *by social actors* proceeds. This imputation and avowal of motives by actors are social phenomena to be explained' (Mills 1940: 904). Intentions and purposes, which might be stated prior to an action, refer us to an awareness of anticipated consequences but not to the specific situated action that ensues. 'Motives are accepted justifications for present, future, or past programs or acts' (ibid: 907). As a result, the degree to which a motive (intention, plan) is consistent with an actually produced situated action can be made, *in any and every case*, only after the fact (Suchman 1987).

To take a concrete example, consider a situation from the Australian classroom analyzed in chapter 1 (Bellocchi and Ritchie 2011). The authors describe that the student Trev was looking over another student's shoulder (Mal) amd present a transcript that included the following lines.

```
Fragment 7.1
 37  Trev:  Shouldn't that whether have a 'H' after the w?
 38  Mal:   Trev let's not worry about grammar in chemistry
 39  Louise: But yes it should
```

The authors then write: 'he noted that Mal had incorrectly spelt the word "whether". Trev intervenes as seen in Extract 1 to correct Mal's spelling'. When we compare what is actually in the transcript with what the authors suggest is there, then we realize that motives have been attributed to the action. Thus, for example, Trev does not say that he had seen an incorrect spelling; he does not say that he is correcting the spelling. Both what has been noticed and what the intention of turn 37 is have been ascribed to Trev. *In the situation*, we see that the turn pair realizes a statement about grammar that is not to be worried about. The second turn pair is a statement | counter-statement pair concerning whether to worry about grammar in chemistry. The two turn pairs, rather than being about the specific issue of the 'h' that should follow the 'w' in 'wether' is actually enlarged to the question of grammar in general. It is precisely in ascribing motives and intentions that the authors 'remedy' the indexicality of the talk: the authors tell their readers what the social actors in the transcript definitely intended to do with their action.

Technically, these researchers conflate what speech act theorists denote by the term *illocutionary act*, the intention that an individual actor might have, with the *locutionary* (fact of speaking) and *perlocutionary act* (the effect of the act). Rather than attending to the turn pair and, therefore, to the irreducible *social* (speech) act – which consists of the speaking | active receiving (or evaluating) pair (Vološinov 1930) – the authors reduce to individualistic psychology what properly is a social phenomenon and, therefore, a sociological problem. To get at the internal 'machinery' that drives this event, we have to look at the work of the actors that endogenously produces the social structure of the situation. The actors themselves do not have access to the intentions and motives of other actors, even though they may ascribe such to the latter in the privacy of their thoughts. But here we are not concerned with what actors harbor in the privacy of their thoughts; we are concerned with what is objectively available for everyone to observe and to account for. Thus, whatever Trev, Mal, Louise, and their mates may have been cogitating in the privacy of their individual minds, what they hold each other to account for are the public actions. From the perspective of the actors, turn 37 is a statement about grammar made in a chemistry lesson, and the predicate in turn 38 is constituted as an assertion about worrying.

This case exemplifies the common practice of ascribing actions to actors, that is, to those who effectuate them – whether these are practical, when something in the material world is manipulated or whether these are discursive, when something is being brought about through talk. 'Motives' and 'intentions' constitute and are constituted, in any specific context, by a particular *vocabulary* or *vocabularies of motives* (Mills 1940). As a result, the motives and intentions of a person, that is, specifications of who someone is, is based on the mobilization of particular vocabularies of motives, which are a function of the particular situated practices in the context of which these are mobilized at a particular point in cultural history. Thus, for example, Freudian 'motives are those of an upper bourgeois patriarchal group with strong sexual and individualistic orientation. When introspecting on the couches of Freud, patients used the only vocabulary of motives they knew; Freud got his hunch and guided further talk' (ibid: 912). Those who have been converted then will see all non-Freudian vocabularies of motives as self-deceptive. In a similar way, and pertinent to the issue of the preceding chapter, to those avowing to a Marxist discourse – i.e., the 'terminology of power, struggle, and economic motives' – all other vocabularies of motives 'are due to hypocrisy or ignorance' (ibid: 912).

A suitable alternative from the perspective articulated in this book is this: 'Rather than interpreting actions and language as external manifestations of subjective and deeper lying elements in individuals, the research task is the locating of particular types of action within typal frames of normative actions and socially situated clusters of motive' (Mills 1940: 913). Motives, beliefs, emotions, personal characteristics, or psychological states are of interest only when they are integral and constitutive part of some situation, which itself requires analysis. Thus, for example, the following fragment derives from the post-lesson debriefing interview that the researcher conducted with Carrie. We can hear them talk about Jane's level of engagement, her apparent enthusiasm, and the use this enthusiasm was made of.

Fragment 7.2[22]
```
010   C:   jane never really engaged in any of it much.
011   R:   did that surprise you?
012   C:   maybe the extent, like she was quite enthusiastic to
           begin with but it didnt carry her very far. she didnt
           take any of that enthusiasm and apply it to anything.
```

Rather than taking the content of this talk as saying something about Jane, we need to consider it in the context of the ongoing activity. This activity belongs to research about science lessons. It is this research activity that comes to be realized in and through the speech activity. We can then learn about the sympractical work in and as part of which personal characteristics of some other person come to be constituted in an accountable way. The request for such an account can be heard in turn 011, which both accepts the preceding statement and requests an articulation of the quality of the perception described in turn 010. It is in and out of the turn pair 011 | 012 that the reason that the extent of the phenomenon was surprising comes to be articulated: there had been evidence for the presence of enthusiasm, but Jane 'didn't take any of that enthusiasm and apply it to anything'. Here, then, certain personality traits of Jane come to be attributed to her in and through the interview talk. In that talk, the two interlocutors are accountable to each other for the production of intelligibility both of the situation itself and the topic that they are producing in and through their talk.

---

[22] For this transcription and those appearing in Fragments 7.4–7.7, the soundtrack was not available. The punctuation is that of the transcriber and, therefore, need to be understood as the transcriber's hearing of what is on the tape.

From the Shop Floor

In this section, I show that we can take the actor's point of view without having to appeal to interpretive processes in the minds of individual actors. To this, we need to enact a decentering approach that moves our analysis away from the discourse of individual action and the associated discourses about motives and intentions. There are two steps required. First, to get at the actor perspective, we have to get down to the shop floor, where the work is being conducted, and describe how the actors themselves take up, react or respond to a preceding action. Second, we have to do so *without* taking this take up, reaction, or response as an individual action in its turn – either constituting an interpretation or being the result of an interpretation. The researcher would in that case interpret what the actors interpreted, attempting to get at their 'meanings' even though nothing of this sort is available in the transcript or on the tape. A further step is required, which, as I show throughout this book, is the shift to describing and analyzing the turn pair. Moreover, we are focusing on the structure constituting *work* rather than on the *structure* as revealed in and through the interpretive analysis of the researcher. This approach, then, does not require a special method. The researcher simply has to be competent with shop floor talk and action. One and the same methodical move – the analysis of turn pairs – therefore gets us onto the shop floor, provides us with the view from within, and decenters from the individual interpretive view (both on the part of the actor and on the researcher's part) to a social view.

Some readers might now suggest that it is the researcher who interprets the turn pair. But such readers would commit the error in assuming that the researcher is giving definite and definitive status to a turn. This is not so, however, because analysts, as the staff in the phenomena they study, are confronted with an openness whereby each phrase both says more and less than it states in so many words. Any phrase can always be articulated as having said something other than it actually has said; and in this, any phrase says less than what it can be reported to have said. Each turn, as we see in the preceding chapters, is bound up with two other turns. It completes the turn pair that has been initiated before and it initiates another turn pair in turn. That is, on the one hand, it frames the reception of what has been said and done; but this framing itself is not accessible to us, if we take the shop floor perspective, because only the next turn allows us to hear how the framing has been framed. The definiteness of an expression always is available a posteriori: 'The definiteness of expressions resides in their consequences; definitions can be used to assure a definite collection of "considerations" without providing a boundary; the definiteness of a collection is assured by circumstantial possibilities of indefinite elaboration' (Garfinkel and Sacks 1986: 160). Our analysis needs to leave open the nature of a phrase until it is determined, from within the setting, to the extent that it can or has been determined. To concretize this discussion, we take a look at the instant where the talk is about having the 'wax bit' in the report as an experiment that was not actually conducted.

What has happened prior to the fragment may be glossed as the announcement of a change of plans, that is, a change of task conditions available on Moodle, which involves adding hot air to the Chinese lantern or heating the air in the lantern by means of a hairdryer. During the post-lesson interview, Carrie glosses the events in a statement that also adds motives inherently taken to be intelligible on the part of the interviewing researcher: 'I approached her with the idea that I wanted her to feel that it was a good thing rather than meaning she'd done all this work and it was wasted etcetera, etcetera'.

The first turn pair, which extends over several, even overlapping turns, consists of a statement | counter-statement pair concerning the relation of theory and experiment. The first statement ('S>') involves a conditional: 'if you have theory, [then] you can still put it in', which is elaborated by means of the statement 'it can be an experiment you didn't do' and a restatement of the condition 'but you still have theory on it' (turns 089, 092, 094). If we were to attribute what Carrie (definitely) has done to her independently of the situation, then we would introduce intentions and motives to the situation from the outside. To get the shop floor perspective, we need to attend to the reception available in the composite turn pair.

Fragment 7.3
```
S> 089   C:    .hh if you hAve thE:ory for the wAX bit (0.17) you
               can stILl put it in
   090         (0.32)
   091   J:    un
S> 092   C:    and it can be an experiment you didnt dO, but.
C> 093   J:    no i need to [do the experiment            ]
S> 094   C:                 [<<all>you still have theory on it.>]
C> 095   J:    to get the theory because theres nobody whos dONe an
               expERiment like that.
   096         (0.40)
   097   C:    yea but you should have a rEAson wHY: it chANges.
               ((Jane's face pensive))
   098         (0.93)
   099   J:    well it could [    (??)    ]
   100   C:                  [because if] there is nO rEAson whY
               then theres nOT much point dOing it.
   101   J:    if gonna be (.) <<p>its gonna be hotter so it takes
               the little cup>
   102         (0.83)
   103   J:    and then the wax (0.46) or whether its going to be
               cool (0.38) cool and thirty minutes its cool wax and
               it burn faster. (0.28) or whether if its hotter it
               will rise mORe because of the hEAt.
```

The replique also stretches over several turns: 'I need to do the experiment to get the theory because there's nobody who's done an experiment like that'. We observe that the second, counter-statement reverses the order between theory and experiment that the statement proposes. In fact, the denotation of the second turn as 'counter-statement' ('C>') has to be tentative, for we do not know the work that the turn does, as seen from the shop floor, unless we consider the subsequent turn. It, too, stretches over several turns in the fragment (turns 097, 100): 'but you should have a reason why it changes, because if there is no reason why then there's not much point doing it'. This next turn includes an oppositive or contrastive conjunction 'but' and the auxiliary verb 'should', which tends to appear in advice, recommendation, obligation, and expectation turn pairs. In articulating that there *should be* a reason, the phrase also marks that the interlocutor possibly has no reason for doing the experiment; the second part of the speaking turn elaborates the issue in saying that there is no point for doing an experiment in the absence of a reason.

We therefore observe a shift here, whereby the talk moves from the contrast between the sequence 'theory → experiment' and 'experiment → theory' to a statement 'reason → experiment'. This last statement therefore constitutes an acceptance of the preceding turn in that it states an obligation to have a reason such that the course of action proposed is 'reason → experiment → theory'. In stating the obligation that there should be a reason, the turn also marks that there currently is none. Again, whether the turn is heard as an obligation *on the shop floor* depends on the next turn. In fact, the selection of the term 'obligation' among the possible descriptions is the result of considering the phrase spread across turns 97 and 100 with the corresponding next phrase spread across turns 099 and 101, which begin to state reasons ('it could ...'; 'it's gonna be hotter ...').

In the preceding chapters, the analyses proceed *as if* the second turn *definitely* told us what the preceding turn had done. In this section, we see that this second turn, because it is a first turn of the subsequent turn pair, itself has to remain open as to what it is really doing until considered in the context of the associated second-turn replique. Each turn is taken as a statement about what the preceding turn 'really means to say' without actually saying so, a procedure that is applied to the turn itself. We thereby get a view on social events from the shop floor without actually having to speculate about the contents of the minds of the actors, any motives and intentions that they may ascribe to their practical actions before, during, or after actually performing them.

Formal analytic approaches – whether quantitative or qualitative, in telling us what an actor is doing and what motives, intentions, and interests – substitute objective expressions to remedy the indexical properties of natural language: 'Wherever and by whatsoever practical sociological reasoning is done it seeks to remedy the indexical properties of practical discourse; it does so in the interests of demonstrating the rational accountability of everyday activities; and it does so in order that its assessments be warranted by methodic observation and report of situated, socially organized particulars of everyday activities, which of course include particulars of natural language' (Garfinkel and Sacks 1986: 161). That, as the authors note, provides professional research 'with its infinite task'.

The present approach, on the other hand, may initially appear disconcerting. We can never fix with any definiteness what an actor is really saying or doing, *as perceived from the shop floor*, until we have available the next performative turn in that situation. That is, this form of analysis introduces uncertainty. But, and this is possibly the most interesting part of it, this approach inherently introduces the properties of life: openness and continuous change just as we experience these in our day-to-day affairs. We actually get at the event(ful)ness of the act as a microevent, which is available to us always only after it has been completed and when its effect is known as exhibited in and through its social consequences. With respect to talk, we may express this situation in terms of the distinction between the *Saying* (speaking event in the making) and the *Said* (content of the speaking event). There always is a delay between the Saying and the Said, and this delay is itself constitutive not only of movement and time but also of knowledge. We do not know what is being done until the doing has come to its end and something has

been eventuated. But this knowing of what has been eventuated is itself a performance, which can be known only when the performance has ended. It is this continuous delay that eternally returns as the same: the eternal flow of time and the
continuous change of what we know. To understand the conversation, from the
shop floor, we must not impose the content of the Saying – i.e., the Said – from the
outside, through the interpretive effort of the researcher, but as addressed within
the conversation, that is, from the shop floor where the conversation is actually
made.

Identity Talk

Identity is an important construct in science education. Thus, in the pages of professional journals we may read phrases such as 'students define their identity
through coping strategies', 'students move to a more comfortable identity', 'teachers have beliefs about their identity', 'pseudonyms are used to protect the identity
of participants', 'students try identities', 'students author identities', and 'students
author identities by performing certain behaviors, speech, and perceptions'. Without going into the details of an analysis of the textual work that authors perform
with and through the mobilization of the 'identity' concept, we may recognize that
all the examples listed are evidence of the following definitions,[23] which are but
two of 15 entries in the chosen dictionary:

> **identity, n. 2. a.** The sameness of a person or thing at all times or in all cir-
> cumstances; the condition of being a single individual; the fact that a person
> or thing is itself and not something else; individuality; personality.
> **b.** Who or what a person or thing is; a distinct impression of a single person
> or thing presented to or perceived by others; a set of characteristics or a de-
> scription that distinguishes a person or thing from others. (OED 2012)

The definitions show that identity refers us to a self-same entity, here, the human
being. Even though a person changes – e.g., from infant to toddler to child to ado-
lescent to adult – something is recognized as being the same. In formal analytic
approaches, the questions of who and what a person is comes to be answered by
the researcher, who, using interpretive methods specially identified in the appropriate sections of a research article, chapter, or book, extracts identity from the
data. Although it would be interesting to investigate the professional researcher's
work by means of which identities come to be constituted, I focus here on identity
talk on the part of the researcher in the field and a research participant (Carrie).
That is, I focus on a shop floor perspective on the issue of who someone is, where

---

[23] This would be done by means of the documentary method (Garfinkel 1967; Mannheim 2004),
whereby the concept of identity would be defined by the totality of all concrete statements about
identity. There is then a whole | part relation, whereby the totality of statements is defined by all
constitutive parts, but these parts are parts only because of the entire collection of statements
about identity.

the shop floor now is precisely there where interviews unfold producing talk that subsequently results in 'transcriptions', data sources to be analyzed.

We begin by taking a look at a part from Carrie's gloss (see chapter 2) in which she talks about what has happened in the episode that she had identified as standing out from the lesson. The account glosses what happened as 'Jane balking' 'at it all', where the 'it' can be heard (following Sacks' maxim) as pertaining to the change of plans from heating the air in the lantern by means of a candle to heating it by means of a hairdryer. We then find the articulation of a motive, in fact, an intention and a motive. First, the statement 'as much as it makes life easier for her' constitutes an intent to the change of plans: to make life easier for Jane. Such statements could be used to support suggestions that Carrie and the department head Andrew 'want' or 'intend' to help the students doing the lantern experiment generally and Jane specifically. Second, it attributes a motive to Jane: 'she wants to do her own thing'. Later, we find that Jane 'is not as interested in physics as she is in singing, music and ...'. There are further motives attributed to Jane such as not wanting to be seen to not know things and an attribution to the emotional state ('I sort of knew she wouldn't be happy').

> So and Jane did balk at it all. As much as it's making life easier for her, she wants to do her own thing so hopefully it doesn't put her off too much and she does get on with it. She's also not working with anyone. ... I don't think she is as interested in physics as she is in singing, music and ... when she does do a little bit of something she'll let you know, 'cause it's rare. Anyway so that was probably a fairly important thing that happened today and yes, I'll try and give her more guidance to try and get her doing things so she can get to ... It appears to me that she doesn't want to be seen to not know things. This is the whole point, they don't know things and they're meant to be trying to find things out and the other girls will say, I don't know. Whereas she spouts all these words that, when you add them up, don't say much at all. I was, I sort of knew that she wouldn't be particularly happy with it. (Carrie, in the conversation with the interviewer)

We can understand such statements as glosses of the *sym*practical work that the speaker previously has been part of. It is her a posteriori constituted view – in conversation with the researcher and *for* him. We can then take each gloss and ask for situations in which work was performed on the basis of which the speaker, Carrie, could justifiably, accountably, and demonstrably ground her gloss with all the etceteras that accompany any such narrative. But if we extracted what Carrie said then we would be no further than in formal analytic approaches. To understand 'identity', we need to understand the *sym*practical work that produces 'identity', *identity work*. Such work may be observed when those involved talk about their own identities – such as when an African American student makes a Powerpoint presentation in which he talks about himself, his life, who he is, and who he identifies with (Roth and Hsu 2010) – or when interlocutors talk about someone not actually present, her motives, intentions, beliefs, and so on. To get a handle on this issue, 'what is needed is to take all these *terminologies* of motive and locate them as *vocabularies* of motive in historic epochs and specified situations' (Mills 1940: 913). In this way, 'motives are of no value apart from the delimited societal situations for which they are the appropriate vocabularies' (ibid: 913). That is, to understand identity talk we need to look at the societal situation in and for which such talk is produced in an accountable manner.

The foregoing quotation of phrases Carrie produced must not be ascribed to her as if this were her (singular) ideas about Jane. These phrases have been excerpted form a societal situation, which also was constituted in and through this talk. The talk, therefore, not only reflects some content attributed to it but also the societal situation: a researcher who interviews a new teacher, Carrie, who previously also received her teaching degree under his supervision. The lesson-debriefing interview is conducted under the auspices of the agreement that they had reached and signed concerning participation in the research. The conversation constitutes sympractical work so that its results must not be reduced to the intentions, ideas, beliefs, inclinations, or motives of individual speakers. In the following, I analyze the interview talk in which aspects of Jane's identity – i.e., of who Jane will come to be – is constituted in institutionally relevant, accountable talk.

Fragment 7.4 begins with the statement concerning Jane's balking and with the statement of (teacher) intention and (student) motive. We then hear a statement about Jane not working together with someone else (as the other students in the class), the active reception of which is articulated in the replique: 'is that by choice', a querying statement that is affirmed in the next turn (turn 024). The next turn begins with an affirmation of having had the same impression, followed by a statement of the evidence that actively accounts for the reasons of having such an impression: 'she said she wanted to do it by herself' and 'she wants to be proud of her own work' (turn 025). Whatever Jane had said, the turn attributes particular motives to Jane – e.g., 'she wants to be proud' – in the context of accounting for an impression.

Fragment 7.4
```
022   C:   so and jane did baulk at it all. as much as its
           making life easier for her, she wants to do her own
           thing so hopefully it doesnt put her off too much and
           she does get on with it. shes also not working with
           anyone.
023   R:   is that by choice?
024   C:   yes.
025   R:   i got that impression. she said she wanted to do it
           by herself because she wants to be proud of her own
           work i think.
026   C:   she and ruth and sally whos working (?) sally or
           sally they tend to sit with each other and ruth and
           sally often try to push her back on track when
           they=re working out problems or whatever it is cause
           shes pretty easily distracted.
027   R:   okay. so jane gets distracted?
```

The next turn does not directly pick up from the preceding one but constitutes a statement about what happens when Jane works together with two other young women: the others push Jane back on track. They do so because 'she gets easily distracted', which thereby constitutes a particular character trait to Jane. The next turn picks up precisely on that statement about Jane, thereby exhibiting the subject currently salient from the shop floor perspective.

Whatever social situation he witnessed, it allowed the researcher to observe a particular social fact, or to get the impression to have observed it: Jane, by choice, does not work with anyone. The researcher provides details of the observation that constitute the warrants for the account provided: 'she said she wanted to do it by herself because she wants to be proud of her own work. The researcher ends by adding 'I think'. We do not know what he might have intended to say and whether pride in the work is an explanation or an instance of in/direct speech. For the purposes of the analysis, it does not matter, because we need to hear it through and in terms of the next turn with which the phrase forms a pair.

Turn pair 27 | 28 constitutes Jane's distractibility as the topic. In the second turn of the pair, distraction is co-articualted with a lower interest in physics as compared to singing and music. In conjunction with the next turn pair 29 | 30, Jane's musical ability comes to be affirmed. The remainder of the talk may be heard as an expansion of the issue of interest, the quantity of work that Jane is actually perceived as doing, and about Jane's 'letting you know' that she had done 'a little bit of something' (turn 030).

```
Fragment 7.5
  027   R:   okay. so jane gets distracted?
  028   C:   yes. i dont think she is as interested in physics as
             she is in singing, music and-
  029   R:   is she good at that?
  030   C:   yes. she tries and she does occasionally say things
             like, i did all those questions. well yes, so did the
             rest of the class but yes, she=ll be, when she does
             do a little bit of something she=ll let you know,
             cause its rare. anyway so that was probably a fairly
             important thing that happened today and yes, i=ll try
             and give her more guidance to try and get her doing
             things so she can get to-
  031   R:   so give her more guidance than some of the others?
  032   C:   yes. some of the others are giving themselves more
             guidance. i think you recorded my conversation with
             (?) with the rocking bottle.
  033   R:   i did too.
```

At the end of the turn, we find an assertion involving an intention for future action: 'I'll try and give her more guidance to try and get her doing things'. This is the current topic, as reified by the next turn. This intention is articulated against and set into relief by the next statements, which describes other students as 'giving themselves more guidance'. The final statement refers to the conversation with another young lady, which the researcher is noted to have recorded as confirmed by the next turn. At this point, articulated by the turn pair, another student is becoming the topic of the conversation.

The confirmation 'I did [record the conversation] too' is treated as an invitation to talk about the conversation and the student. It constitutes a generalizaing statement about the student, attributing to her the saying of a lot of words that do not say much. It then glosses the student's way of talking as a 'presentation' rather than just plain talk ('other girls will just talk'). The following turn adds to this account by stating an observation that followed the concrete conversation referred to: 'After the [recorded] conversation, you know what she did: She went "Aaah", as if it was the end of a presentation'. That is, we have a statement | affirmation pair,

where the second part of the pair provides further details to account for the qualifi-
cation of the student to talk as if she were making a presentation rather than just
talk. That is, a particular motive comes to be attributed: something of the likes of
disingenuous, pretensional, and supposititious. That comes to be further affirmed
by means of elaboration in the next turn, which uses again talk about motives: 'she
doesn't want to be seen not to know things'.

Fragment 7.6
```
033   R:   i did too.
034   C:   she=ll say all the words and she=ll say a lot of
           words and not say much and thats (?) she=ll try and
           the way she sort of talks to me is very like as if
           shes doing a presentation. she=ll present it to me
           whereas other girls will just talk.
035   R:   i noticed that, because after the conversation, you
           know what she did, she went, aaah, as if it was the
           end of a presentation.
036   C:   it appears to me that she doesnt want to be seen to
           not know things. this is the whole point, they dont
           know things and they=re meant to be trying to find
           things out and the other girls will say, i dont know.
           whereas she spouts all these words that, when you add
           them up, dont say much at all.
```

Talk may also make the psychological states of one of the speakers the topic,
either in the present or some preceding situation. For example, shortly after the
preceding fragment, the conversation (qua *sym*practical work, that is, even the
change of topic involving *both* speakers) returns to Jane. The first statement is
about not having 'spent a huge amount of time with' the student, and then, drawing
on the motive repertoire of language, articulates the presence of a concern. This
concern is about Jane 'keeping on with it, "I know what's going on", and then have
nothing to write about'. Again, an attribution is made that the student knows or
pretends to know what is going on and, as a consequence, may not have anything
to write about (in her report).

Fragment 7.7
```
040   C:   i probably didnt spend a huge amount of time with
           jane, other than the discussion about whats changed
           in it but yes, i am concerned that (jane?) will keep
           on going with, i know whats going on and then have
           nothing to write about.
041   R:   how did you feel when you approached jane?
042   C:   i think i was, i sort of knew that she wouldnt be
           particularly happy with it and i guess i approached
           her with the idea that i wanted her to feel that it
           was a good thing rather than meaning she=d done all
           this work and it was wasted etcetera etcetera.
→ 043  R:   is that an intentional strategy on your part?
044   C:   that was the aim of the conversation to let her know
           that this was what was happening but have her feel
           that it was okay.
045   R:   how did you feel then?
046   C:   okay. i know that during that lesson she switched
           off. at the end she was over chatting with rita, not
           doing anything. i had another little discussion.
           there are things that she can be doing but i think
           she=ll get back on track.
```

Rather than taking up on the preceding thought, as realized in the predicate of the statement, the next turn offers up a query about the feelings of the interlocutor when she approached the student. The offer comes to be reified in the next turn in the form of a replique that includes the 'idea' of 'wanting [the student] to feel that it was a good thing rather than meaning she'd done all this wark and it was wasted'. That is, although the preceding utterance could have been heard as a query about feelings, it comes to be reified as a query about knowing in advance the emotional reaction of the student and approaching the latter in a way so that she could feel the change of topic was a good thing. The next turn is interesting, because it is apparently offered as a question about the intentions underlying the descriptions in the preceding statement. That is, by explicitly posing the question about whether 'wanting the student to feel that it was a good thing' was the intended action, the turn also constitutes the preceding statement as providing two hearings. The first would simply be an after-the-fact justification of what was done; the second would be the intention for engaging the action described by the statement. That is, in the actual speech situation, intentions may not only be attributed to an action a posteriori but this attribution itself may be queried as one of accidental or intentional nature. As the next turn 044 shows, this is precisely the hearing realized in this conversation. There is a confirmation in stating that 'that was the aim' followed by the re-articulation in a different way what the preceding statements have said: 'have her feel that it was okay'. We therefore see that it is not only one or the other party to this exchange who is drawing on psychological language to account for practical actions, but that the talk is sustained by all parties and is done so in a sympractical way: one for the other and thus for the self.

The next turn repeats an earlier turn, but now offers up the question about feelings concerning the end of the episode ('how did you feel *then*'). Again, we may hear this question to be answered by means of the word 'okay' but used – distinctly from the adverbial use discussed in chapter 6 – in the adjectival way: a description of the quality of feelings. This statement is followed by a gloss of what she observed to have happened during the remainder of the lesson: Jane switched off. This gloss is follwed by the statements that the young woman was not doing anything and was chatting with someone else. All these subsequent statements in fact constitute evidence that justify the characterization of Jane as 'having switched off', as if the speaker had been held *accountable* for the gloss and as if Carrie had been asked to provide justification. The 'okay' becomes 'okay' with the final statement transcribed here, which *formulates* the thought that Jane 'will get back on track' (turn 046).

Reflexivity and the Ethnomethods in Formal Research

Subsequent to their time in the field, researchers write up their findings for publication in scientific journals. They provide detailed descriptions of the methods. These methods have to be specified if and only if they are different from what people can be seen as doing in the events reported. That is, the research methods for arriving at the reported understanding of what has happened are explicitly articulated as different from the methods that the people in the reports exhibit. If the methods were the same, then the research reports would be highly duplicitous in stating the methods twice. However, as studies of coding showed, knowledge of the organized, accountable ways in which social situations are sympractically produced is actually presupposed. One such study asked graduate sociology students to code the folders of an outpatient psychiatric clinic to inductive arrive at 'what characteristics of patients, of clinical personnel, of their interactions, and of the [career path] tree [diagram] were associated with which careers' (Garfinkel 1967: 19). The graduate students received a coding sheet and conventional training in reliability procedures. They then coded the 1,582 records that constituted the database. The results revealed, however, the need to question the inductive procedure that would have uncovered the answers to the research questions from the data. This was so because 'in order to accomplish the coding, coders were assuming knowledge of the very organized ways of the clinic that their coding procedures were intended to produce descriptions of. More interestingly, such presupposed knowledge seemed necessary and was most deliberately consulted whenever, for whatever reasons, the coders needed to be satisfied that they had coded "what really happened". This was so regardless of whether or not they had encountered "ambiguous" folder contents' (Garfinkel 1967: 20). In fact, the coders used their knowledge to read the relevance of the coding instructions. That is, what the coding instruction meant to say was available only when the coders could recognize their relevance in and to the situation. That is, in the practical use, the instrument itself was irreducibly bound up with knowledge of the situation, which the research had intended to uncover. That is, the research method – which researchers tend to describe and account for in great detail – *presupposes* knowledge of what it reports to have been its results. We may now turn to look at the present situation through this lens.

The researcher who appears in the interviews may subsequently report about the emotional states and other psychological characteristics of Carrie. He may write about the 'semiotic resources' that the participants make available and about the use of a coding system to categorize Carrie's facial expressions. However, those coding methods are impossible unless the researcher already is familiar with the ethnomethods of accounting for emotions, intentions, motives, and other psychological states. In fact, much of what will be described in articles about the psychological constructs related to Carrie or other teachers derives from the in situ talk that the researchers have previously engaged in with participants themselves. This talk presupposes the mutual intelligibility that the researcher subsequently claims to have extracted by means of special methods.

The methods descriptions in research journals, therefore, presuppose the very performative competencies that produce the social facts that researchers say they have identified by special methods. If these performative competencies were not to exist, this researcher, when he writes journal articles, literally would not know what he is talking *about*. Researchers in some educational fields might then be talking about the *symbolic* rather than real mastery and practical understanding.

The analysis of the post-episode interviews not only provide the glosses that the actors themselves use to say what has happened as they understand it after the happening has ended but also allow us to understand that the researcher himself is accountable for the endogenous constitution of the interview situation and, therefore, the endogenous production of an intelligible conversation. He is integral to the sympractical work of producing the interview and, therefore, he must not be abstracted from the interview as outcome. What we hear in the interviews goes beyond Carrie's thoughts about Jane. Rather, we hear forms of talk in which the behavior of people in situations is explained, described, and accounted for. Even though a particular turn is associated with the speaker who has actually produced the sound-words with his/her vocal cords, every word, every phrase, has to be considered as sitting on the intersection of all the interlocutors, language more generally, and the endogenous production of the social situation more specifically.

8

Planned, Enacted, & Living Science Curriculum

> Curriculum is all the planned, guided and implemented learning that occurs
> in a school. Queensland state schools develop school curriculum plans using
> the Key Learning Area syllabuses or New Basics organisers. (Aussie Educa-
> tor, 2012)

The (state, provincial, national) syllabus is an integral aspect of the school curriculum generally and a teacher- and course-specific curriculum more specifically.
However, it does not determine what will actually take place in the classroom. This
is so because there are many courses of actions that can be said to have followed
the syllabus after the fact. As a physics teacher, I have had personal experience.
Although all the fellow physics teachers from other schools that I met while teaching high school physics used lectures, assigned textbook word problems, and used
standard prescribed laboratory exercises to realize the official Ontario provincial
syllabus, my students spent 70% of their time in class on designing experiments,
conducting experiments, analyzing the data using sophisticated statistics software,
and wrote research reports (e.g., Roth 1995). Because I had moved to Ontario from
outside of the province, I had to undergo official inspection to be certified in the
province as a public teacher (though I did not need it for teaching in the private
school where I worked). After the inspector had come to one of 'my' lessons to
evaluate it and 'me', he not only wrote a glowing report, noting its 'exemplary
nature', but also recommended to physics teachers in other schools to visit and
spend some time in my lessons. That is, even though the lesson was very different
from what the inspector would normally see, he assessed it not only as meeting the
expectations set out by the provincial syllabus but also as doing so in an extraordi-
nary way. I am certain that there were other physics teachers in private schools
where he would have made remarks about their exceptional status. One of the lessons we can draw from this is that there are different enacted science curricula that
can be said to have followed the syllabus generally and the planned curriculum
more specifically.

Standard Approach to Curriculum

Throughout this book, I focus on the work and practices of social actors in a science classroom that produce the observable objective order of social facts that participants and spectators alike are able to witness. At the same time, there are also documents that individuals such as the teacher Carrie are aware of that describe the physics curriculum as intended. Whatever happens in a classroom, the teachers subsequently are held to account for it with respect to what is stated in the state syllabus generally and the curriculum specifically. Or rather, what can be said to have happened, the enacted curriculum, is compared with official documents to see the extent to which the latter describes the former. The analyses provided throughout this book, however, show how creative, generative, and ad-hoc the work is from which the lesson as fact emerges, that is, as a thing that can be assessed after the fact. We are thereby alerted to the difference between the syllabus or curriculum as a plan that exists prior to the lesson, the actually enacted curriculum as a lived (past tense) finished product that is assessed a posteriori, and the actual living sympractical work that produces the social facts that are after the fact assessed. This chapter focuses on the relation between these three aspects of the curriculum, that is, the planned (intended), enacted and after-the-fact-assessed, and living curriculum. Three different perspectives on the curriculum are involved: one anticipates future events, one looks back at completed events, and one witnesses happenings that will be denoted as this or that curriculum event (without being in a position to definitely say what is happening until after the happening has ended).

Science education curricula, as the curricula in other subject matter areas, is prescriptive and normative in the sense that they specify what should be observed after a course or a series of lessons on a particular topic has been completed. In some instances, such as the Queensland where the events reported in this book (as those in the study analyzed in chapter 1) were recorded, the curriculum specifically states what students 'must' do (Table 8.1). But the syllabuses are not written for students; they are written for teachers – often by teachers. Teachers subsequently 'translate' them into specific curriculum either at the school level, in the attempt to coordinate what is happening in classes taught by different teachers at the same grade level, or at the teachers level. In the independent school that participated in the study from which the data presented in this book were culled, the department head made decisions about specifying just what the students are expected to be doing for their extended experimental investigations.

The lesson episode analyzed in an exemplary fashion throughout this book took place in a context framed by these documents, here the state syllabus (Table 8.1) and the statement of the problem as Andrew, the department head, had published it on Moodle for teachers and students alike. But the actual events that follow should not be thought of as somehow caused by the documents. In fact, drawing on the documents in the interpretation of the events will mislead science education researchers because they would inherently look at what actors actually and accountably do and exhibit to and for each other through the lens of the document and, therefore, through the teacher's eyes (i.e., taking a psychological lens). Just as a recipe does not specify and determine the situated actions of the person who uses it

Table 8.1   Definition of extended experimental investigation and specified student actions. (QSA 2007: 22)

What is an extended experimental investigation?
Within this category, instruments are developed to investigate a hypothesis or to answer a practical research question. The focus is on planning the extended experimental investigation, problem solving and analysis of primary data generated through experimentation by the student. Experiments may be laboratory or field based. An extended experimental investigation may last from four weeks to the entirety of the unit of work. The outcome of an extended experimental investigation is a written scientific report. *Aspects of each of the three criteria should be evident in the investigation.* For monitoring, the discussion/conclusions/evaluation/recommendations of the report should be between 800 and 1000 words. This should be increased to 1000 and 1500 words for verification.
What must a student do to complete an extended experimental investigation?
– develop a planned course of action – clearly articulate the hypothesis or research question, providing a statement of purpose for the investigation – provide descriptions of the experiment – show evidence of modification or student design – provide evidence of primary and secondary data collection and selection – execute the experiment(s) – analyse data – discuss the outcomes of the experiment – evaluate and justify conclusion(s) – present relevant information in a scientific report.

to cook a meal so a syllabus or curriculum does not specify and determine the situated, sympractical (social) actions from which the enacted lesson will have emerged. The difference between these three perspectives has been documented in a study of Yucatec Mayan midwives who attended training workshops in using UNICEF midwifery kits, courses that the Mexican Ministry of Health and the National Indian Institute organized and that doctors and nurses from the regional hospital and ministry representatives taught (Jordan 1989). These lessons specified, like plans, what the traditional birthing attendants were to do (planned, intended curriculum). When the workshops were later assessed, the midwives accounted for what they were doing in terms of the language that they had learned in the workshop. That is, they accounted for their completed actions between workshop and assessments in terms of the discourse that they had learned and that was used to frame what should happen as part of the job of a midwife. When observed in the field, however, the midwives were doing precisely what they have done before receiving the training: their practices, which were supposed to have changed actually had not changed a bit.

Such results should not be taken as an occasion to be ironical about the midwives, training providers, or policymakers. In each instance, participants are situated in particular settings where they contribute to the accountable sympractical work that produces the social facts in the settings. In training, in the field, and in subsequent assessment, the midwives are part of, and constituted by, situation-specific conversational practices and situated actions. As shown throughout this book, the conversations and practical actions as social fact transcend the individual. The case of the midwives is interesting because it can be seen as an analogy to the teaching situation, where the contents of the training courses function like a syllabus that specifies what is to be done, when, and how. Thus, for example, the Mayan midwives are told something like this: 'How is the IUD positioned? The IUD is positioned in the uterine cavity, preferably when the woman is menstruating ...' (Jordan 1989: 926). Similarly, the Queensland syllabus includes statements about what a teacher *must* do when planning and implementing an extended experimental investigation (Table 8.2). Such statements may be used – and are used, as I know from temporarily supervising a foreign doctoral student completing a three-month stay in my research laboratory – as a standard against which the actual performances of (beginning) science teachers are held. This practice is common in teacher training, evaluation of teaching within school systems, and science education researchs. The evaluation renders judgment as to the fit between a planned curriculum and an enacted curriculum or between what a teacher says he would be doing or has done with what researchers say they have actually done (when compared to some non-articulated standard). This can be observed in one of the first ever qualitative studies from and about science teaching.

> 'Hoskin Named Teacher of the Year by Science Group'. So read the headline of the local newspaper. The members of our research team were attracted to the banner headline and the photograph of a teacher in a familiar pose, his right hand poised at the blackboard as he explained some aspect of science to one of his five science classes at Rural County High. We were pleased at the recognition that has been given to a hard working teacher we had come to know and respect over a period of six weeks of intensive observation and interviews. At the same time we were perplexed. What we had seen in Mr. Hoskin's class was not always what you would associate with exemplary science teaching. As we scanned the columns of the newspaper, we read that Mr. Hoskin was a popular choice for the award, and had been the recipient of similar awards during the past six years. Convincing evidence was provided to support his claims to the award; his teaching was held in the highest regard by his students, his colleagues and professional educators throughout the state. (Tobin et al. 1988: 433)

In the report, the authors state that they had anticipated the displeasure of the teacher because they 'had highlighted a number of concerns about his teaching and the learning environment in his classes' (ibid: 434). They describe that there was little in the paper that was judgmental but subsequently acknowledge that 'everything in the paper was judgmental in an implicit way. Even though we set out to describe the classes in an objective manner, every observation and every interpretation of data reflected our perspectives on teaching' (ibid: 434). After the authors had shown their initial report to the teacher, the latter wrote a 17-page written reaction stating, among others that 'there is no way that university personnel can understand the school process if they are not in the classroom every day'. The researchers had used grounded theory method from a constructivist perspective on learning to explain their observations, i.e., reportable and justifiable social facts.

Table 8.2   Prescribed teacher actions according to the Queensland syllabus. (QSA 2007: 22)

What do teachers do when planning and implementing an extended experimental investigation?
– The teacher suggests topics/issues and provides some stimulus to trigger student interest. – Teachers can provide the research question or it may be instigated by the student. In those instances teachers should negotiate with students to ensure safety and the possibility of success. It is more likely that students will be able to generate their own research questions the further they progress in the course of study. – Teachers must allow some class time and provide some supervision at times for students to be able to effectively undertake each component of the extended experimental investigation. Teachers may allow elements of the extended experimental investigation to be conducted in small groups or pairs. However, independent student time will probably be required to complete the extended experimental investigation. – Teachers must implement strategies to ensure authentication of student work. Some strategies are annotated notes in response to issues that emerged during research (e.g. journals, experimental logs), teacher observation sheets, research checklists, and referencing and reference list. – Teachers must consult, negotiate and provide feedback before and during the research process to help ensure occupational health and safety requirements are followed, to provide ethical guidance and to monitor student work. Feedback and assistance should be provided judiciously, gradually being reduced with the development of student experience and confidence. – Scaffolding must be provided. When an extended experimental investigation is undertaken for the first time, the scaffolding should help students complete the assessment by modelling the extended experimental investigation process and familiarising students with the expectations for the written scientific report. However, the scaffolding provided should not specify the physics, or lead the student through a series of steps dictating a solution. Scaffolding should be reduced from Year 11 to Year 12 to allow the student to better demonstrate independence in the research process. When an extended experimental investigation is revisited (most likely in Year 12) the scaffolding should be reduced and could be a series of generic questions.

In such reports, an attribution of the entire event is made to the teacher; the entire curricular event is considered once completed and the event known (i.e., can be *re*presented, made present again); and a judgment is rendered about the attainment or non-attainment of a specified or unspecified norm. In such reports, research is concerned with the *enacted* curriculum, that is, the curriculum as end product of what the actors *have done*, which implies that the effects are known. The enacted curriculum is a finished product, like a game of football that has been completed. Those who have seen it talk about the 'losers' and the heroes, the 'most valuable player', or 'the best goal'. This is equivalent to an approach to 'education' that focuses on outcomes, which, after the fact, are attributed to this or that actor.

The approach championed in this book is rather different because it is oriented toward the identification of the actual, living sympractical work that endogenously produces the social facts to which all members to the setting orient. The approach is to take the actor's point of view but in a sociological rather than a psychological manner. A lesson, the living science curriculum as an event-in-the-making, does not just depend on the teacher. It is a happening from which the event, qua social fact that can be named and pointed to, emerges as end result from the social practices typical of schooling. The enacted curriculum is the outcome of practices that in any specific case is staffed by the participant teachers and students. That is, the research question is in regards to *how* the members pull it off to make social facts available to each other and, thereby, endogenously produce the rationality and intelligibility of the setting. In other words, the question concerns the particular natural language game within which what the social actors do is *the* reasonable and defensible thing to do. But these actors do not have available to them an a posteriori perspective. They are in the middle of a game, the game of life. In the way football players act in relation to their current situation (rather than like someone with a God's-eye view or like a Monday morning quarterback), doing what can be done within the room to maneuver *in this situation and without time out for reflecting*, social actors contribute to unfolding practice relative to the openings (i.e., room to maneuver or Spielraum) that the current situation provides. In this approach, there is no place for judgment.

Re/Living Curriculum: Temporality, Rhythm, Pathos

> [T]hese social facts ... will be found in that their *lived analysis* – their *lived accountable production* – 'lands the analyst in the midst of things'. (Garfinkel 2002: 249, emphasis added)

In the preceding chapters, I by and large focus on the analysis of natural language employed in the episode for producing the situation from within. However, communication does not only occur by means of words: there are gestures, prosody (pitch, speech volume, speech rate, rhythm), hand and head gestures, and body position and orientation (Roth 2000). Even perceptual gestalts and pauses need to be taken into account when it is apparent that talk occurs only in troublesome situation so that the speaking pauses constitute the evidence for the alignment of the actors as to what is happening (Roth 2004b). The words alone do not do justice to what actors are oriented to, which is why chapter 3 also includes some images that provide an indication as to how the two actors were oriented with respect to each other as seen from the witnessing camera's perspective. In chapter 5, I also add images that exhibit how the hands were involved in the communication. All of these different communicative means need to be taken into account to understand, for example, the emergence and disappearance of conflict or solidarity among social actors (Roth and Tobin 2010). In this section, I expand on the discussion of the endogenous production of the *living* curriculum by exemplifying the role of other communicative means – those that contribute to our understanding of the affective qualities apparent in a situation. When I refer to affective qualities, I do not mean to embark on an individualistic psychological endeavor. Rather, I expand the forms of analyses that have been developed in ethnomethodological circles to include what is known from the *sociology* of emotion (Collins 2004). That is, only what is apparent in and relevant to the *con*versation as *social* fact is of interest rather than attributions to the singular interior of persons that is inaccessible to other social actors. This, thereby, allows us to work toward an understanding of the living curriculum, that is, as something unfinished, affectively charged, with particular speed, temporality, and rhythmicality.

Before providing some exemplifying analyses, a note is required concerning the 'reading' of transcripts. Ethnomethodological writers often make the explicit point that the reader has to do the work described. To authenticate Sir Isaac Newton's and Johann Wolfgang Goethe's theories of prismatic colors, the reader is encouraged to work with a prism to look at images that are provided in and with the text (Bjelic and Lynch 1992). The reader thereby does what the text describes or rather, in doing discovers the relevance of the textual descriptions. In another place, the author suggests taking the descriptions of the work of lecturing chemistry and attending a lecture such as to find the practical relevance of the descriptions in the actual observation (Garfinkel 2002). This is similar to knowing what a recipe *actually* rather than possible says *in* any *concrete case*. Rather than just reading the ingredients and instructions, we need to actually engage in making the dish. It is only in the making of the dish that we discover what the recipe really says without being able to say it in so many words.

What are the implications for science educators who focus on classroom talk? In the context of (hands-on) mathematics education, I have suggested not merely providing text but producing more inclusive transcripts that capture some of the other communicative dimensions, like rhythm, gestures and their temporality and rhythms, and intonations (pitch), speech intensity (Roth and Bautista 2011). These transcripts should then be used like musical scores that readers can perform, in fact have to perform, to feel, hear, and sense what members to the setting could feel, hear, and sense. The 'reader' no longer solely accesses the situation by symbolic means – open to interpretations that require methodological justification as to their soundness – but in some sense *lives* (aspects of) the situation again in and through the performance of the communication. In the following examples, the 'reader' is invited to approach the transcriptions like musical scores that are to be performed to re/live what any text can only gloss.

The first example comes from the very beginning of the member-identified episode where Carrie announces the 'change of plans', its reception, and the reaction to the reception. I also 'transcribed' the soundtrack by plotting speech intensity and pitch across the turns marked by the arrow ('→') (Fig. 8.1).

```
Fragment 8.1
    001   C:   okay. (0.24) OH; ((moves toward
               Jane)) i better talk to JAne first.
               (0.24) okAY:. (1.63)
→            changef plA:Ns.
→ 002           (0.26)
→ 003   J:   U::M::: ((head sideward, gloss: dis-
               appointment on face))
→ 004           (0.76)
→ 005   C:   uMM::tmake dlIfe EA:sier;
               (0.31) <<all>okay>; ..HHH UUm (0.42) <<len>it has
               (0.22) bin=decided that it is too dIFficult.> kAY:?
               ((187→300 Hz)) ((head sideward, gaze down))
```

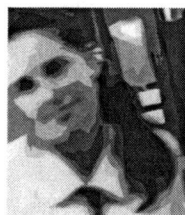

The analysis provided in chapter 3 articulates the 'uMM' in turn 005 as 'reporting', that is, directly taking up, referencing, and 'commenting' upon what the preceding

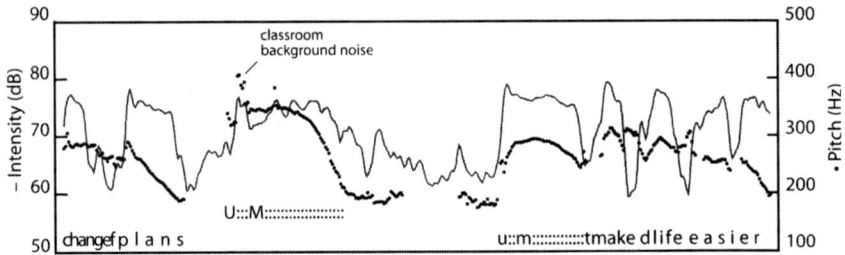

Fig. 8.1   Intensity, speed, temporality, pitch, and pitch contours of speech are available in this 'transcription' of the soundtrack.

turn provided. The transcription in that chapter already contains an image that communicates the position of Jane's head and the gloss that disappointment can be perceived as being played out. Carrie's repetition of the interjection 'um' provides a clue to an empathetic uptake underscored by the statement that accounts (provides reason) for a change of plans: 'to make life easier'. We can get a better sense of this stretch of communicative work when we also attend to some of the prosodic features.

We first note that in 'change of plans', the last sound-word is drawn out whereas the first part is spoken more rapidly. The pitch drops by over 100 Hz (from 287 → 183 Hz). Re/producing the 'changef pla:ns' in this way allows re/living the constative nature of the locution. It is a statement of fact that produces a sense of finalization. The effect of this locution can be 'read off' the ensemble of signifiers made available to the situation. First, the 'um' that follows lasts for about 0.8 seconds, while its pitch initially rises, is held for a while, then dramatically drops towards the end (387 → 187 Hz) as does speech intensity (mean 75 → 70 dB), which also allows us to hear the 'phrase' in constative form. Rather than just trusting the foregoing description, readers should produce this 'um' themselves, while holding the head in the position depicted, until their own pitch and pitch contour representation matches those displayed here.[24]

Some readers may ask, 'But is this of relevance?' Yes, if it matters whether we can *feel* what is happening rather than just read *about* it. This is what happens to the participants in the situation, as we can see when we investigate what happens next. The transcription of the sound shows that what we hear as 'um' involves a similar pitch and speech intensity profile, though with some changes: the pitch differences are smaller, especially because the 'um' is 'cut short' by the immediately following, rapidly unfolding statement 'to make life easier'. Important here is the pitch contour. When we perform it, we can hear that it, too, 'picks up' the preceding contour, repeating it to a certain extent, and thereby also reliving it. That is, in the situation, we observe the reproduction and therefore reliving of the embodied aspects of communication, those aspects that differ from cognitive content.

---

[24] The software package for doing the prosodic analysis, PRAAT, is freely available for Macintosh, PC, and a variety of other platforms (www.praat.org). To re/live a speaking situation, I record my voice, save the soundtrack in one of the acceptable sound formats (aif was used here), and import it into the PRAAT software.

This points us to a form of consciousness that is different from intellectual consciousness but operative nevertheless; it also points us to the collective aspect, marked by the 'con-' – from Lat. *con*, with – in 'consciousness'. Carrie not only hears the sound quality but also reproduces and thereby exhibits reliving an aspect of it. She can feel the sound and, feeling being related to pathos, she can experience emphathy.

The remaining part of the transcription exhibits prosodic features that also produces the 'tmake dlife easier' what we would transcribe into proper English by means of the phrase 'to make the life easier' (Fig. 8.1). We first note that the initial part is very rapidly spoken, in fact 'attached to' the 'um' sound, which is not allowed to come to its full completion by returning to the baseline pitch. We note that rather than a full pronunciation of the sound-words 'to' and 'the', what can actually be heard on the tape are 't' and 'd' sounds. In this way, what would have been four syllables of 'to make the life' has been reduced to two syllables; the potentially three syllabic 'easier' is reduced to two syllables (Fig. 8.1). Both pairs of syllables are performed at the same rate over about 0.6 s of duration. We hear this as a slowing down and drawing out of the last word, the pitch of which falls together with an already overall descending pattern. The phrase can be heard in a constative form, making a statement of fact. The maximum intensities in the beginning part of the phrase are actually higher than that of the 'um', which we therefore here as less loud, perhaps even calming, just as we can hear the ending of the phrase on 'easier'.

Prosodic features of communication are closely associated with affect, that is, with the pathic aspects of life. It is through these pathic aspects that emotions are and become collective phenomena that are of *sociological* rather than psychological interest. Em*pathy* and sym*pathy*, as the words show, are based on pathos. Sympathy – etymologically derived from the Greek σύν [sun] *sym*-, with, + πάθος [pathos], suffering – literally means suffering with another. Empathy, built on the same principle as the word sympathy, has the sense of feeling what another person is feeling (German *Einfühlung*). The re/production of prosodic features therefore is what is of sociological interest, because there is now a collective phenomenon across two turns that we may denote by the term 'production | re/production', where the re/production is not mere repetition but a full production in its own right that can be heard as being the same (but not identical) across speakers.

We may gain further insight into the affective dimensions of this opening part, which are later glossed in various ways by those present to the situation. Thus, for example, Carrie says 'I had to tell Jane that we've changed the topic' and 'I sort of knew that she wouldn't be particularly happy with it and I guess I approached her with the idea that I wanted her to feel that it was a good thing rather than meaning she'd done all this work and it was wasted'. Jane glossed the episode by saying that the 'back to the drawing board' 'sucks' and that it is 'annoying'. (Of course, we take these descriptions as after-the-fact glosses provided in and for the context, that is, the interviews with the researcher.) Further insight comes from the investigation of the distribution of energy in the sound spectrum, which, besides pitch (technically F_0) contains many other frequencies the intensities of which can be seen in the spectrum (Fig. 8.2).

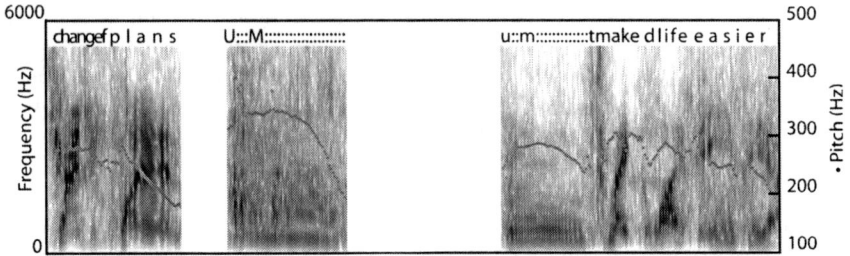

Fig. 8.2   The darker areas in this frequency spectrum represent greater speech energy. Background noise has been left out here and the pitch has been added for comparison and cross-referencing purposes.

The first aspect we may observe in the spectrum are the dark areas in Carrie's articulation of 'change', 'plan', 'make', and 'eas/ier'. These dark areas correspond to higher frequencies near the middle of the spectrum. (We also note the high frequency energy associated with the explosive 't' in 'tmake'.) This differs from the distribution of energy in Carrie's 'um', which resembles that of the 'um' that Jane has produced just before. There is more energy in the lower part of the spectrum and a more even distribution in the middle frequencies. But whereas in Jane's 'um' the energy is maintained for even higher frequencies, there is a drop off in the spectrum of Carrie's 'um'. In part these differences will be heard as the quality of the voice referred to as timbre, which is the most singular of all aspects in sound production and allows us to hear 'who' is speaking even if we do not see the person or that allows us to identify the type of instrument playing a melody. The effect is that there are similarities between Carrie's and Jane's 'um' sounds and between the way this as compared to other sound-words are produced. It is in and with the 'um' that we hear something like sympathy produced, not as something merely denoted symbolically (e.g., by saying 'I feel with you'), but as something re/lived in its expressive qualities.

Some readers may say that we are overly concerned with sounds that do not 'mean' anything in themselves, especially because these do not refer to concepts and conceptual content. However, even the most conceptual of words may not 'mean' anything and have no relevance in and to the conversation because they may only be carriers of intonation. Thus, the literal transcription of a sound-word may deceive the analyst, who focuses on content when the real communication occurs in a different dimension. There are now classical discussions of this phenomenon. The novelist Fyodor Dostoevsky wrote in his *Diary of a Writer* a little story in which six drunken workers, one after the other, pronounce the same word that is too bad to be reproduced in formal writing. There exist at least two famous analyses by cultural-historical scholars, both of which point out, consistent with the author's own comment, that there was a real conversation going on (Vološinov 1930; Vygotskij 2005). In this conversation, the sound-word itself did not matter. Everything was communicated by means of the intonation: contempt, rejection, contradiction, put-down, and pleasure concerning the contents of a preceding locution. In the context of this book, we hear each of these as social facts – i.e., contempt, rejection, etc. – that require bracketing so that we become oriented to the

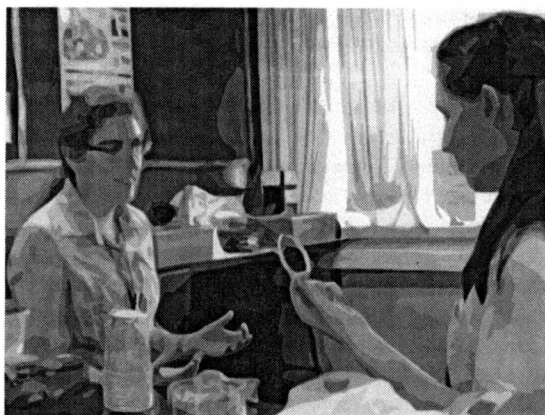

Fig. 8.3   Artistic rendering of the instant when Jane articulates a phrase about having found a way to do it. (From Fig. 2.2)

sympractical work that produces each in this situation. In science, a student may produce a phrase containing science words, but whether this phrase is a reply to a query, an insult, a query, an uncertain answer, a joke, or some other social event does not tend to be contained in the phrase itself – which is why it might be followed by another, often quickly spoken phrase, 'just joking [kidding]'. We saw an instance of this not only in Jane's replique 'breath into it?' (turn 012) or Carries 'the wire?' (turn 051) but in all cases, for example, where one or the other produced 'okay' or a variation thereof was put into play.

The second example is taken from the video immediately following the preceding one. We are interested in the sequence, highlighted by means of arrows ('→') from the instant that Carrie articulates a phrase about a decision that 'it' is too difficult (turn 005) to the beginning of her following turn at talk (turn 008). Following the statement that it is too difficult is paired with a counter-statement where the speaker, Jane, announces that she has just found a way to do it. At the same time, she brings up a paper ring into the line of sight between Carrie and herself (Fig. 8.3). The transcriber glosses the speech as 'plaintive'. The transcription glosses the speech as words running into words (see equal signs connecting words) without clear separation (turn 006). To find out more about the affective quality that marks this transaction ritual, we take a look at some of its prosodic features.

Fragment 8.2
```
    005   C:   uMM::tmake dlIfe EA:sier; (0.31) <<all>okay>; ..HHH
→                UUm (0.42) <<len>it has (0.22) bin=decided that it is
→                too dIFficult.> kAY:? ((187→300 Hz)
→ 006   J:   <<plaintive>i=just=found=out=a=way=to='dO=`it.>
→ 007          (0.30)
→ 008   C:   ((200 Hz)) EE::: umm::::; (0.85) BUT (0.50) <<all>but
→                it might still work for chAnge of plANs.> (0.22)
                 .hhHH its (0.36) ↓'O::N:: (0.52) mOO:dl, the new
                 stAtement, (0.24) but it is to dO with (0.21) .hhhhh
                 <<len>hAVing a lANtern,> (0.50) with hOt AI::r (0.23)
                 <<all>added to it> (0.26) by means other than using
```

```
the flA:Me, (0.91) suchA:s;
<<all>can=you=think=of=anything⁻>
```

We note that the pitch levels of the two speakers are very different (Fig. 8.4). The mean pitch in the latter part of turn 005 is 192 Hz and it is 229 Hz over the course of the interjection 'ee=umm' (turn 008). On the other hand, the turn between – which completes the first turn pair considered here and begins the second turn pair – has a mean pitch of 460 Hz before dropping off to 300 Hz. We observe similar differences, for example, when Jane produces the statement 'that means I can't experiment with waxes' (mean pitch over 430 Hz) and the replique (mean pitch below 260 Hz). In cases of contrast in conceptual content of two turn pairs, we observe, as in other reported cases such as children arguing over a game of hopscotch (Goodwin et al. 2002), sharply contrasting pitches within the same turn pair. As it would in music, such different pitches are heard as disharmony rather than harmony, which is based on a continuity of pitch from speaker to speaker (Roth and Tobin 2010). That is, the differences in conceptual content of two phrases in the same turn pair are accompanied by hearably different pitch levels. In fact, if an argument develops over several turns, the pitch levels of each next turn tends to rise above that of the preceding turn until an instant where the lower pitched voice of another speaker 'calms' the situation. Although in arguments the speech intensity tends to increase as well, the mean intensity of the present locution (75 dB) is not much different than that in other turns Jane takes (e.g., in 'breath into it', the mean speech intensity is 74 dB).

There is something about the quality of voice, however, that clearly stands out. We may get an inkling of what makes the voice quality stand out from the spectrum (Fig. 8.5). When the part corresponding to Jane's voice is compared with that of the preceding 'um' (Fig. 8.2), which could be heard and glossed as expressing disappointment, we note the darkness for higher frequencies. This means that there is much more energy for these higher energies, which makes for the voice to sound more shrill than normal.

We now focus on the next turn pair, in which Jane's turn comes to be paired with its reception on the part of Carrie. We notice that the pitch in the replique is low, only slightly above what it has been before. We can hear this as 'taking things up where they were', as an expression of equanimity. That is, what could have given rise to an expansion of conflict if the pitch had risen above that of the preceding turn does not happen here. However, we cannot say that it has a 'calming' effect until we hear the next turn, for there are instances in life where such equanimity actually may accelerate the conflict (e.g., because the person is seen as not 'really debating the issue').

The beginning of the second turn in the pair, 'ee=umm', does not translate into an English word. Part of it may be heard as the interjection 'um', which tends to be associated with the production of hesitation and doubt but also of assent. In the first sense, it is a production within a replique by means of which a turn is taken without actually saying a specific word. It makes and gives the speaker time for the production of words without giving up the turn. In the second sense, the interjection constitutes a second-turn part of a statement | doubt pair. In the third sense, the interjection, especially when the elongated 'mm' part stands out, is another interjection that can express satisfaction, approval, or assent as well as hesitation, re-

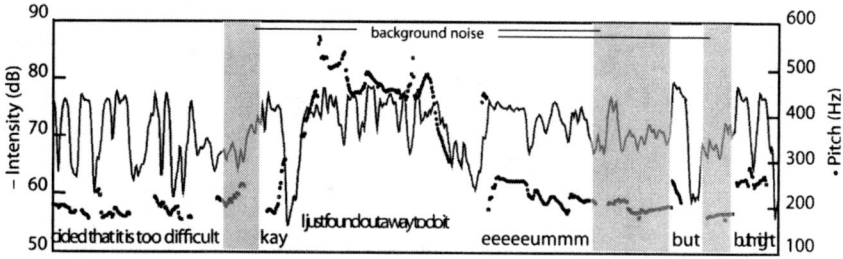

Fig. 8.4 There is a stark contrast in the pitch levels of the three turns, the first and second being of similar level. (Grey shaded areas correspond to background noise from the classroom.)

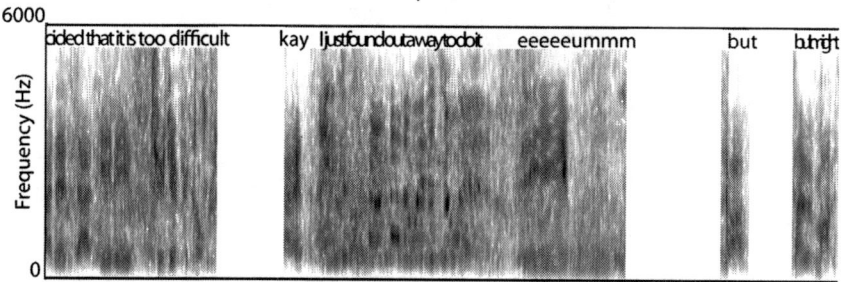

Fig. 8.5 The spectrum shows that there is a lot of high-frequency energy in the articulation of having found a way to do it (getting the Chinese lantern to lift off).

flection, and interrogation. We note that the pitch in the production of 'ee' first rises to plateau at a mean of 258 Hz and then descends to a mean of 216 Hz on 'mm'. The beginning of the replique, therefore, is significantly higher in pitch than the preceding speech, which presents a contrast and then returns to a value closer to the surrounding norm. Moreover, the spectrum shows considerable energy in the mid- to upper frequency range, which make the voice sound more strident.

We may develop an even deeper sense of the replique when, together with the voice, we re/produce some of the bodily gestures. Thus, for example, while articulating 'ee::: umm::::', Carrie's head moves sideward and then back near the original position (Fig. 8.6). This head movement, where the sideward position falls together with the more strident production of 'ee:::' may be seen as the gestural equivalent to the gloss 'maybe' or a doubting 'well'. Across the different moments of the performance of the replique, we perceive and – when we actually use the information provided here to perform the replique – empathically feel the doubt. The next part of the turn begins with two statements of the contrastive conjunction 'but', followed by the statement that 'it might still work for change of plans'. That is, the turn pair now is '"I just found a way to do it" | doubt' followed by a turn-internal contrast manifested in the pair 'doubt | "but it might still work for change of plans"'.

A final aspect of the situation to be articulated here concerns their physical orientation. We observe that the two speakers are not directly opposite to each other. Whereas Jane is rotated slightly to her left and towards the laboratory table on

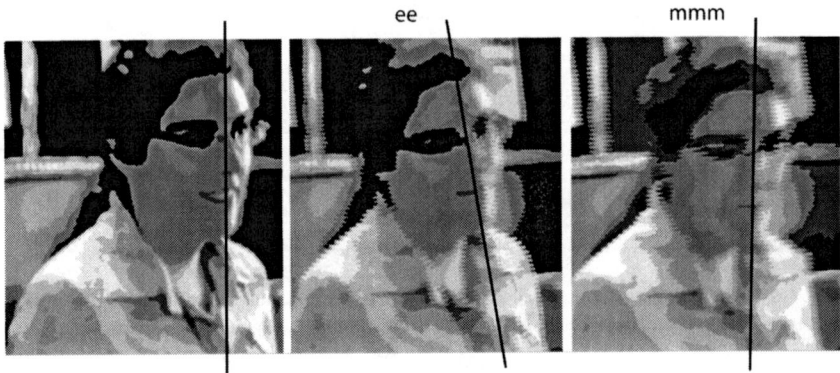

Fig. 8.6   Artistic rendering of the instant when Carrie's head moves sideward while producing the sound transcribed as 'ee:::' and then, while articulating 'mm', returns back near the original position but with the chin further towards the floor. (The line falls on center of chin and point between eyes.)

which her materials are placed, Carrie is also oriented to her left from the axis that is defined by connecting their respective body centers. The two literally do not exactly 'see eye to eye' (a gloss) with each other, that is, they are not of one mind with respect to the issue discussed.

We can understand all the communicative aspects other than what we hear as words with intellectual content as an important dimension of the production of the social relation and of the production of the performative aspects of the sympractical social work. As suggested, rather than just looking at the different types of transcription provided, readers are invited to actually view these as part of a score that requires being played by an instrument, here the entire human body, to *feel* and *hear* what is being communicated. Rather than having and considering symbolic forms, which require intellectual consciousness only, the reader then re/produces the communicative instant. It is precisely when some of the key features of the reader's production coincide with the originally recorded production on the part of Carrie's and Jane's productions, that the situation comes to life again. The reader performs and thereby re/lives part of the situation, including aspects of its affective qualities. The materials provided here will then have had the same kind of relation to the actual performance as that which exists between a recipe and the making of a meal or, more generally, between any form of instruction (plan) and the corresponding situated actions.

The present section therefore articulates a very different stance with respect to the science curriculum than the one that precedes it. There, the curriculum was defined in symbolic terms either as a plan (intended curriculum) or as a set of after-the-fact observation (enacted curriculum). Here, the living curriculum comes to the fore, as it is performed without the benefit of hindsight. We are thrown into the thickets of things, into the happening, without knowing where we will end up. In performing the transcripts, we experience the temporality, the hesitations, the accelerations, the shrillness of the repliques, or the equanimity in the consecutive turns of the same speaker.

Where Is the Content?

In the science education peer review process, one can frequently hear the complaint that studies focusing on communication insufficiently attend to the issue of conceptual content and content issues of the curriculum. Such complaints warrant attention in the present context. The two preceding sections provide us with a contrast that allows us to understand the very different foci of (a) those who are interested in the living curriculum, the work that brings about science lessons and whatever lasting changes it leaves in participants and (b) those interested in plans and outcomes. We may consider the latter, plans and outcomes, as social facts. These social facts can be reported. They tend to require special interpretive methods on the part of the researcher to assure readers that the social facts correspond to the observed realities. These clearly are abstractions, which have very little to do with the actual labor of learning, that is, the performances in and through which human beings change. Only descriptions of the actual performances of people will allow us to understand the coming about of these social facts. But the actual performances are 'governed' not by special methods, not by psychological schemas or underlying rules that cannot be observed. Rather, social facts such as 'concepts', 'content', and 'conceptions' are the result of endogenous productions on the part of the members to the respective settings. That is, if Jane ends up failing the course, we need to know the entire range of performances that will lead to a failing grade. This range includes what happens in classrooms but also other events in which social actors engage in accountable performances that contribute to the production of the grade.

Evidence for Having Enacted the Planned Curriculum

The approach advocated here is consistent with a cultural-historical approach to learning. Accordingly, every higher psychological function is first lived in and as a societal relation (Vygotskij 2005). If there is anything such as conceptual learning that can be ascribed to an individual, then it is the result of the work that produces the societal relations. The higher function is not something the individuals construct on their own following a societal relation. Rather, the relation, qua performance, *is* the higher function.[25] If much of what Jane participates in during the lesson are relations of the kind presented here – Carrie later suggested that she did not have many more exchanges with Jane during this lesson – then this is also the

---

[25] Doubting readers might want to think for an instant in terms of neurons required for participating in sympractical work (i.e., in 'co-construction' or 'social construction'). Those neurons and neuronal collectives that are required to perform in the collective situation also fire when persons later perform the work on their own. During the original performances, together with the associated firing of neurons, other neurons come into play that 'mirror' the performance of those required in performance. Neuroscientific research shows that we can *recognize* actions and objects only when these mirror neurons are in place. These neurons are also required for producing some action independently from the situation where they were it was first experienced.

place where we need to look for any concepts that teachers and researchers later attribute to her as the outcome of the curriculum.

In chapters 1 and 2, I elaborate on the ethnomethodological position concerning the relation between performances, the actual 'doing', and the corresponding glosses, that is, articulations or glosses that are used to denote the work and thereby constitute accountable social facts. This relation, for the present curriculum topic of extended experimental investigation, may be expressed in the form 'doing {investigating a phenomenon by means of self-directed inquiry}'. Research on instructions and plans suggests that these may serve, after the fact, as accounts for describing what an individual actually has done or for describing the distance between intended and situated actions (Suchman 1987). When the outcomes match what was anticipated, the relevance of each instruction or intended step is found together with the outcomes. When the outcomes differ from those anticipated, then the person might search for those situations in the process where the instructional gloss might not describe the situated action.

We know that Jane told Carrie when she had done something: 'She tries and she does occasionally say things like, "I did all those questions". Well yes, "so did the rest of the class". But yes, she'll be, when she does do a little bit of something she'll let you know, cause its rare'. In the present instance, we actually might ask Jane to do something similar: to take a look at the prescribed curriculum and reflect on her practical actions, her doing, in relation to the glosses. We take a look at the first four statements of the Queensland syllabus that constitutes the planned curriculum for the present lesson concerning what a student must do pertain to planning an extended experimental investigation. For each of the resulting work | gloss pairs, we might then ask Jane to produce accounts of her 'doing' that would warrant the gloss.

– doing {develop a planned course of action}
– doing {clearly articulate the hypothesis or research question, providing a statement of purpose for the investigation}
– doing {provide descriptions of the experiment}
– doing {show evidence of modification or student design}

Jane may then refer to the conversation that she has had with Carrie quoting and pointing to particular parts of the conversation. In the context of the conversation, there is evidence for 'doing' {developing a planned course of action}, for example, when she tells Carrie that she had gone out and bought materials or when she explains how to use a paper ring and tinsels to mount the candles so that the Chinese lantern could actually rise. In the conversation, we do hear a statement that could be mobilized in support of 'doing' {clearly articulate the hypothesis or research question, providing a statement of purpose for the investigation}: in the statement that relates the height of the candles and lift off. We do find descriptions of parts of the anticipated experiment, and Jane would be able to provide clear evidence that she had engaged in the modification of the original design to make it work. In fact, Jane may want to argue that she 'was not allowed to do' the investigation in the way it was intended and she was thereby never given the chance to make it work or to gather the kind of data she was really interested in. She could find evidence of having been right in saying that she needed to do the experiment without having a hypothesis because nobody had done the investigation before and that there was no theory. That is, a lot of the sympractical work done is useable for making the case that Jane did the work that the syllabus intended. If she nevertheless failed the course, there are other places where we would have to study the work involved in the production of the failure qua social fact.

Losing the Phenomenon

The foregoing discussion further comes into relief given the possibilities that the pursuit of the investigation as Jane had planned it would have set up opportunities for experiencing an important dimension of science: Losing the phenomenon. Thus, 'being able to lose the phenomenon is essential to scientific practice' (Garfinkel 2002: 264). In an explanatory note, the editor of the book notes: 'In science the essential point is that you can lose the phenomenon. Other studies of Galileo's inclined plane experiment concentrate on figuring out how Galileo got from start to finish in doing a proof. They proceed to a foregone conclusion. What they don't attend to is that Galileo would have faced the problems of losing his phenomenon. Some ways of setting up the experiment would not produce the required phenomenon. Galileo would have to figure out that this was not because the experiment wouldn't work, but because there were contingencies that he still needed to deal with' (Rawls, in Garfinkel 2002: 264, note 2). With respect to Jane, Carrie, and the planned curriculum (as stated in the state syllabus), there were opportunities for learning precisely this perhaps even more important aspect of science then eventual successes. Thus, describing the experiment and investigating the conditions that did not allow the lanterns to rise is just as important to a scientific investigation and understanding a phenomenon as the actions that actually do produce the science. In fact, scientists routinely set up 'control' conditions in their accounts to ascertain that what they report as a fact is not an artifact. The scientific fact arises as such precisely in contrast to all those other conditions in which the phenomenon is lost. And even when they do not want it to happen, losing their phenomenon is a routine experience in scientific laboratories.

'Losing a phenomenon' is not something that one comes to practically understand until one has come across it in one's own practical performances. (See also the comments in chapter 1 on how what science educators have to do to lose their phenomena'.) Then 'all these *topics* we had come upon as topics to talk about – "losing the phenomenon", "wasting time", "getting the phenomenon out of your data" – would instead, in the workplace become the *looks* of things; we would have to come upon it – *if we were lucky*' (Garfinkel 2002: 266). In the same way, Jane would have had the opportunity of 'spending more time trying to make it work', experience 'difficulties' and 'complications' involved in actually making it work, and perhaps even 'wasting time' pursuing a line of research that does not lead to apparent results. To actually experience 'losing a phenomenon' one has to 'do something, to wait around for a while, to see what the thing looks like when in fact it hits' (ibid: 266).

This is not the place for producing judgment nor is it my intent to judge what did or did not happen. The important point we can get from this is that students can learn (about) science whether the experiment 'works' or 'does not work' in the intended way. Whatever they do, it is a form of human investigative engagement in the course of which students may contribute to the production of everything that the intended curriculum (syllabus) states. That is, even if the lantern were not to rise, the events would have provided an occasion for actually living *extended experimental investigations* that could be accounted for, once finished, by means of the normatively functioning instructions of what a student 'must' do to complete this part of the state syllabus. The experience, qua experience, would be no more and no less authentic in terms of inquiry. And not getting the lantern to rise – even though there is ample evidence on the Internet that the Chinese get these to rise in massive amounts – is an occasion for performing the work in 'doing {science}' as an investigation where some actual correlation between two variables comes to be measured.

9

So *What* (More) Is in It for Science Education?

What more is there in and for science education to do in terms of researching science lessons? A lot, I suggest, if research turns from studying science education extracting social facts using special methods, which journal articles require to state, to studying the work and ethno-methods by means of which participants themselves create their structured world of science lessons. This book presents, with concrete materials from an inquiry-oriented physics course, a way of doing science education research that radically differs from existing approaches. I articulate this approach for a science education audience, where this approach is by and large unknown, and where the primary literature is often experienced as impenetrable and as requiring years of work to gain entry. Consistent with this different approach, the very kind of concrete materials are used that constitute the only way in which reflexive production of social order is observed by the actors (teachers, students) themselves.

The analyses provided in this book exhibit the work required for producing social order, here, that students do as they are asked to do as reported in chapter 2: 'Study the bubble ...', 'Students were required to design ...', and 'they were required to write and submit ...'. In the approach proposed here, all such descriptions are taken to be prospective or retrospective glosses. The present case study shows even for a part of this curriculum, the change of research topic, requires a lot of work that teachers and students accomplish together – though, when there is immediate compliance, such work tends to be and become invisible. The choice of *this* episode was mediated by the fact that what normally remains hidden is made visible when there is trouble, such as in this for the teacher difficult situation of having to announce a change of topic to a student who apparently has invested a lot in her project.

Science education, as other social sciences, are premised on the idea that special methods are required to extract the order – i.e., the 'structures' associated with 'agency' in sociological theories of social phenomena – said to underlie social phenomena such as teaching and learning in science classrooms. This approach, for self-evident reasons named the *formal analytic* approach, has yielded a vast body of literature about identifiable patterned and methodological specifications of what to do to observe these patterns in any concrete case. This book is designed to present a radical ethnomethodological alternate to the existing approach for doing research in science education. This alternate does not question the results of existing research on social structure (patterns) but instead shows how in any concrete case, order is an endogenously produced and reflexively accounted for collective achievement irreducible to individuals and their psychological characteristics. It is a radical alternate, because once specified, the work allows us to understand the *what* and *how* of the order accomplished, whereas knowing orderly properties of social phenomena does not allow us to get to the work that actually produces it and that is required, though generally unacknowledged, on the part of the analyst to see the order in the first place.

When we enter the classroom, in the background of the video showing Jane and Carrie, we see students in the process of conducting different inquiries. A comment out of the natural attitude would be to explain the observation by reference to the type of school, the particular school, and the type of students that attend this school, its elite status, and many other forms of explanation of the same ilk. This is precisely what the researcher in the field had done when he first introduced me to the videotapes. But in the approach presented here, these forms of explanations and their scientific derivatives are explicitly bracketed and put out of circulation. These do not have any explanatory function whatsoever and, in as far as these are matters of fact, are but other aspects of the natural attitude and what it makes to be known.

In this book, I exhibit the collective, sympractical work done to bring about what participants glossed as a 'change of plans', which from one perspective 'sucks', but from another perspective is in the interest of the student who is more likely to get good data that are suitable for analyses, all of which lead to a 'good mark'. I do not draw on a special method that would be required for extracting patterns from otherwise unordered events or events in which the order is not visible. Rather, focusing on the actual work being done, I only have to rely on what this work makes visible as order to the members of the setting themselves. To do so, I have to rely on the practices of the people that results in the accountable production of the orderly conduct and ordered world. To be able to do so, I need to be sufficiently familiar with *such* situations and phenomena to hear and see what is going on in the way any other insider can hear and see them. That is, unlike the formal analytic approach to method, which presupposes the lack of visible order in the social world, and, thereby presupposes the need of a special method, I take as my starting point the observation that social phenomena exhibit their order to those who staff them. Just as I recognize a queue when I see it, and recognize when there is trouble in the queuing leading to work to fix it, there is order produced in science lessons that is accessible to its staff ('students', 'teachers'). There is indeed 'order in the most ordinary activities of everyday life in their full concreteness, and that means in their ongoingly *procedurally* enacted coherence of substantive, ordered phenomenal details without loss of generality' (Garfinkel 1996: 7).

In this form of analysis, we actually do not have to draw on 'teacher' and 'student' as resources for explaining the unfolding event that is currently in the making. The minimum unit focuses us on *social* processes, and, therefore, on *relations*. These social relations are the loci of the higher psychological functions, the loci where a learner first lives them. But we do see asymmetries being produced in the course of the unfolding event. For example, a change of plans is being announced to one person, the other already knowing about it. The content and form are known to one person as much as that a statement announcing and specifying this change is already available in the Moodle environment.

As we follow the event, the arguments for and against a change of plan, until the change of plan has been accepted. One particular instance where asymmetries come to the fore is in the turns 020–022. We have an explicit attribution of what one speaker can do and not do. It is not that the 'teacher' forbids a particular action; the locution 'that means I can't experiment with waxes' attributes the interdiction to the other. The second speaker asserts affirmatively, 'No. You can't experiment with different waxes'. The after-the-fact effect is that both speakers appeared to have attended to the respective mutual roles of teacher and students, when in fact the social fact of the different roles or positions is produced right there in the here and now of the situation. There is a direction where a change of plans is announced on the part of one speaker has implications for the actions of another; and this other eventually complies with the change of plans, though reluctantly (i.e., by 'balking at it all'). There is also a change in topic from the nature of the experiment to the role of theory. The changeover is unremarkable and immediately accepted de facto in the next turn that constitutes the reply to the offered question that also contained the change of topic (turn 074). Differences are written all over the transcript, and experienced analysts do not require any information about the background of a transcript and the roles of the participants to figure out just from the internal dynamic of what *kind* the situation is, the most likely distribution of roles, the setting, [meanings] behind the words or in the minds, and so on. The analyst sticks with what is on the page and does not do – as can be found frequently in reviewer reports – asking for additional context that would explain a situation. The experienced analyst can take the transcript *as* the sole available evidence and will, always pointing to the specific location in the transcription, that support a particular finding.[26] Like in an actual detective case, not anything goes. When a dective gets the wrong person, the latter could end up, in certain countries including the US, on death row. This does not mean, however, that people merely fill slots. My analyses take great care to show that at each stage a locution taken as a first turn makes an offer for a particular turn unit without ever having the change of definitively determining the nature it will have had once we look back.

From the sequentially ordered transaction ritual, each turn is a second turn to a preceding one, even in the case where a turn appears to be the first one, such as turn 001. But, this is not a first turn at all. It already is a response to a double histo-

---

[26] In my graduate methods seminars, I ask students to bring a piece of transcript to class but not say anything about it. In real time, I then read the transcript, articulating as much as possible about what is going on, the kind of situation the transcript has been recorded in, the social roles and ranks of the participants, and so on. In the end, the graduate students 'evaluate' my performance by publicly comparing my reading to all the background that they have for original event. Extended descriptions and analyses of this method are available (Roth and Hsu 2010, 2012). (See also note 20, chapter 6.)

ricity: of schooling in general and of this physics course in particular. It is offering an opening to a conversation that is understood only in the larger context of the inquiry curriculum not only in this class but also in all classes in that school, where other students have been doing the same experiment as Jane. Moreover, the turn is an offering to a conversation, which is accepted in this case. But alternative continuations are easily imaginable, such as those that would have occurred had Jane said something like 'I got to go to the bathroom' or, 'I am in the middle of something I can't stop right now'. In this case, new possibilities and constraints would have to be dealt with *by the conversation*, with quite uncertain outcomes – which does not preclude science educators to speculate that an 'assertive teacher would have forced the conversation' or a 'weak teacher might have given in to Jane', or whatever else the natural attitude has available for making projections in such cases. I implement that approach *radically* in the sense that every subsequent fragment begins with one or two turns that constitute the end of the preceding fragment. In this way, every turn explicitly has a preceding turn, even if it apparently does not relate to it such as in a sudden change of topics, which itself constitutes a form of work that the interlocutors collectively produce. There is no change of topic unless the topic changes at the conversational level, which is, when the interlocutors produce it *collectively*.

Science educators may ask: What can be done with such a form of analysis? Moreover, one of the question reviewers of journal articles frequently ask, 'What is specifically science educational about the phenomena described?' The question assumes, in fact, that it makes sense to separate out science education and to postulate that it has a distinctive existence and structure from everything else we do in society. One lesson we can learn from the analyses presented here is that anything special in science education is the result of order production that is pervasive in society rather than special about science education. The structure of classroom talk that pertains to atoms may not differ at all from one in which students learn to balance a chemical equation or to create a motion graph. In the course, many potentially interesting phenomena in our field are overlooked and glossed over as uninteresting. In the present situation, the analyses actually show what we might take as a sophisticated work of argumentation in the course of moving activity from one task description to another task description, with the correlative abandonment of all the work that the student has put into her project so far. The analyses offered throughout this book show that there are very interesting possibilities that arise in the sequentially organized 'change of plans' that are not actualized. These include the testing of hypotheses and production of theory in an area 'where nobody else has worked before'.

It turns out in the end that the student (Jane) fails physics – she is the only one to fail this course. Going beyond the analytical approach chosen here, science educators who are responsible for the situation will orient in a normative way to what *ought* to be achieved. We may then ask, normatively: 'Is this what science education should be about?' Or might there not have been more positive outcomes if Jane had been supported in pursuing the experiments and tests that she had planned, in part executed, and purchased the materials for? But such normative questioning would not be in the spirit of the analytic approach articulated and explicated here.

It appears evident that the episode could be glossed in a variety of other ways and the form of analysis would show how the gloss is being achieved. For example, science educators interested in investigating open inquiry would show that in the present case, it is not so open at all. In fact, a change in the experiment is announced and compliance is achieved in the change despite the fact that the student has had many ideas for alternative experiments, each of which would have provided a range of data that could have been analyzed. What is achieved, then, is the fact that not experimenting is the real issue, but some of the other things that the participants describe: getting data that can be analyzed, knowledge of an existing theory that is to be confirmed, getting a good grade, making life easy, and so forth. Although the Queensland curriculum states that there be a possibility of a negotiation, here we see that there is no way that the student can pursue any of the alternative routes that all would have led to forms of experimentation and inquiry, and, if Jane is right that 'nobody has done it before', would have been 'open' in the way that the adjective is used in connection with 'inquiry' (Roth 1995). Moreover, in this case the student is 'scaffolded' and 'helped' – apparently against her will, given that she repeatedly pleads to do the experiment she has been designing and begun to prepare for.

This form of analysis, therefore, allows us to learn about the sympractical work underlying a particular way in which 'open inquiry' comes to be instantiated in schools. In contrast to other forms of research, which make liberal use of natural accounts to explain phenomena, I present here a way to focus on the actual (conversational) work, which not only produces social facts as 'things', but also, correlatively, deal out differential subjectivities (in the making). Changes of plan are the result of work that require, among others, compliance when the changes or in the interest of people other than who are subject to the changes. The change of plan and compliance are the result of this lesson fragment, and the analysis elaborates the manner in which this is achieved. This elaboration is not merely a singularity. If it is a process possible for one setting or set of persons, then it is possible for all social settings and persons: 'It can be seen that ... what is recognizable to one ego has to be, *on principle*, recognizable to *every* ego' (Husserl 1976: 102, original emphasis). This is so not in the least because any recognition of something as something requires a language-mediated concept, and thereby, because of the social nature of language, a possibility for every language user. As in other social phenomena, the individual user is only part of the staff that produces the phenomenon as social fact. The concepts and language do not depend on the particular user.

Appendix A: Transcription Conventions

The transcription conventions are those of standard conversation analysis enhanced for the transcription of prosodic features (Selting et al. 1998). Unless modified, all words are written with small letters.

Notation	Description	Example
(0.14)	Time without talk, in seconds	okay. (0.24) OH
((turns))	Verbs and descriptions in double parentheses are transcriber's comments	((head sidward))
(.)	Period in parentheses marks a hearable pause less than 0.1 seconds long	NO. (.) <<assertive>you
::	Colons indicate lengthening of phoneme, about 1/10 of a second per colon	U::M:::
[ ]	Square brackets in consecutive lines indicate overlap	J: wa[xes.] C: [wAX?] (0.93)
<p> >	Piano, lower than normal speech volume	<<p>like we get hot air from.>
<<pp> >	Pianissimo, a lot lower than normal speech volume, almost inaudible	<<pp>kay.>
<<all> >	Allegro, words are uttered with faster than normal speed	<<all>okay?>
<<len> >	Lento, slower than normal speech	<<len>it has (0.22) bin=decided that it is too dIFficult.>
<<plaintive> >	Transcriber's glosses are provided for ways of speaking	<<plaintive>i=just=found= out=a=way=to=`dO=`it.>
JAne	Capital letters indicate emphasized sounds.	change of plA:Ns
.hh	Noticeable in-breath	..HHH UUm (0.42)
hh	Noticeable out-breadth	
-,?;.	Punctuation is used to mark	T: so can we tell a shape

	movement of pitch (intonation) toward end of utterance, flat, slightly and strongly upward, and slightly and strongly downward, respectively	`      by its color?`
		`T: does it belong to anoth-`
		`    er group (0.67) O:r.`

↓↑	Downward and upward arrows indicate pitch jump downward and upward	`(0.36) ↓'O::N::; ↑IT (0.30)`
=	Equal sign indicates that the phonemes of different words are not clearly separated	`loo::ks=similar`
˅ˊˋ	Diacritic indicates movement of pitch within the word that follows – down-up, up, down	`˘buthh`

Appendix B: Transcripts[27]

Lesson Episode: Carrie (Teacher) and Jane (Student)

```
001   C:   okay. (0.24) OH; ((moves toward Jane)) i better talk
           to JAne first. (0.24) okAY:. (1.63) change of plA:Ns.
002        (0.26)
003   J:   U::M::: ((head sideward, gloss: disappointment on
           face))
004        (0.76)
005   C:   uMM::tmake dlIfe EA:sier; (0.31) <<all>okay>; ..HHH
           UUm (0.42) <<len>it has (0.22) bin=decided that it is
           too dIFficult.> kAY:? ((187→300 Hz) ((head sideward,
           gaze down))
006   J:   <<plaintive>i=just=found=out=a=way=to='dO=`it.>
           ((318Hz))
007        (0.30)
008   C:   ((200 Hz)) EE::: umm::::; (0.85) BUT (0.50) <<all>but
           it might still work for chAnge of plANs.> (0.22)
           .hhHH its (0.36) ↓'O::N:: (0.52) mOO:dl, the new
           stAtement, (0.24) but it is to dO with (0.21) .hhhhh
           <<len>hAVing a lANtern,> (0.50) with hOt AI::r (0.23)
           <<all>added to it> (0.26) by means other than using
           the flA:me, (0.91) suchA:s;
           <<all>can=you=think=of=anything¯>
009        (1.11)
010   C:   <<all>hotair> (1.88) <<p>like we get hot air from.>
011        (0.75)
012   J:   breath INto It?
013        (1.25) (('yea' gesture))
014   C:   EAsier=than=thA:t¯
015        (2.11) ((Carrie grins/laughs))
016   J:   i would say fIre but its a flame.
017        (0.30)
018   C:   yea::. (0.64) <<all>hairdryer, (0.77) somethI:Ng¯
019        (0.54)
```

---

[27] Pseudonyms have been used throughout.

```
020    J:   that means i cant experiment with the wa[xes.   ]
021    C:                                              [wAX?  ]
            (0.93) NO. (.) <<assertive>you cA:nt experiment with
            different wA[xes.]>
022    J:
            [u:m:] ((nose, head as if propped up by hand))
023         (0.44)
024    C:   BUT; (0.45) youcA:::n .hh and its going to bEE::
            (0.42) investiga:te (.) how you can hA:ve (0.60) a
            lANtern, (1.47) rI:::se (2.79) ((glances toward ceil-
            ing as if thinking)) <<all>in the lEAst amount of
            time for two meters> .hh with a:: (.)
            twen:ty:grammass=on=it.
025         (0.90)
026    C:   .hhhhkay?
027    J:   <<subdued, p>kay.
028    C:   .hhh SO:; (0.50) makes it easy for you: and OTher
            thing is to (.17) un to: hOld ↑IT (0.30) untI::L:
            (0.81) you fINish up. (0.33) hEAting (0.22) the air?
029         (0.75)
030         kay?
031         (0.46)
032         remOVe the hEAt sOUurce (0.28) <<all>then let it go.>
033    J:   <<pp>kay.>
034         (0.94) ((Jane nods))
035    C:   kAY? (0.23) .hhh (0.17) sO:::; (0.38) yes, ((facial
            expression of sorry)) you wONt be able to test dif-
            ferent tYPes of WAxES=
036    J:   =i just went out and bought heaps of stuff last night
            for it.
037         (1.95)
038    J:   went out and bought all the candle bASes and (?)
            things and i=ve gone and (0.35) ordered wAXes and
            stuff.
039         (0.30)
040    C:   yea. (0.15) but you can sEE thats (.) its been rEAlly
            difficult to actually get a lANtern [t go;]
041    J:                                       [yea, ]
042    C:   hAsnt [it.]
043    J:         [but] (0.25) i worked out that (0.77) if you
            use a paper ring,
044         (0.46)
045    C:   u::::n?
046         (0.56)
047    J:   and possibly on top of the cup use baking paper;
            (0.58) and just use a lIGhtweight tINsel?
048         (0.56)
049    C:   [yEA::::?    ]
050    J:   [and put the] tINnsel OUtside, the inside of the tin-
            sel=
051    C:   =the wIre?
052         (0.31)
053    J:   that chANges make it prop up. and its only going to
            be at this weight and it will go up really EAsily.
054         (1.10)
055    J:   cause its [full of air. ]
056    C:             [will it bURn?]
057         (0.75)
058    J:   <<all>oh=no cause i=m making it out of baking paper.>
059         (0.98)
060    J:   <<all>baking paper dOEsnt burn.>
061         (0.74)
062    C:   wE:ll: it can bURn but it chA:Rs and gets hOLes in
            it.
```

```
063          (0.96)
064    J:    but i can experiment on how tall it has to be.
             ((Smiles at Carrie))
065          (2.08)
066    C:    can you use the sAMe setup (0.36) with (1.01) adding
             hotair?
067    J:    but i wanted <<all>it how tall it is to go UP.>
068          (0.61)
069    J:    <<all>it doesnt even matter if its a paper cUP it can
             go up. t can go up.> ((Smiles, as if she had made a
             'good play'))
070          (1.59)
071    C:    so have a think about (0.98) what you can do with
             that. (0.20) <<len>i kno:w that youve put thought in
             what we were doing;> but.
072          (1.67)
073    C:    the:::ee (0.79) variATions in whats hAPppening;
             <<all>and the complicATions and dIFficulties in ACtu-
             ally> making it wO:::rk.
074    J:    <<all>if i get it to work can i do it> plEA::se.
075          (0.24)
076    C:    .hhhh but then youll be spending mORe time trying to
             make it wORk.
077    J:    but
078    C:    [and if doesnt youll run out of time.]
079    J:    [but if this time it doesnt work     ] (0.30) some
             (1.00) i promise i=ll: (0.17) go back (0.39) and
             (0.22) do: (0.44) <<all>the hairdryer one; but if
             this works (0.26) can i do it plEAse?
080          (0.75)
081    C:    so you:: (0.19) I:: wou:ld=suggest fr todA:Y: (0.48)
             you work on that (0.68) sort of (1.06) what ideas you
             can change for the other one .hhh and at hO:Me
             ((Jane's face changes to sad expression, averts gaze
             heretofore straight forwardly directed at Carrie's
             face)) (0.23) try:ing (0.41) <<all>try and get your
             wAX one to work.> ((Jane's face goes from smile to
             sadness))
082    J:    <<subdued, p>kay.>
083          (0.48)
084    C:    <<all>kay?>
085          (0.82)
086    C:    'hows your thEOry wrIting gOing.
087    J:    <<unconvinced>s=alright.> ((gaze on to desk, avert-
             ed)) (0.18) avnt done (0.16) i didnt get a chance to
             do any more. <<pp>???>
088          (0.27)
089    C:    .hh if you hAve thE:ory for the wAX bit (0.17) you
             can stILl put it in
090          (0.32)
091    J:    un
092    C:    and it can be an experiment you didnt dO, but.
093    J:    no i need to [do the experiment             ]
094    C:                 [<<all>you still have theory on it.>]
095    J:    to get the theory because theres nobody whos dONe an
             expERiment like that.
096          (0.40)
097    C:    yea but you should have a rEAson wHY: it chANges.
             ((Jane's face pensive))
098          (0.93)
099    J:    well it could [    (??)    ]
100    C:                  [because if] there is nO rEAson whY
             then theres nOT much point dOIng it.
101    J:    if gonna be (.) <<p>its gonna be hotter so it takes
```

```
                    the little cup>
102                 (0.83)
103     J:          and then the wax (0.46) or whether its going to be
                    cool (0.38) cool and thirty minutes its cool wax and
                    it burn faster. (0.28) or whether if its hotter it
                    will rise mORe because of the hEAt.
104                 (0.38)
105     C:          <<dubitative>n yea:h.> ((gloss: perhaps; or 'whatev-
                    er.))
106                 (3.25)
107     C:          kAY?
108                 (0.22)
109     J:          <<subdued, p>yap.=
110     C:          =yup? (0.42) so look up (.) on::; (0.53) moodle the
                    document has been edited (.) to have a new statement.
111                 (0.22)
112     J:          <<subdued, p>yes.> ((Eyes averted downward))
113                 (0.29)
114     C:          okAY?
115     J:          (1.52) ((Jane nods slightly))
116     C:          makes life way easier for you. ((Jane nods slightly))
117                 (0.75)
118     C:          and youll get dA:ta and you can analyze it
119                 (0.62)
120     C:          and you can get a good mark for your analysis.
121                 (0.68)
122     J:          does it matter how much heat
123                 (0.31)
124     C:          does that
125                 (0.28)
126     J:          where you can measure how much AIr you put into it?
                    (.) .hhh (0.24) because with the hairdryer you ca:nt
                    blow.=
127     C:          =well (0.24) itll have whatever volume your lANtern
                    is.
128                 (1.09)
129     J:          <<p>like> (0.30) no=like (0.63) well certain (0.75)
                    like (.) the (0.82) spEEd.
130                 (1.86)
131     J:          <<insistent>you=know like if you put more air in it
                    it will go Up faster.>
132                 (1.40)
133     C:          but it can only fIT the amount of AIr that fit inside
                    the lA:Ntern.
134     J:          but if you push it up with hot air it will move fast-
                    er, it will go faster=
135     C:          =you gonna hold it in its plACe if youre going to
                    hold it in its place
136     J:          un
137     C:          until youve added (0.75) the air and then let it go.
138                 (1.51)
139     J:          <<p>kay.>
140     C:          kAY?
141     J:          do I turn it off you turn it off
142     C:          yea.
143     J:          after you add the air?
144     C:          yea.
145                 (0.40)
146     J:          oo kay.
147                 (1.00)
148     C:          so you need to add it, you are not really (0.54) i
                    guess you can look at ADding hot air or hEAting the
                    AIr thats thEre.
149                 (0.66) ((Jane nods))
```

```
150   J:   kay. but wouldnt that heat the air thats around the
           outside?=
151   C:   ^NN. thats an interesting pOINt you mIght lIke to (.)
           commENT on that.
152        (0.87)
153   J:   <<pp>kay.>
154        (0.36)
155        kAY?
156   J:   <<subdued,p>yup.> ((Averted gaze toward paper cups on
           lab desk))
157        (2:06) ((Carrie gazes at Jane, who still has averted
           gaze))
158        ((Carrie turns, gets up, and leaves Jane))
```

Post-Episode Debriefing: Jane and Researcher[28]

```
001   R:   is that back to the drawing board for you jane?
002   J:   ((Nods.))
003   R:   how is that?
004   J:   its sucks
005   R:   how does that make you feel?
006   J:   its really annoying because i had everything planned
           and i knew what exactly i wanted to do, and its like
           when i first got it, i was like yes this is the one
           that i want to do out of all of them, and now its
           sort of ... you know ... but
007   R:   what was the main problem?
008   J:   well, i was trying to get the right weight so that
           the candle could lift it off and i found something
           that would do it last night but, i mean, mum and i
           went shopping and bought all these stuff, and it was
           fun and like, yeah
009   R:   i guess you can still do it at home, cant you?
010   J:   yeah ... like ... now that its sort of you know, i
           dont know ... i have to come up with a good reason
           for a science experiment so ... i mean i can do it at
           home but like I just ... i dont know what to do now,
           so
011   R:   you know they have a lantern festival in Taiwan ...
```

Post-Lesson Debriefing Interview: Carrie and the Researcher

```
001   R:   does anything stand out from that session?
002   C:   i had to tell jane that we=ve changed her topic.
003   R:   i=m glad I recorded that.
004   C:   And then you had a chat with jane did you?
005   R:   Just at the end I wanted to hear her take on what she
```

---

[28] The two post-episode interviews are presented almost exactly as a graduate student has transcribed these, that is, without following conversation analytic conventions. The sound to spelling transcription follows the conventions in Appendix A. The punctuation, however, is that provided by the transcriber: it has to be read as an outsider's gloss of what can heard listening to the tape. The punctuation therefore includes the transcriber's competence in attending to a conversation rather than reflecting the prosody or how the interlocutor heard and acted upon a preceding turn.

```
                    was going to do.
006    C:    jane is sort of, towards the bottom of the list as
             far as physics achievement in that class goes.
007    R:    oh really. so what would that be? sound or something.
008    C:    scraping a sound. technically linda has a lower mark
             but she was ill and almost didn't do a piece of as-
             sessment but did it. so discounting that, which was
             sort of abnormal, wanda and jane are lower down. so
             jane is really just scraping through. and shes doing
             physics because her dad wants her to do physics, i
             think, really and she struggles with it, which is, i
             always thought that that topic wasnt the best for her
             because its not as straight forward and the other
             groups doing the same topic in other classes have
             also had a lot of trouble getting anything to work at
             all. they=re meant to be making a lantern rise
             through tee-light candles. we have simplified the
             problem and adding hot air to the lantern, seeing how
             quickly it can rise.
009    R:    how did you come about to make the decision that you
             need to change because you seemed to approach her
             with that decision in mind?
010    C:    oh no. its been re written. the wording of her
             problem has been changed. i didnt change it.
011    R:    she changed it?
012    C:    no. andrew ((department head)) changed it because
             theres a dozen other classes doing that problem who
             havent been able to get anything done so andrew
             decided that something had to be done about it, so
             changed the kind of direction of it all. yes it was
             very specific what now is the direction and her
             variables are still up to her. whether she changes
             the volume of the lantern or the shape of it or the
             temperature which she gets the air to before she lets
             it go or whatever.
013    R:    or the mass of the candle?
014    C:    well theres no candle any more.
015    R:    thats standard? no candle any more.
016    C:    yes no candle. so adding hot air through a hairdryer
             or something like that. or heating it by passing air
             over a hot element which is a hairdryer. we havent
             specified using a hairdryer but how else do you heat
             air without using a flame.
017    R:    i dont know how the chinese do it. i was there in
             taiwan festival. i just cant remember the structure.
018    C:    dont know.
019    R:    i think they might have had very small candles.
020    C:    with maybe many wicks or something.
021    R:    yes spread out over a large area but not in terms of
             density. like paraffin or something  yes.
022    C:    so and jane did baulk at it all. as much as its mak-
             ing life easier for her, she wants to do her own
             thing so hopefully it doesnt put her off too much and
             she does get on with it. shes also not working with
             anyone.
023    R:    is that by choice?
024    C:    yes.
025    R:    i got that impression. she said she wanted to do it
             by herself because she wants to be proud of her own
             work i think.
026    C:    she and ruth and sally whos working (?) sally or
             sally they tend to sit with each other and ruth and
             sally often try to push her back on track when
             they=re working out problems or whatever it is cause
```

		shes pretty easily distracted.
027	R:	okay. so jane gets distracted?
028	C:	yes. i dont think she is as interested in physics as she is in singing, music and-
029	R:	is she good at that?
030	C:	yes. she tries and she does occasionally say things like, i did all those questions. well yes, so did the rest of the class but yes, she=ll be, when she does do a little bit of something she=ll let you know, cause its rare. anyway so that was probably a fairly important thing that happened today and yes, i=ll try and give her more guidance to try and get her doing things so she can get to-
031	R:	so give her more guidance than some of the others?
032	C:	yes. some of the others are giving themselves more guidance. i think you recorded my conversation with (?) with the rocking bottle.
033	R:	i did too.
034	C:	she=ll say all the words and she=ll say a lot of words and not say much and thats (?) she=ll try and the way she sort of talks to me is very like as if shes doing a presentation. she=ll present it to me whereas other girls will just talk.
035	R:	i noticed that, because after the conversation, you know what she did, she went, aaah, as if it was the end of a presentation.
036	C:	it appears to me that she doesnt want to be seen to not know things. this is the whole point, they dont know things and they=re meant to be trying to find things out and the other girls will say, i dont know. whereas she spouts all these words that, when you add them up, dont say much at all.
037	R:	and is she in the same range of achievement level as jane?
038	C:	she is higher achieving than jane. puts probably more work in but shes probably second bottom in the class, not counting Linda. thats a bit different.
039	R:	it sort of makes sense then, that today you would have spent most of your time with those two students i think.
040	C:	i probably didnt spend a huge amount of time with jane, other than the discussion about whats changed in it but yes, i am concerned that (jane?) will keep on going with, i know whats going on and then have nothing to write about.
041	R:	how did you feel when you approached jane?
042	C:	i think i was, i sort of knew that she wouldnt be particularly happy with it and i guess i approached her with the idea that i wanted her to feel that it was a good thing rather than meaning she=d done all this work and it was wasted etcetera etcetera.
043	R:	is that an intentional strategy on your part?
044	C:	that was the aim of the conversation to let her know that this was what was happening but have her feel that it was okay.
045	R:	how did you feel then?
046	C:	okay. i know that during that lesson she switched off. at the end she was over chatting with rita, not doing anything. i had another little discussion. there are things that she can be doing but i think she=ll get back on track.
047	R:	that instance stood out today?
048	C:	i guess. yes it was different to the run of the mill kind of trouble shooting type things that are going

```
          on.
049   R:  when you interact with somebody like erna, how does
          that make you feel compared with what happens with
          the interaction with somebody like jane?
050   C:  its always going to be different, so i guess, if i=m
          talking to erna, the sorts of questions shes probably
          asking arent ones about, i guess are more straight
          forward and physics based or equipment based sort of
          thing. so I guess, theres not much emotion from
          either side of us in that sort of conversation, its
          just, this is my question. whereas jane, i guess i
          feel, i feel a bit more aware of making sure i say
          things that wont, i guess, upset her in a way,
          whether its how i say it or how i try and put things
          to make sure she doesnt get off track.
051   R:  so deliberately try not to upset jane but theres no
          need to even think about that.
052   C:  not so much upset jane but not have jane upset.
053   R:  i understand. so that she doesnt walk away feeling
          upset cause but shes not on the right track or
          something.
054   C:  yes.
```

References

Aussie Educator. (2012). A total education page for Australia. Accessed August 14, 2012 at www.aussieeducator.org.au/curriculum/curriculum.html

Bakhtin, M. M. (1979). *Estetika slovesnogo tvorčestva* [Aesthetics of verbal creation]. Moscow, Russia: Iskusstvo. (French: Esthétique de la creation verbale, Éditions Gallimard, Paris, France, 1984)

Bakhtin, M. M. (1993). Toward a philosophy of the act. Austin: University of Texas Press.

Bellocchi, A., & Ritchie, S. M. (2011). Investigating and theorizing discourse during analogy writing in chemistry. *Journal of Research in Science Teaching, 48*, 771–792.

Bjelic, D., & Lynch, M. (1992). The work of [scientific] demonstration, respecifying Newton's and Goethe's theories of prismatic color. In G. Watson & R. M. Seiler (Eds.), *Text in context* (pp. 52–78). London, UK: Sage.

Boden, D. (1994). *The business of talk: Organizations in action*. Cambridge, UK: Polity Press.

Bourdieu, P. (1992). The practice of reflexive sociology (The Paris workshop). In P. Bourdieu & L. J. D. Wacquant, *An invitation to reflexive sociology* (pp. 216–260). Chicago: University of Chicago Press.

Carambo, C. (2005). Learning science and the centrality of student participation. In K. Tobin, R. Elmesky, & G. Seiler (Eds.), *Improving urban science education: New roles for teachers, students, and researchers* (pp. 167–184). Lanham, MD: Rowman & Littlefield.

Chrétien, J.-L. (2007). *Répondre: Figures de la réponse et de la responsabilité* [To respond: Figures of response and responsibility]. Paris, France: Presses Universitaires de France.

Collins, R. (2004). *Interaction ritual chains*. Princeton, NJ: Princeton University Press.

Deleuze, G. (1968). *Différence et repetition* [Difference and repetition]. Paris, France: Presses Universitaires de France.

Dewey, J. (2008). *Later works vol. 13*. Carbondale, IL: Southern Illinois University Press.

Dewey, J., & Bentley, A. F. (1999). Knowing and the known. In R. Handy & E. E. Hardwood, *Useful procedures of inquiry* (pp. 97–209). Great Barrington, MA: Behavioral Research Council. (First published in 1949)

Durkheim, E. (1919). *Les règles de la méthode sociologique septième édition* [Rules of sociological method 7th ed.]. Paris, France: Felix Alcan.

Foucault, M. (1975). *Surveiller et punir: Naissance de la prison* [Discipline and punish: Birth of the prison]. Paris, France: Gallimard.

Garfinkel, H. (1967). *Studies in ethnomethodology*, Englewood Cliffs, NJ: Prentice-Hall.

REFERENCES

Garfinkel, H. (1988). Evidence for locally produced, naturally accountable phenomena of order*, logic, reason, meaning, method, etc. in and as of the essential quiddity of immortal ordinary society (I of IV): An announcement of studies. *Sociological Theory, 6*, 103–109.

Garfinkel, H. (1991). Respecification: Evidence for locally produced naturally accountable phenomena of order*, logic, reason, meaning, method, etc. in an as of the essential haecceity of immortal ordinary society, (I)--an announcement of studies. In G. Button (Ed.), *Ethnomethodology and the human sciences* (pp. 10–19). Cambridge, UK: Cambridge University Press.

Garfinkel, H. (1996). Ethnomethodology's program. *Social Psychology Quarterly, 59*, 5–21.

Garfinkel, H. (2002). *Ethnomethodology's program: Working out Durkheim's aphorism*. Lanham, MD: Rowman & Littlefield.

Garfinkel, H. (2007). Lebenswelt origins of the sciences: Working out Durkheim's aphorism. Book two: Workplace and documentary diversity of ethnomethodological studies of work and sciences by ethnomethodology's authors: What did we do? What did we learn? *Human Studies, 30*, 9–56.

Garfinkel, H., Lynch, M., & LIviginston, E. (1981). The work of a discovering science constructed with materials from the optically discovered pulsar. *Philosophy of the Social Sciences, 11*, 131–158.

Garfinkel, H., & Sacks, H. (1986). On formal structures of practical action. In H. Garfinkel (Ed.), *Ethnomethodological studies of work* (pp. 160–193). London, UK: Routledge & Kegan Paul.

Goodwin, C., Goodwin, M. H., & Yaeger-Dror, M.. (2002). Multi-modality in girls' game disputes. *Journal of Pragmatics, 34*, 1621–1649.

Greiffenhagen, C., & Sherman, W. (2008). Kuhn and conceptual change: On the analogy between conceptual changes in science and children. *Science & Education, 17*, 1–26.

Guba, E. G., & Lincoln, Y. S. (1989). *Fourth generation evaluation*. Newbury Park, CA: Sage.

Have, P. ten (2004). *Understanding qualitative research and ethnomethodology*. London, UK: Sage.

Heidegger, M. (1977). *Sein und Zeit* [Being and time]. Tübingen, Germany: Max Niemeyer.

Husserl, E. (1976). *Husserliana Band III/1. Ideen zu einer reinen Phänomenologie und phänomenologischen Philosophie: Erstes Buch: Allgemeine Einführung in die reine Phänomenologie* [Husserliana vol. III/1. Ideas pertaining to a pure phenomenology and phenomenological philosophy vol. 1. General introduction to a pure phenomenology]. The Hague, The Netherlands: Martinus Nijhoff.

Husserl, E. (1993). *Husserliana Band XXIX. Die Krisis der europäischen Wissenschaften und die transzendentale Phänomenologie. Ergänzungsband. Texte aus dem Nachlass 1934–1937* [Husserliana vol. 29. The crisis of the European sciences and transcendental phenomenology. Supplementary volume. Texts from the estate (1916–1937)]. Dordrecht, The Netherlands: Kluwer Academic Publishers.

Husserl, E. (2008). *Husserliana Band XXXIX. Die Lebenswelt: Auslegungen der vorgegebenen Welt und ihrer Konstitution. Texte aus dem Nachlass (1916–1937)* [Husserliana vol. 39. The lifeworld: Interpretations of the given world and its constitutions. Texts from the estate (1916–1937)]. Dordrecht, The Netherlands: Springer.

Jefferson, G. (1989). Preliminary notes on a possible metric which provides for a "standard maximum" silence of approximately one second in conversation. In D. Roger & P. Bull (Eds.), *Conversation: An interdisciplinary perspective* (pp. 166–196). Clevedon, UK: Multilingual Matters.

Jordan, B. (1989). Cosmopolitical obstetrics: Some insights from the training of traditional midwives. *Social Science Medicine, 28*, 925–944.

Koschmann, T., & Zemel, A. (2009). Pulsars and black arrows: Discoveries as occasioned productions. *Journal of the Learning Sciences, 18*, 200–246.

Leont'ev, A. A. (1969). *Jazyk, rec', recevaja dejatel'nost'* [Language, speech, speech activity]. Moscow, Russia: Prosveščenje.

Levinson, S. C. (1983). *Pragmatics*. Cambridge, UK: Cambridge University.

Livingston, E. (1987). *Making sense of ethnomethodology*. London, UK: Routledge & Kegan Paul.

Lynch, M. (1985). *Art and artifact in laboratory science: A study of shop work and shoptalk in a laboratory*. London, UK: Routledge and Kegan Paul.

Lynch, M., Livingston, E., & Garfinkel, H. (1983). Temporal order in laboratory work. In K. D. Knorr-Cetina & M. Mulkay (Eds.), *Science observed: Perspectives on the social study of science* (pp. 205–238). London, UK: Sage.

Lynch, M., & Macbeth, D. (1998). Demonstrating physics lessons. In J. G. Greeno & S. V. Goldman (Eds.), *Thinking practices in mathematics and science learning* (pp. 269–297). Mahwah, NJ: Lawrence Erlbaum Associates.

Macbeth, D. (2000). On an actual apparatus for conceptual change. *Science Education, 84*, 228–264.

Mannheim, K. (2004). Beiträge zur Theorie der Weltanschauungs-Interpretation [Contributions to the theory of worldview interpretation]. In J. Strübing & B. Schnettler (Eds.), *Methodologie interpretativer Sozialforschung: Klassische Grundlagentexte* (pp. 103–153). Konstanz, Germany: UVK.

Marion, J.-L. (2010). *Certitudes négatives* [Negative certitudes]. Paris, France: Éditions Grasset & Fasquelles.

Marx, K./Engels, F. (1962). *Werke Band 23: Das Kapital* [Works vol. 23: Capital]. Berlin, Germany: Dietz.

McDermott, R. P., Gospodinoff, K., & Aron, J. (1978). Criteria for an ethnographically adequate description of concerted activities and their contexts. *Semiotica, 24*, 245–275.

Mills, C. W. (1940). Situated actions and vocabularies of motive. *American Sociological Review, 5*, 904–913.

Nietzsche, F. (1954). *Werke Bd. 3* [Works vol. 3]. München, Germany: Hanser.

Oxford English Dictionary (OED). (2012). Online version. www.oed.com.

Queensland Studies Authority (QS). (2007). *Physics senior syllabus.* Spring Hill, QLD: Author. Accessed March 26, 2012 at www.qsa.qld.edu.au/downloads/senior/snr_physics_07_syll.doc

Roth, W.-M. (1995). *Authentic school science: Knowing and learning in open-inquiry science laboratories.* Dordrecht, The Netherlands: Kluwer Academic Publishers.

Roth, W.-M. (1996). Teacher questioning in an open-inquiry learning environment: Interactions of context, content, and student responses. *Journal of Research in Science Teaching, 33*, 709–736.

Roth, W.-M. (2000). From gesture to scientific language. *Journal of Pragmatics, 32*, 1683–1714.

Roth, W.-M. (2002). *Being and becoming in the classroom.* Westport, CT: Ablex.

Roth, W.-M. (2004a). Activity theory in education: An introduction. *Mind, Culture, & Activity, 11*, 1–8.

Roth, W.-M. (2004b). Perceptual gestalts in workplace communication. *Journal of Pragmatics, 36*, 1037–1069.

Roth, W.-M. (2006). *Learning science: A singular plural perspective.* Rotterdam, The Netherlands: Sense Publishers.

Roth, W.-M. (2007). Emotion at work: A contribution to third-generation cultural historical activity theory. *Mind, Culture and Activity, 14*, 40–63.

Roth, W.-M. (2008a). Bricolage, métissage, hybridity, heterogeneity, diaspora: Concepts for thinking science education in the 21st century. *Cultural Studies in Science Education, 3*, 891–916.

Roth, W.-M. (2008b). The nature of scientific conceptions: A discursive psychological perspective. *Educational Research Review, 3*, 30–50.

Roth, W.-M. (2009a). Radical uncertainty in scientific discovery work. *Science, Technology & Human Values, 34*, 313–336.

Roth, W.-M. (2009b). Specifying the ethnomethodological 'what more?' *Cultural Studies of Science Education, 4*, 1–12.

Roth, W.-M. (2010). *Language, learning, context: Talking the talk.* London, UK: Routledge.

Roth, W.-M. (2011a). *Geometry as objective science in elementary classrooms: Mathematics in the flesh.* New York, NY: Routledge.

Roth, W.-M. (2011b). Researching living/lived mathematical work. *Forum Qualitative Sozialforschung/ Forum Qualitative Social Research, 12* (1). Accessed January 1, 2013 at http://nbn-resolving.de/um:nbn:de:0114-fqs1101318.

Roth, W.-M. (2012). *First-person methods: Toward an empirical phenomenology of experience.* Rotterdam, The Netherlands: Sense Publishers.

Roth, W.-M. (2013). Toward a post-constructivist ethics in/of teaching and learning. *Pedagogies: An International Journal.*

Roth, W.-M., & Barton, A. C. (2004). *Rethinking scientific literacy.* New York, NY: Routledge.

Roth, W.-M., & Bowen, G. M. (1994). Mathematization of experience in a grade 8 open-inquiry environment: An introduction to the representational practices of science. *Journal of Research in Science Teaching, 31*, 293–318.

Roth, W.-M., & Bowen, G. M. (1999a). Complexities of graphical representations during lectures: A phenomenological approach. *Learning and Instruction, 9*, 235–255.

Roth, W.-M., & Bowen, G. M. (1999b). Digitizing lizards or the topology of vision in ecological fieldwork. *Social Studies of Science, 29*, 719–764.

Roth, W.-M., & Bowen, G. M. (2001). 'Creative solutions' and 'fibbing results': Enculturation in field ecology. *Social Studies of Science, 31*, 533–556.

Roth, W.-M., & Bautista, A. (2011). Transcriptions, mathematical cognition, and epistemology. *The Montana Mathematics Enthusiast, 18*, 51–76.

Roth, W.-M., & Gardner, R. (2012). "They're gonna explain to us what makes a cube a cube?" Geometrical properties as contingent achievement of sequentially ordered child-centered mathematics lessons. *Mathematics Education Research Journal*.

Roth, W.-M., & Hsu, P.-L. (2010). *Analyzing communication: Praxis of method*. Rotterdam, The Netherlands: Sense Publishers.

Roth, W.-M., & Hsu, P.-L. (2012). Analyzing verbal data: An object lesson. In B. J. Fraser, K. Tobin, & C. McRobbie (Eds.), *Second international handbook of science education* (pp. 1501–1513). Dordrecht, The Netherlands: Springer.

Roth, W.-M., & Lee, Y. J. (2006). Contradictions in theorizing and implementing "communities". *Educational Research Review, 1*, 27–40.

Roth, W.-M., & Lee, Y. J. (2007). "Vygotsky's neglected legacy": Cultural-historical activity theory. *Review of Educational Research, 77*, 186–232.

Roth, W.-M., Lee, Y. J., & Hwang, S.-W. (2008). Culturing conceptions: From first principles. *Cultural Studies of Science Education, 3*, 231–261.

Roth, W.-M., & Middleton, D. (2006). The making of asymmetries of knowing, identity, and accountability in the sequential organization of graph interpretation. *Cultural Studies of Science Education, 1*, 11–81.

Roth, W.-M., & Radford, L. (2010). Re/thinking the zone of proximal development (symmetrically). *Mind, Culture, and Activity, 17*, 299–307.

Roth, W.-M., & Thom, J. (2009). The emergence of 3d geometry from children's (teacher-guided) classification tasks. *Journal of the Learning Sciences, 18*, 45–99.

Roth, W.-M., & Tobin, K. (2002). *At the elbow of another: Learning to teach by coteaching*. New York, NY: Peter Lang.

Roth, W.-M., & Tobin, K. (2010). Solidarity and conflict: Aligned and misaligned prosody as a transactional resource in intra- and intercultural communication involving power differences. *Cultural Studies of Science Education, 5*, 805–847.

Roth, W.-M., McGinn, M. K., Woszczyna, C., & Boutonné, S. (1999). Differential participation during science conversations: The interaction of focal artifacts, social configuration, and physical arrangements. *Journal of the Learning Sciences, 8*, 293–347.

Roth, W.-M., Lawless, D., & Masciotra, D. (2001). Spielraum and teaching. *Curriculum Inquiry, 31*, 183–207.

Roth, W.-M., Tobin, K., Elmesky, R., Carambo, C., McKnight, Y., & Beers, J. (2004). Re/making identities in the praxis of urban schooling: A cultural historical perspective. *Mind, Culture, & Activity, 11*, 48–69.

Sacks, H. (1974). On the analyzability of stories by children. In R. Turner (Ed.), *Ethnomethodology: Selected readings* (pp. 216–232). Harmondsworth, UK: Penguin.

Sadeh, I., & Zion, M. (2009). The development of dynamic inquiry performances within an open inquiry setting: A comparison to guided inquiry setting. *Journal of Research in Science Teaching, 46*, 1137–1160.

Schegloff, E. (2007). *Sequence organization in interaction: A primer in conversation analysis vol. 1*. Cambridge, UK: Cambridge University Press.

Scherer, K. R. (1989). Vocal correlates of emotion. In H. L. Wagner & A. S. R. Manstead (Eds.), *Handbook of psychophysiology: Emotion and social behavior* (pp. 165–197). London, UK: Wiley.

Selting, M., Auer, P., Barden, B., Bergmann, J., Couper-Kuhlen, E., Günthner, S., Meier, C., Quasthoff, U., Schlobinski, P., & Uhmann, S. (1998). Gesprächsanalytisches Transkriptionssystem [Conversation analytic transcription system]. *Linguistische Berichte, 173*, 91–122.

Sherman, W. (2004). Science studies, situatedness, and instructional design in science education: A summary and critique of the promise. *Canadian Journal of Science, Mathematics, and Technology Education, 5*, 443–465.

Smith, D. E. (1990). *The conceptual practices of power: A feminist sociology of knowledge.* Toronto, Ontario: University of Toronto Press.

Suchman, L. A. (1987). *Plans and situated actions: The problem of human-machine communication.* Cambridge: Cambridge University Press.

Tobin, K. (1990). Research on science laboratory activities: In pursuit of better questions and answers to improve learning. *School Science and Mathematics, 90*, 403–418.

Tobin, K., Espinet, M., Byrd, S. E., & Adams, D. (1988). Alternative perspectives of effective science teaching. *Science Education, 72*, 433–451.

Vološinov, V. N. (1930). *Marksizm i filosofija jazyka: Osnovie problemi soziologicheskogo metoda v nauke o jazyke* [Marxism and the philosophy of language: Essay on the application of the sociological method in linguistics]. Leningrad, Russia: Priboii.

Vygotskij, L. S. (2005). *Psyxhologija razvitija čeloveka* [Psychology of human development]. Moscow, Russia: Eksmo.

Vygotsky, L. S. (1978). *Mind in society: The development of higher psychological processes.* Cambridge: Harvard University Press.

Waldenfels, B. (2006). *Grundmotive einer Phänomenologie des Fremden* [Fundamental ideas of a phenomenology of the foreign/strange]. Frankfurt/M, Germany: Suhrkamp.

Index

CPSIA information can be obtained at www.ICGtesting.com
Printed in the USA
BVOW05s1445210314

348389BV00003B/63/P

9 789462 092525